TORTURED
GENIUS

Other books by Joseph Romanos

Chris Lewis: All The Way to Wimbledon

Lois Muir on Netball (with Lois Muir)

Dybvig on Basketball (with John Dybvig)

Fastbreak (with John Dybvig)

Makers of Champions – Great New Zealand Coaches

Famous Fullbacks

Famous Flankers

100 Great Rugby Characters (with Grant Harding)

A Sporting Life (with Peter Sellers)

Great New Zealand Cricket Families

The Big Black Book of Netball (with Gael Woods)

The Innings of a Lifetime (with Walter Hadlee)

A Century of Great New Zealand Cricketers

We Knocked the Bastard Off

I'm Absolutely Buggered

Arthur's Boys

TORTURED GENIUS

BY

JOSEPH ROMANOS

HODDER MOA BECKETT

Published in 1995 by Hodder Moa Beckett Publishers Limited,
[a member of the Hodder Headline Group]
28 Poland Road, Glenfield, Auckland, New Zealand

ISBN 1-86958-187-3

Printed by Griffin Paperbacks, Australia

Acknowledgements

Acknowledgements pages usually start with the writing side of a book, so, just for variety, I would like to begin by thanking the people who have helped me with the illustrations. John Blackwell and Don Neely both made available their vast collections of cricket photos, Martin Hunter assisted me further, and caricaturist Murray Webb provided his own touch of class to add distinction to the book. In a few instances, I have been unable to accurately source photos, and offer apologies for any omissions.

During the course of my research, I have interviewed more than 90 people. I appreciated the generous way they gave of their time and offered opinions without fear or favour. Each has contributed significantly, whether to add information about a particular period of Martin Crowe's life, or to help place his cricket in a historical perspective.

Some deserve particular thanks. John Wright, Richard Hadlee, Ian Smith, John Parker, Lance Cairns, Bruce Edgar, John Bracewell, John Morrison – the makings of a fairly useful XI – gave me extended interviews, which I appreciated. Darryl Sambell spoke at length about his time as Martin's agent; Peter Roebuck was as thought-provoking and lucid as ever in discussing Martin the county player; John Graham was able to provide rare insight into Martin's development from a schoolboy to a man; Don Neely offered a selector's viewpoint; Greg Chappell spoke as the first test captain to oppose Martin, and as a valued advisor to him. Some of my friends in the media were particularly helpful, notably Trevor McKewen, Murray Deaker, Keith Quinn, Duncan Johnstone, Grant Nesbitt, Bryan

Waddle, Peter Williams, John Coffey, David Leggat and Doug Golightly.

Many others added a particular snippet, a memory or a fact which helped shape the overall picture. They included James Harding, an Auckland Grammar First XI teammate of Martin's; national team coaches Glenn Turner, Bob Cunis and Geoff Howarth; people who captained him, such as John Wiltshire, Graham Vivian, Jeremy Coney and Ken Rutherford; his personal coach of recent years, Harold Whitcombe; and current players such as Lee Germon, Andrew Jones, Gavin Larsen, Shane Thomson and Mark Priest.

I would like to thank Finlay Macdonald for lending me some particularly useful material and for pointing me in the right direction, and Jim Greenhough, who, when I was weighing up the project, provided me with a piece of sound journalistic advice.

As this is an unauthorised biography, I have not spoken to any of the Crowe family during the preparation of this book. However, I have spoken often to Jeff and Martin over the years and have quoted extensively from those interviews. I also dealt with the Crowe family in some depth while writing Great New Zealand Cricket Families in 1992, and have used a lot of material I gathered at that time.

Also included in this book are quotes from interviews I have conducted with well-known sportsmen, such as Mark Greatbatch and Grant Fox, during my time as a sports journalist.

Peter Marriott deserves praise for his extensive and meticulous statistical contributions, editor Gil Dymock's professional skills were much appreciated and thanks are due to Francis Payne for running his eye over the text.

Finally I would like to thank my wife, Gael, who continues to provide me with direction and inspiration, and who is still the best appraiser of a book I know.

Dedicated to
my backyard cricket boys,
Dominic and Alexander

Contents

Introduction

Martin Davidson Crowe is the nearest thing New Zealand sport has had to John McEnroe during my time as a journalist. Not that Crowe is foul-mouthed as McEnroe was during his tempestuous time at the top of the tennis rankings. But Crowe has in him the same perfectionist streak as the man who was nicknamed Superbrat. (A case of the Superbrat and the Superbat.) Like McEnroe on the tennis court, Crowe aims for perfection. As Don Neely says: "Crowe and excellence go together."

Crowe is meticulously organised, very aware of his grooming and appearance. It is difficult to imagine Martin walking out to field wearing grass-stained creams. Equally, there is nothing slap-dash about his attitude towards his cricket. He prepares as thoroughly as he can, and he expects others to do the same. That's where problems can arise. Very few players are as single-minded and passionate about their cricket as Crowe; almost none meet his high standards. When his teammates fall short, Crowe can be rather intolerant and testy.

McEnroe took out his frustrations on what he perceived as poor officiating in an obnoxious manner: swearing, smashing his racket, belting the ball in rage. Crowe's reactions are more muted, but just as heartfelt. Like McEnroe, he does not like to be challenged. When teammates – or selectors, administrators or umpires – have disagreed, he has argued with them, criticised them in his newspaper columns, even written them personal letters. Like McEnroe, he does not shy away from confrontation. In fact, sometimes he seems to welcome it.

This is the combative, aggressive streak in him, and it is an important part of what makes him a brilliant player. His wonderful batting is the result not only of a refined technique and a constant striving for perfection, but also his willingness, eagerness even, to meet the challenge of pitting himself against an opposing team's best bowlers, and of comparing himself to his opposition's best batsman.

His quest for perfection is especially fascinating as he plays a sport in which perfection is impossible. The weather, the pitch conditions, the state of the ball, the tactics of the opposition all combine to ensure that it is impossible to play a perfect innings. To Crowe's credit, he has never stopped trying, and he has got a lot closer than most batsmen in history. When he falls short of the standards he has set himself, he gets bitterly disappointed. He was furious with himself after being dismissed for 299 in the test against Sri Lanka in 1991. At Melbourne in 1987 he was very downcast after completing his 4,000 runs in a calendar year. While he was being lauded by all about him, he felt he had let himself down by his batting in the last match, the decisive third test of the series against Australia, and so derived less than full pleasure at the time from a notable milestone.

So, on the sporting side, he is an unusual and intriguing mix. But there is much more to Martin Crowe. In fact, he is the most fascinating New Zealand sports personality of the past 15 or 20 years. There have been others we have warmed to more, others who have been more outrageous, and a few who have been as good at their sport as Crowe is at cricket.

But Crowe is the most interesting study. He is so full of paradoxes. He invites the media into his home, then complains about having his privacy invaded; he has a life's ambition to captain New Zealand at cricket, then offers to step down as skipper to shake up the team; he can be moody and surly with teammates, yet the kids love him when he visits schools; he is a superb athlete, yet he has suffered more injuries than any other sportsman I know of.

It's these sort of contrasts that make him such a compelling discussion point for the talkback callers and the letter-to-the-editor writers. How to get a handle on his mass of complexities?

Champion athlete Peter Snell was similarly paradoxical: on the track a killer, a dynamic and ruthless competitor; off it, at least during his time as an Olympic champion, a shy, seemingly insecure person who found it difficult to make a decision. Snell, like Crowe, was a fascinating case study.

But Snell has gone on to find happiness and security not in the glory of his running career, but through his progress in academia at American universities. He is now one of the world's leading exercise physiologists. He is respected as much or more for what he has achieved since retiring from running, and that fact means everything to him.

What is the future for Crowe? Will he one day be revered as a champion cricketer, the way we think of Bert Sutcliffe or Martin Donnelly? Or will there always be a caveat? There has been a swirling mass of drama around Crowe for the past decade – rumours, speculation, injury updates, problems with the captaincy, his dealings with fellow players.

Crowe certainly provokes more criticism than virtually any other New Zealand sports star. Why is this, and is it fair?

Consider the case of Ken Rutherford, one of Crowe's peers. Rutherford has against his name a drink-driving conviction and a broken marriage. He has captained New Zealand through one of the blackest periods in our cricket history. He has criticised the national selectors while captain, he has been suspended for bad behaviour, he has shown bad sportsmanship on the field. Yet Rutherford provokes surprisingly little critical comment. There are a few sniggers about whether he scores enough runs to justify his place in the team, but otherwise he's regarded as a good Kiwi bloke, doing his best. He enjoys life's pleasures – which run the gamut from a social beer to a punt on the horses – like anyone else, and people seem to relate to him.

With Crowe, though, any hint of controversy is seized upon and he becomes the target of ever more vicious criticism on talkback radio. He is a better bat than Rutherford, was certainly a better captain on the field. And yet, to many New Zealanders, he is public enemy No 1.

It seems bizarre. Yet there is a reason. And that's why I have written this book. I doubt whether this sort of book could have been written as a regulation sports biography, or a ghosted autobiography. With Crowe, there are some uncomfortable questions that need to be asked. The author has to explore areas which the subject might happily avoid. It would take a very rare personality to willingly and honestly delve into those areas. Crowe is not that personality.

It has been quite a challenge writing an unauthorised biography. Initially, I was concerned that the people I approached for comment and analysis – Martin's friends, acquaintances, teammates, opponents and others in the cricket world – would feel I was setting out to write a muck-raking sort of book. But their reaction was surprisingly positive. "An unauthorised biography on Martin… a straight, honest book. It should be tremendous," was typical of the reaction I received.

It is a pleasure not to have to include the self-justification, the gloss and pap that is found in virtually all autobiographies. By covering his cricket career – and what a career it has been – honestly and objectively, in words and statistics, due credit has been paid to Martin as a player.

On the other hand, I did not want to rake over any controversy, any dispute, in the hope of creating a headline. I have not printed what I regarded to be gratuitously nasty comments, and have avoided the few stories about Martin which, while mildly unsavoury, have had no bearing on his cricket or the person he has become.

There is a chapter on his dealings with the media for, with Crowe, more than most sportsmen and women, the media has played a pivotal role. He has had columns in several newspapers and undertaken radio and television work. He has developed a testy relationship with many cricket reporters, been chummy with others. The media has played a large part in shaping the public attitude towards Martin Crowe, so it is an area worth exploring.

I've explored the change in his personality; from the bright, enthusiastic, ever-smiling schoolboy to the intense, complex, haunted public figure he is today. And I've been able to examine at some length the much talked-about (especially by Martin) tall poppy syndrome, explaining why he finds solace in attributing criticism of him to that trait.

And the verdict? A genius as a cricketer, without question. But a tortured genius, "always at war with his own publicity" as his county captain Peter Roebuck puts it.

Having studied his career, and his life, what amazes me is the manner in which he has been able to leave behind him all the turmoil and the self-doubts and the controversy as he walks through the dressing room door, bat in hand. He finds sanctuary and peace out in the middle, even if he is being confronted by the best bowlers in the world.

Just another odd twist in this most unusual of personalities.

The essential Martin Crowe, as captured by caricaturist (and former test fast bowler) Murray Webb.

Chapter One

WHERE TO FROM HERE?

JOHN GRAHAM:
> *"At the moment he's the centre attraction even when he's not playing."*

Martin Snedden: "It's just a personal opinion, but I think he'll play until the year 2000."

John Morrison: "He's a mess. He doesn't know what to do. He doesn't like the pressure of fronting up. He could easily never play again."

Those opposing views, from former internationals who have remained close to New Zealand cricket, illustrate the quandary Martin Crowe found himself in at the end of the 1994/95 New Zealand summer. It was a summer of discontent for the New Zealand team, which staggered from scandal to scandal, defeat to defeat. For Crowe personally, a season which promised so much produced only frustration and an increased portion of public scorn.

He damaged his knee again in South Africa and had to have an operation in Auckland in January 1995. There followed weeks of rehabilitation while the West Indies toured. He felt he was fit enough to take part in the centenary one-day series, but pulled a thigh muscle in his first outing and limped out of the team again.

Crowe returned only once more, for an unsatisfactory appearance in the test against South Africa, when he had two failures and was accused of batting selfishly. (A century would have given him a test hundred against every other test-playing country, the first to manage the feat.)

Thereafter Crowe's season slumped into a series of failed fitness tests. It looked like he might just about be fit again for the last couple of one-dayers against Sri Lanka, at the tailend of the season, but Crowe was advised to go away and spend the winter getting properly fit.

What lay ahead – retirement, and soul-searching about what to do with the rest of his life, or renewed determination to extend his test career and write a more satisfactory closing chapter?

So off he trooped to Arrowtown, to regroup. In early May, while New Zealand's sporting public were bombarded with news on All Black selection battles and Australian Super League squabbles, Crowe had a real bonanza bulletin. He'd been granted a testimonial season by New Zealand Cricket – a unique honour. As Crowe announced his availability for Wellington in 1995/96 the late-autumn strolls around his Central Otago property must have been made with lighter tread than he'd enjoyed for many months.

The end of the 1994/95 season was very much the crossroads of his career. On the one hand he has done more than enough to ensure he is recalled forever as one of the great players of New Zealand cricket. Quite apart from a first class average of 56.03 and the small matter of 69 first class centuries (second only to Glenn Turner, who played far more matches), Crowe has performed wonderfully in the test arena. He holds the New Zealand records for the most runs (5394), the most centuries (17) and the highest score (299).

Yet he has a fear of being remembered for the "wrong reasons". He wants the name of Martin Crowe to be recalled for great batting deeds and service to his country, not for injuries and rumours, not for squabbles with fellow players, selectors, umpires, the media. He told Martine Rule of *Woman's Day* in 1994 that, when he does retire, the most important thing to him will not be the records he has broken, but the way his teammates and the public remember him as a professional and a New Zealander. "I still have this concern that I will finish my career and people will have this idea that I'm self-centred and never helped my teammates, that I was only in it for my own selfish reasons and for the money. That would blow me away, because it's just so completely untrue." The fact that Crowe even raised such concerns shows he is aware of how a sizeable section of the New Zealand public perceives him.

Crowe is steeped in the traditions of the game, and one of his great goals is to join the elite group who have scored 20 test centuries. He once explained to Radio New Zealand commentator Bryan Waddle over dinner at Cambridge, England, why he did not regard himself as one of the game's great players. "He wrote down a list of the batsmen he rated highest," says Waddle. "He justified each one, either because of their average, or the number of centuries they'd scored, or for other reasons. I suggested he must come close to that category himself, but he shook his head and said he hadn't done enough to be put on that level. Martin is very aware of cricket history and naturally would want to be a significant part of it."

He has spoken often of his desire to play until after the 1996 World Cup, and perhaps finish after the tour of the West Indies that year. As he told TVNZ interviewer Ian Fraser: "By 1996 I'll have played test cricket for 15 years – I began early. John Wright played for 16, and he had a long career." Crowe has said on other occasions that he would be able to play at least until 1998.

When TV3 interviewer Brian Edwards asked him about retirement during *Sunday,* in April 1995, Crowe said: "I will decide over the winter. It's certainly something to contemplate. It's not far off; it's just whether I want another year or two."

Despite his assurance at the batting crease, and the confident way he can make statements during an interview, Crowe is surprisingly fragile and insecure. During the 1994/95 season, Crowe spoke with a number of former internationals, including John Wright, Martin Snedden, Jeremy Coney and John Parker, asking their opinions on what he should do. He seemed confused, and so lacking confidence that he even went outside the Crowe family for advice.

It was obviously a time of concern for him.

When he wasn't pondering retirement, Crowe would insist publicly that he was eager to play again, which is rather surprising, because there is nothing as soul-destroying for a top sportsman as a bad injury which will simply not go away. A person can have only so many operations, and make only so many comebacks. As his brother Jeff said at the end of the 1994/95 New Zealand summer: "Martin was absolutely devastated at this other [thigh] injury. He didn't know how serious it was. An injury is always the best way to sink the emotions."

He spoke to Coney and Parker during the test against Sri Lanka at Napier, another match he was forced to sit out. Coney and Parker were emphatic he must spend the winter getting fit and healthy, and only then think about playing cricket again.

As Parker says: "It's pointless Martin going away for a few weeks, partially getting over an injury, then being selected to play while only half-fit. What happens is he breaks down again, and the dramas surrounding him – all the talk – start again."

Coney says the problem is that selectors have always reasoned that Crowe at 70 per cent is still better than any other batsman at 100 per cent, so have chosen him as soon as they could. "It's not the right way to go about it," says Coney. "It's bad for Martin and the team."

Interestingly, both Parker and Coney feel Crowe, should he front up fit and well, must be selected as the New Zealand captain. Coney: "He's the best captain in New Zealand on the field, by a considerable distance. Rutherford has shown weaknesses tactically. Martin's trouble has been the dressing room. He's not a good communicator, as everyone knows. So it's important the set-up is right to take that responsibility away from him. As long as the right coach and manager are in place, Martin should be captain." Apparently Glenn Turner, named in May as the new New Zealand coach, is the "right" coach.

But what about the injuries? After all, Crowe has missed nearly all the past two summers because of injury. By the end of the 1994/95 season, he had missed 12 of 26 test matches over the preceding three seasons, plus more than half the one-day internationals. How could a person with that record be appointed captain. What about continuity?

Parker: "You have to forget about what's gone on, and tell Martin he's starting with a clean slate. He has to go away and get properly fit. Then he has to have a proper fitness test. Not just a few stretches and a rubdown, but a proper, rigorous, searching test. If he comes through all that, then, and only then, you pick him. And if you pick him, you make him captain."

Parker and Coney feel that if Crowe passes the correct sort of fitness test he is not likely to be any more prone to injury than anyone else. And, they say, there's a lot less likelihood of him getting injured if he's captaining New Zealand and enjoying the job.

This is a nice, positive scenario. And it is plausible, too, especially if you remember the good times of the Crowe captaincy, like the World Cup in 1992.

Many others feel Crowe is the man to captain New Zealand, still. Bob Cunis says: "Martin was the best captain we've had for many a year on the field. There was never a question of Martin not understanding the game. What he had to learn was man-management skills and they've improved tremendously."

Don Neely's view: "He is capable of losing a game by going for a win. He is bold enough to wander down the unpalatable realms of declaring in search of victory. That's a marvellous attribute. His frustrations came more to the fore in test cricket where he had bowlers unable to bowl out sides. He was used to seeing players like Richard Hadlee bowling out the opposition. There was a core of good bowlers. Then suddenly Danny Morrison was our most experienced bowler, and Martin was second. That made it very hard for him. But I feel he had and has the ability to be a very fine test captain."

This is putting a sunny, positive spin on it. But during his time at the helm Crowe was often a tortured individual. He complained about the media, suffered a staggering array of injuries and illnesses, and struggled to get alongside some of his players plus coach Geoff Howarth. He tried very hard to impose his views at team selection time, and got extremely testy on the rare occasion when he did not get his own way.

John Morrison says it would be an appalling mistake to go back to Crowe. "From the day he was appointed last time, it all began falling apart. He went round the country promoting the new era and all that stuff. There was lots of psycho-babble, then, out on the paddock, things got worse and worse.

"Over the years Martin has got more neurotic, more intolerant, more self-centred. Sadly, the minute he lost, he was like a five-year-old. He won't play any more. So they say, 'C'mon Billy, you're really good, I want you to bat.' So he bats again. If things went well for Crowey, he was all right, but he couldn't survive the cut and thrust. He had a great deal of difficulty in terms of relationships with guys. There was no deep respect there. If he couldn't do the job properly a few years ago, what possible grounds are there for giving it to him now?"

Morrison suggests that if there is to be a change of captain, then someone from outside should be brought in. "It's been such a rotten time for New Zealand cricket that it needs a totally fresh approach. Glenn Turner pushed for Lee Germon to be captain, and there was a lot of sense in that. Germon has shown he can do the job with Canterbury, and is a good player. If he was captain, then Adam Parore would become a specialist batsman, which would be a good idea. If not Germon, then what about Roger Twose?

He is now eligible to play for New Zealand, and is clearly up to test class. He is mature, and doesn't have any of the baggage of that last disastrous season."

John Bracewell, too, doubts Crowe has the personality to be captain: "He's reasonably dismissive of those of lesser ability. He expects everyone to be as gifted as him. He has matured since he gave up the captaincy. He's had his little taste of glory and, hopefully, should now get on with his life."

Some members of the current New Zealand side are sceptical. One said to me: "I'll be bloody disappointed in him if he becomes captain again because he's got the coach he wants, and then has no more problems with injury. While it would be good to have Hogan back and fit, you'd really have to wonder about his desire and motives over the past couple of seasons. There is a degree of scepticism about that in the New Zealand team."

Speculation aside, it seems unlikely the national selectors will be keen to revert to Crowe as captain, for the simple reason that he is perceived to be too much of an injury risk.

Selection panel convener Ross Dykes says, "I belong to the school of thought which hopes desperately that Martin regains his fitness and is able to play a full part in our programme. He is one of the world's outstanding batsmen and New Zealand cricket is all the richer for having him. I felt very sorry for him during the centenary season. He was desperately keen to play and was almost embarrassed that he was unable to get onto the park."

As a captain? "His fitness has to be taken into consideration, in terms of the appointment of a captain. Martin has been an outstanding New Zealand captain, a brilliant tactician. But one would have to be very, very sure of his ability to play consistently before even considering him as a captain."

Gavin Larsen, one of the more stable, solid members of a rather fragile national team, says there is a great desire in the test line-up to have Crowe back on the field. "I think everyone felt sorry for him. It was a crying shame. The guy was batting on one leg and was still world class. It would be great if he was fit." Larsen has watched the "Crowe drama" unfold over the past decade and is able to offer a detached view. "The first thing I'd say is that under Hogan we had a brilliant time of it in the 1992 World Cup. I don't think he had an equal in terms of captaincy on the park. Tactically and strategically, he is without peer. That was in 1992. Then the dramas came, a fistful of them.

"The next thing, I went to England as vice-captain in 1994 and Martin was one of the senior players. I couldn't question his contribution to the team. I think he interacted really well with the younger guys in the team. Early in the tour some of the younger players were nervous about Hogan, almost intimidated. But right through the tour he bent over backwards to help them.

"Hogan is a lot more relaxed these days. He has definitely changed over the years. About the time of the World Cup he was very intense, but like all of us, he's got a little older and wiser. The battering he has taken in terms of the public and the media has made him realise he has to make an attempt to get on with his teammates.

"Whereas he might have had his problems in the previous group, I can honestly say that in the current New Zealand team I haven't seen any animosity, any anti-Martin Crowe feeling."

Though Larsen says he had his most enjoyable time in the New Zealand team under the Crowe - Warren Lees leadership duo, he is doubtful if Crowe can captain the side again. "There are a couple of factors. Martin isn't particularly strong in the dressing room, so he needs to have a coach who complements him. With Lees, it was perfect. Wally was great in the dressing room, in the team environment. He's not intense. Hogan was good on the skills side and the tactics. So he could be captain if he had the right coach, except that there's also his injury problems. To me that makes it too much of a risk. Overall, I'd say there are too many variables, too many peripheral things going on, for Hogan to captain New Zealand again."

Everyone agrees the next New Zealand tour, to India, will be significant. Crowe wouldn't travel to India in 1994 – he bypassed that segment to go straight to South Africa, and was permitted to do so by New Zealand Cricket on the grounds that he was susceptible to viruses and that he would be fitter if he trained in South Africa.

A few months later Crowe said that it was important exceptions no longer be made for any player. He identified this as one of the problems New Zealand cricket has faced in recent times. If Crowe signifies his availability to tour India, and if he gets through the tour without any of the injury problems which have plagued him over the past few years, perhaps the many sceptics in New Zealand cricket will accept he is back.

What no one wants is for Crowe to continue being the exception to the rule. This is what has made him such a divisive factor lately, and has made a section of the public so cynical. "It will just carry on," says John Morrison. "Martin is such an egotist, he thrives on publicity."

John Graham, Crowe's headmaster at Auckland Grammar, and a former All Black captain, puts it strongly: "The best thing that could happen to Martin would be if Dykes and the other selectors dropped him. They'd do that if they had any balls. New Zealand Cricket should sack him, give him no salary and say they want nothing to do with him until he's really ready to play international cricket again. At the moment, he's the centre attraction even when he's not playing. The team must loathe it. He's milking the publicity. Why did John Kirwan turn to league? It's the same thing; they can't move out of a high profile environment."

The Crowe family, who do not take kindly to criticism, or even any suggestion that they are much less than perfect, will not like what Graham says. Yet of all the people I spoke to while researching this book, no-one was keener than Graham to see Martin happy and enjoying life again. He remembers the lad who was such an outstanding pupil at Auckland Grammar and is sad to see the intense, complicated individual he has developed into. Graham is also a straight-shooter, which is what has helped make him so successful in sport, business and as an educationalist.

Like Graham, others feel sorry for Crowe. John Parker says: "I'd say he's quite lonely. He feels ostracised and that he's not getting the support he requires. What Martin is facing now is the question of whether he can live without cricket. It dawns on you that you have to work for a living. Martin will be asking if he can live without cricket.

"He has earned a lot, and that's great. Where is he going to continue earning that sort of money? The media? You must be joking. Promotional talks? They'll last a year until the next superstar comes along. He has to understand he should play cricket until the last day he can because that's where he will earn money, and that to retire would be the easy way out. Except it's not really the easy way. Look at Andrew Jones: he retired, then he found out he'd only been tired.

"The people advising Martin must explain this to him. Then an environment must be put in place – coach, manager, captain – in which he thrives. If that happens, we'll have Martin for some years yet, and he'll be happy. If not, well, he'll continue down a miserable, lonely path."

What could he do if he retired? He has no tertiary qualifications, and has not worked for any period in any job not related to cricket. In addition, he does not have the attractive image many big businesses look for – it's difficult to imagine Crowe replacing Richard Hadlee as the BNZ cricket ambassador.

What about coaching, or administration? says Peter McDermott, the New Zealand Cricket chairman in the Crowe captaincy years and beyond. "I've never found him particularly difficult to deal with. I like him. He and I have had differences of agreement, but I have a high regard for him. Geniuses have eccentricity. He has his moments. His attitude to the game has been focused and maybe that's been misinterpreted.

"Martin's PR is very good. His visits to schools, his attitude to things like Cricket Awareness Week – we couldn't ask for a better ambassador. I hope he stays in the game as a coach or an administrator when he does stop playing."

Like every other person quoted in this book, I have reproduced what McDermott told me and been careful not to take it out of context. However, in view of their turbulent dealings, especially during the early part of the 1991/92 international season, I was surprised to hear McDermott offer such a glowing account of his dealings with Crowe. Crowe has seemingly erased earlier question marks with his work on the public relations side.

This draws a smile from John Morrison. "Martin is at his best when he's not playing, and he's doing the royal tour, visiting schools, doing interviews. It's all the spotlight, and none of the responsibility."

So discussion about Crowe swirls about still, as it has for some years now. Will he want to play? Will he be fit? Will he want to be captain? Will he like the new coach?

Talking to a sampling of leading lights in New Zealand cricket, I get the feeling there are still many who haven't written off Martin Crowe, who hope he will make peace with his own demons and will play out the remaining years of his career happily and profitably. Richard Hadlee emphasises that Crowe was one of the best captains, tactically, that New Zealand has had. "He might have problems in the dressing room relating to people of lesser ability. Perhaps he'd get frustrated if things were not going well. He has admitted that as a captain in the dressing room his man-management skills left something to be desired. But it's a learning thing. He may have learned enough."

Parker is equally up-beat: "He still has the makings of a fine captain. Life teaches you a lot of things. Earlier, he never understood what it's like not to be as good as him. I think he has learnt about having to mix and be part of a team and is more beside the young players. He would certainly do a better job now than before. I mean, how good can your man-management skills be as a 28-year-old? He is an intelligent guy; he will have learnt from the mistakes he made before."

Perhaps the most perceptive judgment comes from a man well removed from the turmoil which has overcome New Zealand cricket: Peter Roebuck, Crowe's captain at Somerset, and these days an astute and entertaining writer about the game. "Martin is a little intense. He always was and that won't change. He's inclined to judge a man's play by his character. But in the World Cup in 1992 he was extraordinary. New Zealand would never have got that far without him.

"In terms of humanity he's easier with some than others. He's good with people he can work with, but not so good with the knockabout types. If you're a highly intense professional cricketer, a perfectionist, this can be frustrating.

"Martin is probably a bit immature in a way. He is an outstanding tactician and reader of other players. But he captained New Zealand after that period of success when expectations were high. He didn't have the great players. It was a freak of timing, the way New Zealand produced so many good players at one time in the 1980s.

"Should he captain New Zealand again? This is the interesting question. Has he grown and matured from his first experience as a test captain? Is there the support for him in the team? These are the questions the New Zealand selectors, and perhaps Martin himself, must ask."

Like most things about Crowe these days, he enters the 1995/96 season with the cricket community divided about him. It's ironic that it should come to this because, when he was a lad, everything was so clear – he was a brilliant young cricketer, a lovely, approachable, enthusiastic boy and a person who had well-wishers everywhere. Where did it go wrong?

Chapter Two

SCHOOLBOY PRODIGY

JEFF CROWE:

"I believe Martin has developed into a magnificent player because of all the obstacles and challenges put in his way ever since he could walk. He has had a tremendous desire to succeed."

Martin Crowe and his older brother Jeff were always going to be keen sportsmen. They and their sister Debbie grew up in a family where sport was very much a way of life. Their father Dave, born in Blenheim in 1933, had a brief first class career in the mid-1950s, playing a total of three matches for Wellington and Canterbury. He wasn't exactly the Bradman of the 1950s – 55 runs, highest score 19, average 11.00. Nevertheless, he spent a lot of time thinking about and watching cricket. He also read a great deal about the game. While he may not have been in the Dempster-Sutcliffe class, Dave Crowe's teammates describe him as a stylish, correct batsman.

Dave's brother Alex played senior club cricket in Wellington, yet water polo, not cricket, was the first sporting love of their father Jack. Besides his cricket, Dave also became a reasonable squash player and a squash umpire at international level.

Audrey Crowe, Jeff and Martin's mother, is also a keen sports follower. As a youngster in Wellington, she was a promising swimmer and a good tennis player and athlete. After the couple married, her tennis progressed and in 1967 she won an Auckland women's hardcourt title. She played Caro Bowl interclub for several years. She also took up golf and got her handicap down to a very respectable level.

So it was only natural Jeff and Martin would be keen young sportsmen. Of course, there are many thousands of youngsters who run, play tennis or rugby or cricket, or swim or whatever. Very few of them progress to a high standard. It takes more than just enthusiasm to become an international sportsman. Jeff and Martin both became New Zealand captains in our national summer game. Clearly they both possessed natural ability well beyond the norm. In the old "nurture versus nature" debate, both elements played a significant role in their success at cricket.

Jeff, as the older brother of one of New Zealand's greatest ever cricketers, has been rather dwarfed in cricketing achievement – he once likened playing cricket with his brother to having a round of golf with Severiano Ballesteros.

Yet it should not be overlooked that Jeff scored 10,233 runs in first class cricket, including 22 centuries, and averaged a shade under 38 an innings. To put it in perspective, his first class figures are considerably better than those of Bevan Congdon, Barry Sinclair and Graham Dowling. At test level, where he tended to be more inhibited, he struggled, managing just 1601 runs in 39 tests with an average of 26.24. He was noted for his grit and courage more than for high run-scoring in international cricket.

Jeff captained New Zealand in six tests until poor batting form led to him being dropped from the team in 1988.

Besides their cricket, the Crowe brothers have shone at a range of other sports – golf, tennis, squash, soccer, rugby. They have natural timing, are extremely competitive (especially with each other, though less so now than a few years ago) and have good sporting acumen, an asset that is too easily overlooked. As both developed into top batsmen with good techniques, a lot of the credit for giving them a sound grounding in cricket must go to their father.

Having Jeff, who shone at sport from an early age, as an older brother was a huge advantage for Martin. Jeff, four years older, provided a role model and a competitor almost from the time Martin could walk.

There was a mini-sized pool table in Jeff's bedroom when he was a youngster. The boys played countless games of pool, often with the same intensity as a world championship final. Things would sometimes get so heated that as one was about to pot the black, and so win the game, he had to also think about self-preservation. While the black ball was still on its way to the pocket, he would be beating a hasty retreat to the far side of the room.

"When we were kids," Martin told his brother during the *Crowe on Crowe* television programme after the 1992 World Cup, "I used to hate your guts. You were the worst friend I could ever have; you were the most competitive brother. I was always Jeff Crowe's younger brother."

Constantly striving to keep up with a talented brother provided tremendous motivation for Martin, who was forever trying to pull more out of himself. Today, the fruits of that striving are clear. As kids, things probably seemed a lot murkier. For instance, the two of them played a tennis match in Piha during the 1970 school holidays. At stake was the Piha Junior Challenge Shield. Jeff was 12, Martin eight. Young Sampras and Agassi battled it out for more than an hour, watched by quite a crowd, until Jeff won 9-7. Martin wouldn't shake hands.

In the cricket matches they played on the road outside their house or on the lawn, it must have been difficult for Martin to bridge that four-year age gap. Being younger, Martin always had to bowl first. One day Jeff scored a double-century and Martin didn't get a bat.

When Jeff was playing schoolboy cricket, Martin would trail along, and occasionally he was asked to field. Once or twice, when he was hardly any taller than the pads, he was allowed to bat. He never seemed to make much allowance for the fact that he couldn't do as well as Jeff, and it bred in him a terrific urge to succeed.

Jeff: "I believe Martin has developed into a magnificent player because of all the obstacles and challenges put in his way ever since he could walk. He has had a tremendous desire to succeed."

Martin recounts in *The Crowe Style* how he played his first game of cricket at Walker Park, when he was five, a fill-in for Jeff's team: "Of course, I had to bat last, but all the other boys were nine and I was only filling in for an absentee. I got into bat and hit the first ball into the covers. Then I discovered what I hadn't realised when I had waddled out to the wicket. The pads were far too big for me to be able to run in them. I had to stand there and watch the other batsman miss the first straight ball and leave me nought not out."

There was no organised cricket at Titirangi Primary School, where Martin began as a five-year-old. But he tagged along with Jeff to Cornwall Park and was eventually permitted by the coach to play, even though he was short of the normal minimum starting age.

"I wanted to develop my batting, but I was having trouble collecting the first run of my life. I had three ducks in a row, Saturday after Saturday. I came home and demanded coaching from dad every night for the next week, to learn how to hit the ball along the ground and to be able to play forward defensively...

"The next Saturday, after those awful three ducks in a row, James Whineray, son of former All Black captain Wilson, and I came together at the crease when we were struggling, and we added 130. I made 80 and that's when I first felt an appetite for runs."

Though Martin played more softball than cricket at Titirangi Primary School and Glen Eden Intermediate, he played Saturday morning cricket at Cornwall Park, which as far as he was concerned could just as easily have been the Melbourne Cricket Ground during the World Series Cricket finals.

Martin is well-known for the intensity with which he approaches his cricket. Anyone watching him as a kid in short pants wouldn't be surprised. Most youngsters enjoy their game on Saturday, then hardly think about it until the following Saturday, except perhaps for the hour or two of team practice midweek. Martin was not like that. He would go home and contemplate what had gone right and wrong, and work during the week to eradicate any problems. He'd practise fielding, often alone. Though it seems absurd, Martin Crowe as a pre-teenager possibly had a better work ethic at cricket than some of New Zealand's test players have shown over the past season or two.

He thrived on the cricket atmosphere. Duncan Johnstone, a couple of years older and later a teammate in the Auckland Grammar First XI, remembers Martin always with a bat in his hand even then: "He'd tag along with Goose Man – that's what we called Dave. He was always in the background, looking to play a bit of cricket."

When he was nine, Martin made his first tournament team. An accident at practice just before the tournament began – he was apparently injury-prone even back then – resulted in him having four stitches inserted over his eye. So he didn't bat, but he did bowl 10 overs. His figures of 2-1 (nine maidens) make Gavin Larsen seem extravagant.

Success came quickly for Martin. Doubtless he was helped by the fact that he was bigger than many of his mates. Those few extra centimetres of height can make all the difference at that age. But it was more than that.

He had a tremendous natural aptitude for cricket. He could bowl and field well and, from very early, he was making big scores. How many kids in short pants would even dream of scoring 151 not out, as he did one day at Papatoetoe? By this time Jeff was in the New Zealand Secondary Schools team touring Australia, so the incentive was always there for Martin.

Besides playing and practising the game, he read a good deal of cricket history, working his way through many of his father's books, including *Wisden*. He is one of the few New Zealand cricketers today with more than even a passing acquaintance with the deeds of former test stars. Later, when he was in the test team, he and Martin Snedden, another student of cricket's history, used to set each other cricket "exams".

When he was 11, Martin came to the attention of Murray Deaker, then First XI coach at Auckland Grammar and a premier cricketer. "I'd heard about this little kid Martin Crowe by then," Deaker recalls. "A lot of us had. I was coaching Jeff at Auckland Grammar and everyone was talking about how Jeff would eventually play for New Zealand. Jeff was outstanding. I think he made a fifty in his first big game for Auckland Grammar. But other people would tell me I was only seeing the second best; wait until I saw Martin. I was very loyal to Jeff and took a bit of persuading.

"I remember the day I first saw Martin batting. I was still playing premier for University and we were playing in a knockout tournament. I was having a few beers inside the Cornwall Park pavilion and the kids were outside playing cricket. Now, at that time I knew a chap named Faulkner Bush pretty well. He was the number one barracker at Eden Park; the rudest man I ever met! He used to hold court at the Carlton Club Hotel at 3.15 each working day and often I'd get along there from Auckland Grammar and talk sport with him. He was a brilliant barracker, very outspoken and never wrong, according to him!

"Well, Bushy burst into the pavilion and said, 'Deaker, come out here and you will see the greatest batsman New Zealand has ever produced.' I did go out, and that's when I saw Martin.

"I'd seen a lot of kids and had played against Turner. I was in the sixth form when Glenn Turner was in the third form. I knew that this time Bushy really was telling the truth. This kid had shots like kids never have. He had power and he was a big kid, bloody big. But he had much more than just size. He had more talent than anyone I've seen in my life.

"Glenn stood out by the length of the straight. We played him in the King's High v Otago Boys match when he was just a third-former. He batted in sandshoes and we gave him hell. He was unruffled, but couldn't hit the ball off the square. Glenn played like a journeyman; Martin played like an aristocrat. He had that private school look. He looked like Peter May when he drove – very upright. And even then he knew he was good.

"After that I never had any doubts about Martin. In a sense you could say I found Danny Morrison. I discovered him and coached him from the third form. But it wasn't until his last year at school that I thought he could play for New Zealand. With Martin you knew the moment you saw him. He was in the First XI by the end of his third form year at Auckland Grammar, which is exceptional."

In 1974 Martin made the Auckland junior reps. He had a useful tournament and was named 12th man for the North Island team. The following season, he captained the reps at the tournament in Gisborne, where he followed two ducks with a century. He finished as one of the outstanding players of the tournament.

He had some large footsteps to follow when he started at Auckland Grammar in 1976 – brother Jeff was First XI captain and a school hero. But Martin's talent was undeniable; hence his rapid elevation into the First XI, coached then by Graham Henry, these days better known as coach of the Auckland rugby team.

From then, it was a story of almost continual success for Martin in school and age rep cricket. (Jeff, by the late 1970s, had decided to live in Adelaide, at least temporarily, and was playing Sheffield Shield cricket alongside famous players like Ian Chappell, David Hookes and Ashley Mallett.)

By the age of 15, Martin was representing Auckland at under-23 level, and he spent so many years in the province's Brabin side he could have qualified for life membership. By the end of 1977, aged 15, he had been picked for the national Brabin side. (John Bracewell, a future sparring partner of Crowe's, opened the batting for the team.) Strangely, he missed selection for the New Zealand Brabin team the next season, despite a solid national tourament. It was to be a rare selection reverse in the career of Martin Davidson Crowe.

Very quickly, word spread about his ability. Not only was he making huge scores, but he batted beautifully, already exhibiting the exemplary footwork and sound technique that have stood him in such good stead since.

Like Jeff, Martin was three times selected for the New Zealand

The chubby chap on the left is Martin, aged three. Pictured alongside him are his cousin Terry and Sean and Kristen Neely, two children of cricket selector Don Neely and his wife Paddianne. Dave Crowe and Paddianne Neely are cousins.

The 1980 Auckland Grammar First XI. Martin Crowe is the captain. On his left is Grant Fox. In the back row, third from left, is Mark Greatbatch.

Crowe and Auckland captain John Reid plotting and planning.

New Zealand skipper Geoff Howarth – "He treated me abominably," says Crowe.

In his younger days, before back problems hampered him, Crowe was a nippy, and sometimes hostile, pace bowler.

John Wiltshire – "He showed he was pretty well ready for the test team in that first season."

Greg Chappell – "He was picked too soon."

New Zealand Woman's Weekly

Proud parents – Dave and Audrey Crowe

New Zealand Woman's Weekly

Crowe at his former home in Eastbourne. Behind him is the Wayne Young painting he called "Tall Poppies".

Jeremy Coney and Crowe share a celebratory champagne after the series win over Australia at Perth in 1985.

Best man at brother Jeff's wedding.

J.G. Blackwell

A singular reverse in the career of Martin Davidson Crowe. He stands on Eden Park No. 2 and hears the New Zealand team for the 1983 tour of Australia named. Brother Jeff has been called in to replace him.

J.G. Blackwell

Crowe sweeps during his maiden test century, against England at the Basin Reserve in 1984. Jeremy Coney, who also scored his first test century, and helped save the test, looks on in approval.

Crowe acknowledges the applause after reaching his century at Guyana in 1985.

A magnificent victory at Brisbane in 1986. From left: Smith, Border (the Australian captain), Hadlee, Snedden, Wright, Edgar, Coney, Chatfield, Martin Crowe, Brown, Jeff Crowe.

Running repairs during his gritty test century at Christchurch in 1986.

Secondary Schools side. After undistinguished batting efforts in 1978 and 1979 (although he topped the New Zealand bowling averages at the Kookaburra Shield Australasian tournament the second time), he came right in 1980. On the full tour of Australia, he scored 649 runs at 81 an innings. He captained New Zealand that last year and was named Player of the Tournament, as his brother Jeff had been a few years earlier.

While climbing to the top of the schoolboy ranks, Martin made progress elsewhere as well. He played senior club cricket and represented Auckland in the Shell Trophy while still at school, and made the national Brabin and Rothmans sides as if by right of birth. Most astoundingly, in 1978, when he was just 15, he accompanied the Auckland team to Christchurch for the Shell Trophy final.

"There I was," he recalled years later, "plucked from nowhere and in with Burgess, Vivian, McIntyre, Stott, Cushen and other old campaigners. I was 12th man, but I'd have been playing if someone had been injured.

"I recall Graham Vivian giving me a hard time in Christchurch over my being late with the drinks. I was intimidated by the Canterbury players, and I was sitting with them while Auckland fielded. The drinks were taken five minutes earlier than scheduled, and I wasn't ready. Vivian wasn't terribly pleased about that.

"The most memorable piece of cricket from that match was Vivian's second innings. He was there 100 minutes and scored just one run. Richard Hadlee pummelled him, but he stayed put and saved the game, so Auckland won the Shell Trophy."

Vivian, himself once touted as a cricketing prodigy (he was taken to India, Pakistan and England in John Reid's 1965 team when he had just turned 19 and had never played a first class match), was impressed with what he saw of Crowe, but wary. "I always thought he was very promising, but a lot of kids are promising at 15 or 16 and don't go on. He came from a pretty solid cricket family with his parents and older brother, and even at 15 he was a pretty mature cricketer. We took him down there for experience, but would have been relaxed about playing him if someone had been injured. We didn't treat him with kid gloves, and he fitted in no problem."

At Auckland Grammar, Crowe was a colossus. Many of New Zealand's future test players are outstanding at school level. But the only one who really compared with Crowe was John Reid, the elder, who was already as physically mature as a man while still at Hutt Valley High School in the 1940s and batted like the test player he became just a year or two later.

Academically, says John Graham, Martin was above average: "He would have bolted in for a university degree. He had a good schoolwork ethic, especially in his earlier years. He was in the top stream, outside the double language (Latin and French) group."

In his third form year at Auckland Grammar he was in Form 3C1, the third of nine third-form classes. He finished fifth in class, three places behind a short, skinny, fair-haired lad named Grant Fox, who was to become quite a handy rugby player and a very good friend of Crowe. Martin won the Japanese prize for his class, and Deaker presented him with the third form cricket trophy – he captained the 5A team and had a top score of 58 and best bowling of 4-15, including a hat-trick. Crowe and Fox also featured in the school junior tennis champs. In the singles, future Davis Cup player Bruce Derlin beat Fox in a quarter-final 6-0, 6-0. In the semis he dealt with Crowe 6-1, 6-0 and in the final he also won without conceding a game. Fox and Crowe reached the semis of the junior doubles.

In the fourth form Martin was in 4C1, the third of 11 classes. But he slipped to 22nd in class (Fox was again second). Of course, by then Crowe was in the First XI and was presented with the Bruce Boaden Cup for the most improved player in the side. Though the youngest player in the First XI, he quickly established himself with a top score of 70 and best bowling of 5-7 and 5-31. In the big game, against Christchurch Boys', he scored 22 and 32.

He was moved down to 5D in his fifth form year, the sixth of 11 classes. He finished fourth in class, won the history certificate and got through School Certificate comfortably enough, passing in five subjects. His cricket raced ahead. Even Graham's rather clinical report in the front of the annual Grammar book notes: "The team [First XI] beat Christchurch Boys' High School by an innings in this highly competitive annual game which was dominated by a great innings of 192 by M. D. Crowe." The previous week he had scored 104. That year Crowe also won the Grahame Thorne Cup for the most meritorious batting in the First XI, the Jenner Scott award for the best batting average in the First XI, the A. M. Haresnape bat for the most meritorious innings in any grade, and the Douglas Cup for the most outstanding performance in any sport. He also played soccer to a high standard, being a centre half in the school under-16 A team. Though only a fifth-former, he was already a big name at school.

Graham recalls: "Martin was extremely ambitious at school, and he was a perfectionist. It showed up in his schoolwork and his appearance.

His grooming was immaculate. He looked as fashionable as a schoolboy could look in an Auckland Grammar uniform. Crowey always looked good."

In his sixth form year Martin gained University Entrance in five subjects, and was one of seven sixth-formers accorded the privilege of being named prefects. By now he was in 6C, the sixth of 11 classes. Graham's report noted: "M. D. Crowe has again represented New Zealand at secondary schools level, this time as captain. In the third term this remarkable young cricketer on three successive Saturdays scored 177 runs, took seven wickets for 67 runs and then scored 247 runs. The last score, we believe, was the first double century hit by a First XI cricketer in the history of the school." He scooped most of the cricket prizes, including the Woolley Cup for the best all-round performance in the First XI, the Thorne Cup and the Douglas Cup. He captained the First XI in 1979 and among his teammates were Fox and a roundish young wicketkeeper/batsman named Mark Greatbatch. Crowe turned from soccer to rugby for his sixth form year and played outstandingly on the wing for the 2A team, earmarking himself for First XV honours the following year. "He added class whenever he played," the school Chronicle recorded. Crowe was also a member of the school squash team.

By 1980, when he finished 14th of 22 in his seventh form class, his schoolwork had slipped considerably and he failed his bursary exams. In fact, this tailing off in academic achievement probably cost him the head prefect position which he cherished – he was named associate head prefect instead. Graham: "Martin saw himself as a natural leader. He once said to me he felt he would have made a very good head prefect, which he would have. Halfway through the year he asked me why he hadn't been made head boy. I felt the head boy had to be an outstanding academic – the school stood for that. David Morris was made head boy. He was a good musician, was involved in athletics, was captain of the Second XV, and was a good scholar. With Marty being a role model in other areas, they were a perfect duo. They've since become good mates."

Crowe's cricket, which absorbed so much of his time, improved further – he again won the Woolley Cup, while Greatbatch took the awards for the most improved and most meritorious batting in the First XI – and he also played in the First XV, on the right wing,where he scored a record number of tries.

Auckland Grammar had some big sporting names in those days – it is now referred to, not really in jest, as the Golden Age of Auckland

Grammar – including the Whettons, Fox, Nicky Allen, Gary Henley-Smith and Bruce Derlin, all of whom went on to play sport for their country. But none stood out as Crowe did.

Finlay Macdonald, a year ahead of Crowe, recalls school assembly being "a regular laugh" when John Graham read out the First XI results. "It was always Martin. Either he had scored a century or a fifty, or he had taken a packet of wickets."

Crowe was a giant in performance and large, too, in physical stature. By his mid-college years he was nearly 6ft tall, and he was one of the biggest names in the school because he was getting so much publicity for his cricketing exploits with various Auckland teams. Auckland Grammar played in the 2A grade of Auckland senior cricket, one level down from senior. So the school First XI was being fed a diet of adult cricket (when not engaged in the traditional inter-school annual fixtures). Most of their opposition had played senior cricket at one time or another.

Yet Crowe hardly faltered. The three consecutive Saturdays Graham referred to in his report were obviously exceptional, but James Harding, who was a year behind Crowe and spent three years in the First XI "as an all-rounder of modest ability", says Crowe dominated the show, through his personality and his deeds. "He very much epitomised the cliche 'a man among boys'. By the time Martin was in the sixth form, he was very mature. He seemed to have worked out what he wanted to do. He set goals at a time when setting goals wasn't very fashionable. I was a sportsman, so I thought he just about walked on water at school."

Crowe and Fox were good friends and together dominated the two major sports. "It was taken for granted that Martin would be a test player pretty soon," says Harding. "Not many people did the sort of things he did, like playing for Auckland while still at school. It was much the same with Foxy at rugby. He was obviously going to be an All Black and had similar stature in the school, though there were a number of very good rugby players in the First XV in those years."

So good was Crowe, in fact, that he advanced beyond most of the typical schoolboy jealousy that surrounds an outstanding player. Harding: "He was so far ahead that no-one thought they were in the same league as him, so any element of competition was removed. There was really just admiration for him. It was great having him in the team. Players like me would be involved in partnerships of, say, 130 and we'd make about 15 of them. Mind you, he was pretty keen on keeping the strike!"

As a captain, says Harding, Crowe made a huge impact: "He'd played under-23 cricket for Auckland for so long, and had mixed with very good cricketers. He had experience beyond the normal years. I suppose having a brother like Jeff helped him too. His team talks were superb. It was a different approach to what we were used to. His words obviously came from the various Auckland and invitation teams he'd been in, so it was on a different level, a bit deeper. A lot of other schoolboys wouldn't have had the benefit of that sort of discussion. His team talks were more along the lines of 'let's work out what we want to do each session' and breaking the game down into bits. There wasn't much of the 'let's do it for the school' stuff. He was analytical. On the field, he always seemed to know what to do. Field placings always seemed logical and well-organised. Even today, the people who criticise his captaincy don't do so for his technical ability or knowledge of the game.

"It's strange he has had problems relating to people. Back then we were young and keen and wanted to do it for the school. I can remember a couple of public sessions where he did his scone a bit, but it was mainly at himself, if he hadn't played well, or if it was a terrible wicket. But you never saw the complex side that has emerged since. Occasionally he'd give a couple of guys stick for not trying, or not using their brains – that was unacceptable.

"But I always found him very encouraging. If you missed out, he'd let you know what you'd done wrong, but then he'd tell you to put it behind you. He didn't dwell on it. He'd say, 'Let's take guard again,' and move on. It was that maturity coming from mixing with older cricketers.

"I've heard people say over the past few years that Martin's a bit up and down, either talking to you or not. But I've always found him pretty genuine."

John Graham recalls Martin as "an outstanding, quite remarkable skipper at school. He would seize the chance. He was inspiring and, looking at him, you felt he was tailor-made to captain New Zealand one day". Graham recounts the time Grammar were playing their needle game of the season against King's High. "Peter Neutze was bowling spinners. He later represented Auckland, but this day he wasn't bowling all that well. King's High were closing in on their target. Some of us were wondering why Martin kept Neutze on. He could have brought back the quicker bowlers and played for a draw. But Martin persevered with Neutze and finally he got a vital wicket.

"Then Martin whipped on a fast bowler but, after one over, he put Neutze back on. Slowly Neutze worked his way through their order, but it was very close. We won by about 10 runs in the end. I remember Martin saying to me later, 'Never in doubt, sir. Always under control!'

"That was a very impressive piece of captaincy for a youngster, considering it was our big game of the year. He was prepared to risk a defeat to go for victory, when most people would have been content to escape with a draw. In those days Martin was a bubbly, buoyant, positive captain who led from the front."

Though Fox never excelled at cricket as he did at rugby, he was a regular member of the First XI. He bowled medium-pacers and batted usefully. He says he has vivid and happy memories of his schooldays with Crowe: "Most people who played with him at school realised it wouldn't be long before he was playing test cricket. But he was good at all sport – tennis, rugby, soccer, squash."

Crowe had a huge influence in those early years on Greatbatch, who is a year younger. It is amazing how Greatbatch has followed the Martin Crowe royal line... Auckland Grammar, Auckland, Central Districts, Somerset, New Zealand. Greatbatch looked up to Crowe at school and used to make friends smile when he told them he was trying to match Crowe as a cricketer. "My reasoning," says Greatbatch, "was that if I only got somewhere near, that wouldn't be bad. Martin and I talked about cricket for hours and hours. I've learnt a lot from watching and talking to him, and I think he's learnt a fair bit from me too."

They joke now that Crowe's main role at Auckland Grammar in 1980 – not forgetting that by then he was in the Auckland Shell team – was school groundsman. Fox: "Marty and I enjoyed talking to John Graham in his office, mainly because we weren't in class. John was very good to talk to. But Marty spent much of his time out there preparing the pitch – he was really a professional curator. Except that he couldn't back a tractor with a roller on it, and I had to do it. I was brought up on a farm."

By his seventh form year, Crowe was playing senior cricket for Cornwall. He played for Auckland Grammar in the big inter-college matches against King's, Palmerston North Boys' and Christchurch Boys'. The school had a policy of giving a player a pair of batting gloves when he scored a century, but Crowe had forced a rethink well before he departed. "He made it standard that he got a bat," recalls Harding. "He'd gone through all the other gear – pads, thigh pads etc. After that we all got a bat too."

As well as his superlative batting, Crowe was an often hostile bowler, a big fellow who could be decidedly nippy and had a useful bouncer. On one occasion, just before Auckland were to play the West Indies in 1980, Crowe and a young Auckland batsman named Peter Webb (soon to represent New Zealand) turned up at the nets at Auckland Grammar. It was decided Crowe would bowl off 18 metres. However, after a few deliveries, Webb confessed Crowe was simply too quick and asked him to go back a couple of metres.

Though he had relatively little experience of rugby, Crowe made the First XV in 1980. Normally there might have been a few murmurings initially when Crowe, who had more soccer than rugby in his Auckland Grammar background, made the side. After all, this wasn't just any old college First XV, but a team which a lot of players were striving to make. However, in typical Crowe fashion, any resentment about his elevation was not allowed to surface when he began scoring vast numbers of tries. Doubtless having Crowe as his surname helped him make the First XV, yet such was his stature and sporting ability that it was taken for granted he could do the job.

Fox reckons that if Crowe had persevered with rugby, he would have become a top player in any company. "He was big, fast, read the game swiftly and had the try-scoring instinct. He scored three in a match against St Paul's; there were qualities there of a game-breaker." Interestingly, not everyone agrees with this assessment. Though he was very fast, especially off the mark, with his quick, short steps, some felt Crowe was not a good defender and was reluctant to involve himself in the physical side, which might have told against him at a higher level.

During his seventh form year, Crowe teamed with Fox again in the school tennis doubles championship. They performed above themselves to lose the final by the narrow margin of 7-5, 7-5 to future professionals Mark and Greg Long. Crowe was awarded the school's prized Torch of Tradition in 1980.

For Crowe, though, rugby, tennis and everything else was little more than a diversion. A thigh injury while representing Auckland Grammar in the Pan Pacific Trophy tournament in Hong Kong and a further injury later in the season served as a reminder that he should focus on his cricket.

Chapter Three

FIRST CLASS CRICKET AT 17

JOHN WILTSHIRE:
"It was obvious then he was destined to be a New Zealand player."

Ces Dacre is still the youngest player in New Zealand first class cricket history. He was just 15 years, 224 days when he turned up at Eden Park with his cricket boots and borrowed long whites wrapped in a paper parcel, having learnt of his selection for Auckland against Wellington in a newspaper the previous day. That was on Boxing Day, 1914. Since then many players have made their first class debuts at the age of 17 and a few even at 16.

But it's getting rarer. Crowe was 17 years, 119 days old when he was bustled into the Auckland team to play Canterbury at Eden Park in the Shell Trophy match beginning on January 19, 1980. Since then only two New Zealand players, Ken Rutherford and Matthew Bell, have entered the first class scene younger, and then not by much. Rutherford was a week younger when he made his debut for Otago a couple of seasons later, and Bell was 12 days past his 17th birthday when he turned out for Northern Districts against the New Zealand Academy XI in February 1994.

Crowe was indeed rushed into the Auckland team for the Shell Trophy match against Canterbury. He'd been in Australia for a couple of weeks, captaining the New Zealand Secondary Schools team, which also included future test players Trevor Franklin and Rod Latham. Crowe was undoubtedly the star of the side. His 649 runs at 81.13 included scores of 92 not out, 78, 58 not out, 142, 80 and 138. In addition to 17 catches he took nine wickets at an average of 21.

The tournament, in which New Zealand placed third, did not finish until January 10. He had not been back a week when he was facing a Canterbury attack in which Dayle Hadlee was the big name bowler. Crowe batted at No 6, part of a revamped Auckland batting line-up in which Phil Horne, Rex Hooton and Austin Parsons were missing from the previous match.

It was a dream debut for the 17-year-old. Cran Bull won the toss for Canterbury and put Auckland in. Dayle Hadlee ripped through the early Auckland batting and, when Crowe arrived at the crease to launch a famous career, Auckland were teetering at 80-4. He and Auckland captain John Wiltshire then added 88 at faster than a run a minute. Crowe batted 93 minutes and hit seven boundaries in his handsome 51 before having his leg bail removed by Vaughan Brown.

Any thoughts that perhaps this first class lark wasn't so difficult after all were dispelled the following week at Tauranga when Crowe became a real cricketer by registering a duck against Northern Districts. He scored a statistically insignificant 17 in the second innings, but his obduracy, during an innings of 75 minutes, helped Auckland to hold on for a draw which had seemed improbable at one point.

That was the end of the Shell Trophy, but there was a lot more cricket for Crowe that season. The world champion West Indies team arrived in early February and opened what became one of the most torrid, controversial tours in cricket history with a one-dayer against Auckland.

Auckland put up a meek performance, replying to the visitors' 196-9 with 137. Crowe was hustled out first ball by off-spinner Derek Parry. "I had scarcely marked my guard when he came in from two yards and slipped it through me before I had time to get my bat up and down!" he later wrote. "It was a lesson for me. Step back if you're not ready."

Despite this setback, Crowe's ability had attracted the attention of national selection panel convener Frank Cameron. "I could see he was an exceptional young cricketer from very early on," says Cameron. "But there is no great credit in that; it was plain for all to see. I had him in the New Zealand dressing room as a reserve fieldsman while he was still at school, to give him a taste of the atmosphere.

"And in 1980 I put him in the Young New Zealand team which had a couple of matches and then met Derrick Robins' XI. Smithy [Ian Smith], Martin Snedden, Andrew Jones and several other promising lads got a run in that side too.

"We tried out Martin as an opener in the big match, against the Robins XI. He struggled… well, perhaps that's not the word. He had to work hard. He got a 40-odd, but he didn't look as if he was comfortable."

The Young New Zealand team, captained by Matthew Toynbee, opened with a match against Central Districts at Wanganui, but Crowe, the youngest member of the side by quite a distance, stood down. He came in for the game against Auckland and made 15 and bowled 11 surprisingly hostile overs.

Against the Robins XI which included future test players such as Bill Athey, Dipak Patel, Christopher Cowdrey, Tony Pigott and Nick Cook, he fought hard for 47 in just over two hours. As he also took two wickets, it was a useful all-round performance in that company. Ian Smith says that, for such a young player, Crowe had handled himself well. "He didn't have a great tour, but his class was obvious. The signs were there. You just knew that at some point he would be in the New Zealand team next to you, if you could get there."

Crowe finished the season with first class figures of 138 runs at 23 an innings.

Though he'd been offered the opportunity to take up a Young Cricketer to Lord's scholarship, Crowe elected to return to Auckland Grammar for a seventh form year in 1980. Clearly sport was the big lure in his seventh form year.

When the cricket season rolled round in October, Crowe, already an established member of the Auckland Shell team, chose to play senior club cricket for Cornwall, and started off staggeringly well. After five innings, which included two centuries, he was averaging a Bradmanesque 340.

He began the 1980/81 first class season with a duck against Canterbury, and by the end of Auckland's fourth match his highest score was just 34. But he came right against Northern Districts at Hamilton, when he scored a pleasant 75 in 165 minutes and added a record 195 runs for the fourth wicket with John Reid, who went on to 173. An unbeaten half-century against Wellington and 81 against Otago lifted his season's haul to 303 runs at 33.66 – good figures for an 18-year-old who'd just left school.

This was John Wiltshire's last season as Auckland skipper and he very much enjoyed having the young Crowe in his side. "Martin and Trevor Franklin were the two young guns, so to speak," says Wiltshire. "We developed a good rapport. We interspersed these two youngsters with Austin Parsons, John Reid, Peter Webb and myself, players who had more experience. It all worked well. I seemed to develop a special affinity with Martin. We got on well and talked a lot about tactics. Martin will surprise you the way he can take in a lot of information and sift through it for what he wants.

"In that first full season, we said to him there was no need for him to get out slogging after quick runs. We wanted him to just go out there quietly and make his runs. But he was in great nick and he made crucial runs. Even then he had a polished style and he was a very good runner between the wickets. He never needed to slog. If he just played his own game, he scored quickly enough. He really was a class player. We weren't used to seeing a 17- or 18-year-old bat like that."

Wiltshire says it was a good time to get into the Auckland team. "Sometimes a team will be dominated by players who know each other from one school or one club. But that year we had a good cross-section from various schools, clubs and teams. So while we had a senior cabinet, as you might say, making decisions, everyone had real input. We had ploys for making sure the young fellows felt at home, getting them rooming with older players, or I'd breakfast with Martin and Peter Webb before we batted together and we'd talk about what we might do.

"We included Martin and Trevor in the team discussions by asking them about the young guys in the opposition. We'd say they knew them from age tournaments and that their advice would be helpful. It gave Martin and Trevor a particular responsibility and made them think more about what was going on."

The innings Wiltshire recalls best was the one at the end of the season against Otago. "We were in the cactus and needed a big innings from him. They had Boock and a steady seam attack and the ball was moving about. But he batted beautifully. He had a maturity beyond his years. It was obvious then he was destined to be a New Zealand player. I felt as his first first class captain that really my job was simply to focus and hone his skills. With Martin it wasn't a matter of if, but when and how quickly. And he showed he was pretty well ready for the test team in that first season."

Wiltshire had followed Crowe's progress up the ladder since he was a schoolboy. "I was a King's boy and one of the big matches was King's against Auckland Grammar, so I kept an eye on the big school matches. I'd seen quite a lot of Martin. One day we were playing a senior club match and on the next wicket he made 240-odd. There he was, just a schoolkid. Some of his shots were unbelievable. The consistency and selection of shot production made him a cut above his contemporaries. We became so engrossed in that innings, we rather drifted away from our own game!

"Martin was a good kid. Even when he was 16 or 17 he would line up the kids and sign autographs. He was a good thinker. I felt even then he would become an outstanding captain. There was never any doubt about that. He'd captained a lot of teams as a youngster because at that level the best player tends to be the captain."

Off the field, Crowe was facing a crucial point in his life. John Graham, whom he admired and respected, advised him to go to university, figuring that not only would Crowe improve his education, but that the university lifestyle would help him. Crowe, though, was devoted to cricket and when the offer to go to Lord's as Young Cricketer of the Year was repeated, he accepted with alacrity. He had toyed with the idea of doing a chiropractor's course in Melbourne, but once the offer from Lord's came through, that was that.

In the cricket sense, it was probably the correct decision. But perhaps if Crowe had spent those early years without such an intense focus on cricket, he may have developed into something other than the complex, tortured personality he is today.

Of course, for a youngster who had read about Lord's, practised imaginary commentaries there, dreamed of scoring a century there, it was the opportunity of a lifetime. He mentioned many times how proud he was when he was able to write "professional cricketer" under the heading "Occupation" on his passport application.

The Lord's head coach was Don Wilson, who proved an important influence during 1981. Not only did Wilson, a left-arm spinner, play six tests for England during an era when the test team could call on the likes of Laker, Lock, Wardle, Allen, Titmus and Illingworth, but he made 392 appearances for Yorkshire, taking more than 1100 wickets, from 1957 to '74. He was an experienced, canny, approachable cricketer, and he immediately saw that Crowe was a special talent.

Wilson tutored Crowe at Lord's, emphasising how important it was to develop the cricket professional attitude towards his game. And Wilson also arranged for Crowe to play for Bradford in the Yorkshire league. Crowe's batting leapt ahead as he learnt how to pace an innings, bat the full 50 overs, take advantage of a weak bowler. During his year in England, Crowe played 36 matches and scored 2013 runs at 69.50. He hit five hundreds and 15 fifties. With 25 wickets and 27 catches, he proved himself a potentially brilliant all-round cricketer.

His most memorable match that season was for Young MCC against MCC at Lord's. After taking 4-21, he struck a rich vein when his side batted and smashed his way towards a century. The match reached an exciting climax so that, with one ball remaining, Crowe was 97 not out and Young MCC needed four to win. The leg side was packed with fieldsmen, and Crowe smashed the last delivery over extra cover for six to raise his century and win the match.

Scoring a century at Lord's was, naturally, a cherished ambition. Like most of Crowe's cricket goals, he faced up to the challenge and conquered it. It's interesting that during his career he scored a century at Lord's against Middlesex in 1983, and test centuries at cricket's headquarters in 1986 and '94.

He returned to New Zealand at the end of the English season, just about to turn 19. Even given the experience he'd gained in England, few would have imagined his test debut would be so near at hand.

Chapter Four

TESTING TIMES

MARTIN CROWE:
> *"The plain fact was that I was 19 years old and out of my depth, and I knew it..."*

"Let's face it," says Greg Chappell, "he was picked too soon. He was like a fish out of water." Chappell is referring to Martin Crowe's selection in his first test series, against the powerful 1981/82 Australian team. He ended that season with 20 runs in the three tests, and a paltry average of just 5.00. Snedden, Hadlee, Cairns and Troup all placed above him. It was no different in the one-day internationals where his two innings produced just 10 runs.

"It was a big ask and no doubt it did cause him some problems for a year or so in his career," says Chappell.

"Possibly against a less potent attack it might have been easier. I suppose it was an indication of how good a player he was that people thought he might handle it. But they were asking a bit too much of him, against that attack. It was too soon for that responsibility, though he was obviously talented."

Just a couple of months earlier you would have got long odds against 19-year-old Crowe donning the black cap against the Aussies. Didn't New Zealand, after all, have such fine batsmen as Edgar, Wright, Howarth, Reid, Morrison and Coney available? Hadn't Crowe played a mere 11 matches for 441 runs at an average of 29.40? Weren't New Zealand due to meet a potent Australian team spearheaded by the formidable fast bowling duo of Thomson and Lillee?

The Australian visit that season was a big one for New Zealand cricket. Wicketkeeper Rod Marsh later wrote that the tour of New Zealand, after a long domestic season, "sounded about as attractive to us as Ethiopia". At the time, though, all New Zealanders knew was that the Aussies, who'd bowled underarm to beat New Zealand the season before, were touring, and that their side included the architect of that underarm fiasco, Greg Chappell, as well as stars like Lillee, Thomson, Marsh, Border, Alderman and Hughes. It was not the sort of environment in which to blood a youngster, even if he was clearly something a bit special.

But Crowe seemed to have advanced two years during the off- season. In his first big outing of the summer he opened for the North Island in a one-day fixture against the South Island at Alexandra. He and his Auckland teammate Trevor Franklin had a picnic, putting on 174 for the first wicket before Crowe was dismissed for 94 in the 37th over.

That set him up for a good Shell Trophy season. In the first three-day match, he scored 36 against Central Districts, handling David O'Sullivan's curly left-arm spinners with surprising comfort. Then he hammered 72, including a six and six 4s, against Otago, adding 134 with John Reid in under two hours. There were a few whispers about him being a possible long-shot test selection, but they became fairly muted after he had two failures against Canterbury.

Crowe bounced back with a fine double at Eden Park in mid-January. Against a useful Northern Districts attack, he battled 244 minutes for 99 before he was caught by John Parker off medium-pacer Stu Gillespie. In the second innings, he played a different sort of innings as Auckland captain Reid chased quick runs before declaring, smashing 60 in 87 minutes. After another double failure, against Wellington, he scored usefully against Canterbury, his 25 and 34 all the more commendable because the formidable Richard Hadlee was in the opposition.

It all came together for Crowe on January 31, 1982, when he scored a majestic 150 against Central at New Plymouth. It was his maiden first class century, and he could not have picked a more picturesque ground on which to achieve the feat. Crowe peppered Pukekura Park with boundaries, hammering five 6s and 18 4s in a run-a-minute display of cultured strokemaking combined with sometimes brutal power.

The impressive century forced his inclusion in the New Zealand team to play The Rest at the Basin Reserve the following week. Suddenly, he had leapfrogged over players like Franklin, Edwards, Blair and Wiltshire, who were all in The Rest lineup. The New Zealand side won with embarrassing ease, scoring 422 and dismissing The Rest for 80 and 182. Crowe batted at No 6 and chipped in with 37. Perhaps just as impressive was a second innings bowling stint of 15 overs for 19 runs. He bowled brisk medium-pacers and was capable of a good quicker one and a nasty bouncer.

So he was pulled into the New Zealand team, initially for the three one-day internationals, and then for the full test series. Selection panel convener Frank Cameron says it was a line-ball decision. "I had to think about whether to put him in then or leave him for the next series. He was a little bit inexperienced and had a slight lack of confidence at that level, as you would expect of a young player. But I felt he was ready, and he was certainly better than the next fellow who would have been picked."

For Crowe, it was the start of a nightmare. When I spoke to him about it 10 years later, he still had vivid and rather bitter memories.

"I didn't bat in the first one-dayer in Auckland, though I got three catches and a couple of wickets. In the second one, in Dunedin, we had to bat first on a real green top. John Reid pulled out 10 minutes before the game and Geoff Howarth put me in at No 3 for some reason. I don't know why. I'd been batting at 5 or 6 until then. I struggled and failed. They kept me at No 3 for the next one-dayer at the Basin. John Wright was out first ball and I got only a few. I was like a lamb to the slaughter.

"I'd had two failures before the test series began. I didn't get a bit of encouragement. The players tended to protect their own position in those days. Then Thommo had a crack at me in the first test. By then I didn't know how I was going to score a run, and I didn't."

In the test series, it should be recorded, Crowe batted at No 6 in all three tests. He did have a horrible time of it in his test debut, at the Basin Reserve. The wicket was green and moist and Thomson and Lillee worked up frightening pace. A bouncer from Thomson dislodged Crowe's helmet and it was clear from that point that he wasn't happy or confident at the wicket. He seemed almost relieved when he was run out for nine.

Crowe says he's always been mindful of those traumatic times: "I've always felt that individuals have to get themselves right, but not to the extent where they feel threatened."

Just as sour about Martin's first test series is his father, Dave, who wrote in the English *Cricketer* magazine: "He had to learn how to play test cricket in the arena, for he was mustered far too early, at age 19, when the incumbent, an average ex-county player named Parker was, allegedly, too scared to face Thomson and Lillee…

"Martin's early international cricket was 'character forming' to say the least. His first test captain never ceased to hassle him, excusing himself on the grounds that he, Howarth, might have become a great player had he been given more discipline, and by God, he was going to make sure Martin didn't have the same excuse."

In *The Crowe Style*, Martin says: "I had an ambivalent attitude towards Geoff Howarth. He had all the trappings of a great captain, and deservedly earned respect in Australia as a leader. Yet he treated me abominably, to the extent that Lance Cairns once confided, 'Crowey, if you weren't such a strong character, you would have gone surfing long ago.' It was years before Geoff revealed his method. He finally admitted that he had a very good reason for his autocratic attitude to me. He himself had experienced a somewhat undisciplined early career, and he felt that my opportunity for greatness should not be missed for want of some correctly applied discipline. He felt he had missed out himself, and didn't want to be the unwitting cause of my possible demise, for a similar reason."

Howarth is unapologetic about his aloof manner with the young Crowe. "Yes," he says, "that was my reasoning early on with Martin, and looking at what's happened since, and with his record in cricket, perhaps I was right!" Recalling the 19-year-old Crowe, Howarth says, "He was very young, almost a schoolboy with a big reputation, but he always had a certain amount of confidence, though not the mana he has now because of his standing in world cricket."

Howarth dismisses as "bullshit, a load of bunkum" suggestions by the Crowes that Martin was treated poorly that first series. "He was thrown in at the deep end in the sense that he was a big talent and we felt that the batting line-up we had behind us meant he could cope. He had the right temperament. But he was not thrown in ahead of the older players. He was nursed – he batted at No 6 in the tests. And he was helped where possible."

Jeremy Coney remembers the teenaged Crowe struggling in that first series. "When he came into the team, Martin was a colt, unsteady on his feet. It was a lot to ask of him, and while he measured up in the field and bowled pretty well – I remember that first day in Auckland when he got three catches and bowled tidily – when he had to come out with the bat, the pressure got to him and it showed. He certainly wasn't the brash, confident guy he is now."

What the Crowes perhaps overlook is that all the New Zealand players – whether they were Wright, Edgar, Howarth and Coney having to face up to Lillee, Thomson, Alderman and Pascoe, or Hadlee, Cairns, Snedden and Chatfield bowling to Wood, Chappell, Hughes and Border, or wicketkeeper Ian Smith trying to match his counterpart Rod Marsh – had their work cut out in that torrid series, one of the toughest New Zealand has ever played. It's all very well for a youngster to arrive and say, "What about me?" but the New Zealanders weren't exactly outshining their opposition to the extent that they could cushion their promising new batsman.

Anyhow, facts don't back up the picture Crowe paints of a young kid being left to fend for himself in a hostile dressing room. John Wright, surely one of the most amiable and popular fellows ever to have played for New Zealand, says: "Martin earned his place that season. He was good enough to take a punt on, one of the few young New Zealand players who, when you see them the first time, makes you think, 'He's class.' He stood above all the other younger players and he was pushed in.

"But the Aussies are tough and it didn't go well for him. It was a hard way to start. I batted with him in the third test. He hit a couple of boundaries in a row and looked a million dollars. But he struggled mentally to get into test cricket. It was a hard baptism."

Wright says he has been surprised by Crowe's claim that he was not helped by his teammates that season. "I made a conscious effort because, when you started in those days, there was no coach to help. I tried to encourage him. I always had faith in him. The first time I saw Martin was at a coaching clinic in Christchurch. I was 22 and he was about 15 or 16. I batted with him. You could tell then there was a lot about Greg Chappell in him. The stance, the strokes. When you see a player that good you just know. I never had any doubts about him from then on. I knew he'd be a great test player."

Of course, having the ability, and feeling you belong in the test arena are entirely different, as Wright points out: "I spent my first 20 tests wondering if I was good enough. It's a terrible situation to be in. Martin was like that against Australia.

"At that stage we hadn't established ourselves as a top team and were battling at home. But he got as much help as anyone else coming into the team in that period, guys like Edgar. We weren't strong in that department. Everyone had to battle."

Wright feels Crowe might have expected to be more the centre of things, given his dominance as a schoolboy player and then at age-level cricket. "When you are very young, like he was, you're bound to feel it more. You are used to a strong backup, then suddenly you're in there on your own. It's hard. But his treatment was no different to what others got.

"Geoff was not a strong communicator and had that earn-your-stripes mentality. He rode the young players pretty hard.

"Martin probably had expectations of coming in and doing well straight up. It didn't happen, and the bottom line is that you have to look to yourself. I thought I tried to encourage him when he was young. People would have a quiet word in his ear. He was certainly not made to feel unwelcome. He was so obviously destined to be a good player. You want to see a young guy do well."

Lance Cairns feels that in the long run Crowe benefited from his struggles that season. "He was a kid who was talked about a huge amount. But even when a young guy has the ability, he has to take the ability and make it work in the test arena, and that's different.

"Martin was talked of as a wonder-kid, but that first series proved to him that there is no easy way. Very few go to the highest echelon of cricket and succeed straight away. He got very, very disappointed with his efforts. He expected success the way he reacted. To fail was foreign to him. But it was a good thing he didn't succeed. You have to find that hardness."

To Crowe's claim that no one offered assistance, Cairns says: "You've got 11 individuals. You have to ask yourself when a guy is out of form, do you help him or preserve your own place. Often players choose to look after No 1. I've never been in favour of that thinking, but it can happen. I remember on my first trip, I couldn't believe how I was left to find my own feet. It was a rude awakening.

"The bottom line in test cricket is that players have to prepare themselves. They don't have a lot of time to worry about others. When you're picked for the New Zealand test side, there is no easy way out. The glare is on you. If you can't hack it, get out."

Bruce Edgar enjoyed having Crowe in the New Zealand side, right from that first series. "I remember he and I going out by ourselves to practise in some nets on a club ground in Dunedin that first season. He wanted to develop his play against fast bowling. We talked a lot about how to play fast bowling, then fired down missles at each other from 16 or 17 yards. He was thirsting for knowledge, listened to anything I had to say and obviously thought a lot about things. I respected him for that because I knew he was good, even then. He'd come into the side with a big reputation; probably he was two or three years ahead of his time. But he wasn't big-headed. He was looking to learn and was keen to get help from me. I felt humble that he asked me, and that he was so receptive. He was prepared to listen. His whole approach was constant self-analysis and development."

Certainly by the end of the season, having had Lillee and Thomson bearing down on him, Crowe was a shell-shocked young kid. Thoughts of being a prodigy had long since vanished.

Edgar, recalling the second test of that series, at Eden Park (when Edgar scored a match-winning 161), says: "Martin absolutely froze. It was only his second test. He bat-padded one to Wood and walked off. It was by no means an obvious catch and I'd have hung around in those circumstances. But he walked as if he couldn't leave quickly enough. Afterwards, he didn't really know why he'd walked. It was just the pressure of the test match getting to a young player.

"When you think about it, he'd probably grown up playing backyard games involving Lillee and Thomson, and then suddenly there he was facing them in a test match."

Crowe, who'd known almost uninterrupted cricketing success from his earliest school days, must have been relieved when the series finally finished. "The plain fact was that I was 19 years old and out of my depth, and I knew it . . . I felt that at least someone might have sat down to offer me some encouragement and advice."

Yet Frank Cameron feels Crowe might have been unrealistic in expecting so much of himself in his first series. "You rarely get success straight away. It took Wrighty year by year and he gradually inched up the statistics. He used to thank me for keeping him in the team and promise the rewards would come. I knew they would. At one stage, Wrighty was barely in the 20s. You have to have a bit of patience.

"Martin was an exceptional player at all ages. A player like that can have a few outs, but not very often a loss of form. I recall even Greg Chappell had a run of ducks one season."

Cameron says there was no consideration given to dropping Crowe. "He did enough in the domestic season to show that if he got in the New Zealand team, he would be there to stay. You can't pick guys for a few games, then choose new ones. All that says is that you don't know your job as a selector. I don't think Martin should have been too shell-shocked after that first series. He probably would have liked to score more runs, but we never considered dropping him. He was too good, an outstanding player."

Crowe was certainly a fairly lonely, unhappy figure by the time the summer finished. He says that he got so little help from the New Zealanders that he sought assistance from Greg Chappell, who recalls a conversation they had in Christchurch. "I did talk to Martin a few times briefly, then in Christchurch we had a chat about things in general, though batting was the main topic. I explained my views on planning and mental preparation etcetera, and he seemed very receptive."

By the end of the series, even Chappell felt a little sorry for the desperate youngster. "I remember him getting a duck in the Christchurch test. As he walked off the situation reminded me of Graham Gooch, who'd made his test debut against us in 1975 and had bagged a pair. The similarity was that they were both obviously very good players picked too soon to do the job asked of them. When I think of my own career, I batted at No 7 on my test debut, and I had some very good players in front of me. It was a much more satisfactory situation."

Chapter Five

BUILDING AN INNINGS

FRANK CAMERON:
"He was the sort of player who you knew that once you picked would be there for a long time."

Only 19 years of age, and already a failed test cricketer, Martin Crowe faced a big salvage job. New Zealand cricket has a long history of blooding youngsters too soon and then never seeing them fulfil their potential.

Think of the 1985 tour to the West Indies. Two young, unproven batsmen – Ken Rutherford and Ron Hart – accompanied Geoff Howarth's team. Rutherford, only 19, was converted into an opener and had the misfortune to play all four tests. His return? Twelve runs at 1.71 an innings. Hart, also 19, never got a test, but for the full tour played three first class matches and scored 34 runs (highest score 8) at an average of 5.66.

After their harrowing tour, Hart never played for New Zealand again and Rutherford had to battle for years to overcome his nightmare beginning to international cricket. He really only began to emerge from his shell at test level in the 1990s.

But Hart and Rutherford aren't the only two. Jack D'Arcy and Trevor Meale went to England in 1958 and were never heard of again at international level. Over the past 15 or so years, a succession of apparently promising bowlers have been tried, failed, then been discarded. Among them: Graeme Thomson, Mark Carrington, Sean Tracy, Brian Barrett, Stu

Gillespie, Richard Petrie, Mark Priest, Mark Haslam and Heath Davis. At the end of the 1995 summer, had Kerry Walmsley become the latest? And it's not just the bowlers. What about Kyle Wealleans and David White?

They were all considered good enough to be selected for New Zealand, then promptly discarded. It's small wonder that, after that jolt to their self-esteem and confidence, most failed to bounce back.

So Martin Crowe, schoolboy prodigy, Young Cricketer to Lord's, had a lot of work to do at the end of the 1981/82 season to retrieve the ground lost during the Thomson-Lillee blitz.

He began his 1982/83 season with a trek around the Australian outback, a member of an under-strength New Zealand side (Wright, Cairns, Hadlee and Turner were missing) which toured the eastern states. Though he scored 77 against Victoria Country at Horsham, he did not have an unduly productive tour, partly because he was pressed into opening in both the first class matches.

The players returned just before Christmas and shortly after most of them were tripping back across the Tasman to tackle the formidable World Series Cricket one-day series, also involving Australia and Bob Willis' England team.

Martin narrowly missed out on this side, his place going to brother Jeff, who had returned from his stint in Australia and was grabbed by the New Zealand team. The selection understandably caused mixed feelings in the Crowe household – elation for Jeff, sympathy for Martin.

"I don't consider we ever really dropped Martin," says selection panel convener Frank Cameron. "He was the sort of player who you knew that once you picked would be there for a long time. But it was a team picked purely for one-day matches and he was shaded by Jeff. In Australia it would be important to force the strokeplay and chase fast runs in an Australian environment. We felt it was too much to expect of a young fellow like Martin. Jeff was in good form and had experience in Australia, so we picked him."

It was to be an exciting triangular series, which confirmed the status of players like Turner, Hadlee, Cairns and Chatfield. New Zealand made the final at England's expense. Unfortunately, the wheels fell off at that point as New Zealand, without the injured Hadlee, were soundly beaten in both finals.

Back home, Martin Crowe prospered in the domestic competitions. As the *Cricket Almanack* noted: "Star batsman, though only 20, was Martin Crowe, whose batting always had a look of class and maturity about it that was remarkable in one so young." Crowe began with a century against Otago, had another against Northern Districts, a third against Wellington and also scored well against Central Districts and Otago. His season's figures of 736 runs at 52.57 (plus 12 wickets at 18) indicated he would not long be out of the national team. He was the season's highest scorer in first class play and finished ninth in the bowling averages. He also played a key role in Auckland claiming the Shell Cup, scoring 54 in the final against Northern Districts. His partnership with Trevor Franklin – 78 in 46 minutes – virtually sealed the match as Auckland chased ND's 210.

Sri Lanka toured that summer and when Crowe scored an unbeaten 70 for Auckland against them, it became obvious a place would have to be found for him in the New Zealand side. But where? Turner, Edgar, Wright, Howarth, Jeff Crowe and Coney were a solidly-performing top six.

Crowe got his chance in the Bushfire Appeal one-dayer at Sydney when Turner was unavailable. His class shone like a beacon. Of a paltry New Zealand total of 138, which included seven single-figure scores, he made 66 at a run-a-ball. Then he took 2-30 and held a catch to inspire a surprise New Zealand victory by 14 runs and scoop the Man of the Match award. In one match, he had removed all doubts about his ability to play at international level.

It was a significant moment in his career. As he said in *The Crowe Style*, "There I was, going out to bat with nothing behind me to suggest I could do anything other than fail again in an international . . . Was this my last chance?

"I had a bit of luck early on, for at three down for 25, I felt I had to go for my shots. Every time I hit the ball in the air, it fell into a gap. The wicket was patchy and very uneven. I could feel the adrenalin flowing, so I figured I just had to go on with it and really do something. The scoreboard told me I scored 66, but my guts told me after that it was much more. A revelation! A dream come true."

Crowe's superb play left the selectors with a dilemma as they pondered the New Zealand one-day team for the remaining two games against Sri Lanka. As it transpired, Howarth, the captain, stood down for the next match, at Napier, where Martin took two wickets, hit an unbeaten 43 and was again Man of the Match. Martin and Jeff batted together in this match, the first time they had done so since a primary school match at Cornwall Park 12 years earlier. In the last one-dayer, in which Glenn Turner batted superbly for 140 off 130 balls, Crowe had time just to hit an unbeaten seven. By then the match was already sewn up.

So the season ended in triumph for the 20-year-old. He was named in the New Zealand side to tour England, where a central part of the programme would be the World Cup. Never again would the selectors countenance omitting him from the national team while he was fit.

This was a very good New Zealand side to come into. Around him he had Turner (in the one-dayers), Edgar, Wright, Howarth, Coney and brother Jeff, a solid core of class players. There was not the pressure on Martin that if he failed, New Zealand were done for.

By contrast, John Reid in the late 1950s and early 1960s, must have often felt if he missed out, the batting would crumble. And even in the 1990s, when the elegant and promising Stephen Fleming was brought into the New Zealand side, the line-up around him, especially with Crowe so often absent through injury, did not look nearly as secure.

Crowe was by now visibly improving every month. His shot selection improved, his technique – particularly his defence – tightened, and he began to wear the assured look of a world class player.

New Zealand did not exactly cover themselves in glory at that 1983 World Cup, squandering a rosy chance of making the semi-finals by losing to Sri Lanka by three wickets. All hope vanished when Pakistan beat them by 11 runs.

Crowe had a good tournament. Though his bowling was too expensive to be a serious proposition at this level, he batted reasonably well to finish with 202 runs at 33.66 an innings. His 97 in the tournament opener against England was the highest New Zealand score of the tournament.

When the first class section of the tour began afterwards, he was invariably prolific in the fixtures against the counties but couldn't fire in the tests. For the full tour, he scored 819 runs at 58.50, including three centuries, but in the tests, his contribution of 163 runs at 20.57 disappointed him.

Until the 1994/95 season, when he failed to register the century he wanted against South Africa to complete his full house, Crowe has shown a remarkable ability to produce big scores in situations where he's particularly keen. And to a student of cricket, well aware of its history and traditions, there was no bigger match than his first class debut at Lord's, the home of cricket. It was the match before the first test and Crowe, after being diddled out by Edmonds in the first innings, was in supreme form in the second. He hit 12 boundaries on his way to an unbeaten 134, pulling the match around when New Zealand had been in some trouble.

Over the next three years, Crowe graduated from talented New Zealand batsman to world class player. He was given such tags as the best white batsman in the world, the batsman of the 1980s and so on. Sobriquets, of course, mean little. All the test team cared about was that they had a batsman who was at least as good as the best on the opposing team. And that, combined with the unique talents of Richard Hadlee, meant New Zealand never went into a test match without feeling they had a good chance of victory.

Among the highlights for Crowe in this period were:

- His first test century, an even 100 at the Basin Reserve against England in 1984. New Zealand trailed by 244 on the first innings, but Crowe batted four and a half hours to lead a fightback that Coney carried on superbly.
- His 188 against the West Indies at Guyana, when New Zealand were replying to the West Indies formidable 511-6 declared. The next highest New Zealand score was Coney's 73.
- His 188 at Brisbane in the first test against Australia. "It all came together for me. All those years of really struggling to build a reputation as a good cricketer. It was technically my best innings, but Paddles [Richard Hadlee] overshadowed it by taking nine wickets in the first innings."
- His 106 at Lord's in the first test against England in 1986. The innings arose in adverse circumstances. New Zealand were 5-2, replying to 307 when Crowe joined Bruce Edgar and they put together a record stand of 210.
- His 137 against Australia at Lancaster Park in 1986. When he was on 51, Crowe was hit a frightening blow on the jaw after missing a bouncer from 6ft 8in Australian left-arm paceman Bruce Reid. He left the field with blood running down his face, yet came back later to bat commandingly, hitting 21 fours in all.

By now, virtually all his great innings came in tests. He still scored heavily in lesser first class games, including a century on his debut for Central Districts in December 1983, 787 runs at 65.58 on the 1986 England tour, and double-centuries in New Zealand and Australia.

But the true criterion was test cricket. At this point one-day cricket held much less appeal, an attitude he rectified when he became captain.

That maiden test century at the Basin showed how good Crowe could look, even under extreme pressure. New Zealand, 79-2 in their second innings, still trailed by 165 runs when Crowe joined Howarth. Early the next day the innings had slumped to 165-4. Then Crowe and Coney came together in a match-saving stand of 114. Both men played attractively. Crowe hit 10 fours in his first 50. On he went until he took a three from Willis just before tea to bring up his century. He turned to the stand to acknowledge the moment to his proud parents.

Though Crowe was out in the next over, Coney went on remorselessly to 174 – a maiden test ton in front of his home crowd and under absolute pressure – and Lance Cairns defended in uncharacteristic fashion for 64 to save the match.

It was an historic series for New Zealand. In 1978 Mark Burgess' team had scored New Zealand's first test win over England. In 1983, to the utter delight of the county pros in the New Zealand side, England had been beaten at Headingley.

But now, in 1984, New Zealand beat England in a series for the first time. The decisive match was the second test at Christchurch where England were bowled out for 82 and 93 and New Zealand won by an innings and 132 runs in the equivalent of just two full days' play.

Besides forging a reputation as an exciting strokemaker, Crowe could defend dourly when the occasion demanded. One example arose in 1984 during the tour of Sri Lanka. Chasing 266 to win, New Zealand slumped to 89-4 on the final day of the second test.

Lance Cairns recalls the occasion: "Martin had a broken thumb. I felt we could still have pushed on for a win, but the captain [Geoff Howarth] decided to block out the last day. So Martin followed instructions. It was a terrible innings, so out of character. But he was batting to instructions." Crowe finished with 19 not out in 217 minutes. It was one of the slowest innings in test history and he set a record for the longest time to reach double figures. The final figures would have been even more stark had he not hit eight off the last three balls he faced.

John Wright noticed a big improvement in Crowe's batting by 1985. "I really respect him for the way he had that bad start to his test career, then came back," says Wright. "He really sorted out his game when he went to England and played for Somerset. He became so good he could go out and bat and, even if he wasn't in good form, he could give you a century."

After a couple of middling series – against Pakistan in Pakistan and at home – and some poor batting in Australia in a centenary one-day tournament, Crowe geared himself for the big tour of the West Indies from March to May, 1985. By this time Crowe was using a novel idea he had taken from Richard Hadlee to help him concentrate. Hadlee, of course, was known to focus on key words – off stump, rhythm, Lillee, hate. After speaking to Hadlee, Crowe decided to devise his own words and wrote them on a card. They were:

P (pride and performance)
A (application)
D (determination)
D (desire)
L (being one of the lads)
E (enjoyment)
S (success)

Hadlee – Paddles to his teammates – spoke to Crowe about the need to think positively. "He was never sure whether to shave in the morning, what to have for breakfast and what bat to use. It was negative thinking and I thought he'd never achieve success like that. I told him he had to get up and decide he would have a shave, have bacon and eggs for breakfast and choose a bat. All credit to him because the next day he came in with a card with PADDLES on it. He had paid me a great compliment, and I think he had come of age. He had not lived up to his full potential, but I was sure he was going to be a great player in New Zealand cricket."

It would be fair to say no New Zealander – certainly no batsman – enjoyed the tour to the West Indies. Marshall, Garner, Holding, Walsh and Davis guaranteed any batsmen a hot time. Jeremy Coney battled hard, but after averaging nearly 50 in the four tests, had his arm smashed by a Garner bouncer. As Richard Hadlee wrote in Rhythm and Swing: "The West Indies may be paradise for the holiday-maker, but it's hell on earth if you're there to play cricket. The unrelenting barrage wears down your emotional and physical resistance until you can stand it no more."

Martin Crowe played one big innings, 188 in nine and a half hours at Georgetown on the flattest track ever seen. It was the same pitch on which Glenn Turner twice scored 259 on the previous New Zealand tour of the West Indies. There were 10 half-centuries among the 22 wickets which fell in the match. Apart from this monstrous effort, Crowe produced little. His other six innings were worth just 28 runs. While Richardson, Richards, Haynes and Greenidge blazed away and averaged over 50, only Coney of the New Zealanders was able to play more than one substantial innings.

Frank Cameron coached that New Zealand side and feels the tour played an important part in toughening up Crowe. "The 188 he made at Georgetown was on a really good pitch, very flat. He still had to score the runs, though. On other occasions he suffered as the other batsmen did because they always had four-top line seamers firing at us. I could contrast that to the 1995 West Indies team here which had one outstanding fast bowler in Walsh. Ambrose was here, but he was only going through the motions and the others were only average.

"Martin gained experience out of that West Indies trip. He had his failures, but still looked a world class player. When you've been through that sort of fire, it makes it so much easier when you get against attacks you once thought were very good. Suddenly you find them so much easier, and that's what happened with Martin."

Cameron's observations seem vindicated by what happened the following season in Australia. Crowe headed the tour batting averages with 562 runs at 112.40 (the next best was Bruce Edgar's 389 at 38.90). He was also dominant in the three tests where his 309 runs at 77.25 considerably outshone even Edgar's 209 at 41.80. Allan Border was the best of the Australians with 279 at 55.80.

After the blistering examination under the West Indian microscope, Lawson, Gilbert, the young McDermott, Bright, Holland and Matthews must have seemed much more mortal.

Crowe began his tour with a score of 242 against South Australia. It was not a formidable South Australian attack, but even so his six and a half hour innings, which included 41 boundaries and one six, was a superb effort. It was his 21st first class century and his highest first class score. Crowe and Coney added 245 runs at a run a minute, and then the Crowe brothers put on a further 127 before the innings was declared. It must have been gratifying to Jeff to return to Adelaide, where he'd really launched his first class career, and to bat well in partnership with his brother.

The first test that summer remains one of the golden highlights of New Zealand cricket history. The bald facts are that Australia made 179 and 333 and that New Zealand, by scoring 553-7 declared, won by an innings and 41 runs. But there were some outstanding individual efforts by the New Zealanders. Richard Hadlee's bowling figures of 9-52 and 6-71 were the fourth best in 108 years of test cricket. Martin Crowe played one of his finest innings, scoring 188 and adding 224 with John Reid, who scored 108. Bruce Edgar describes that 188 as "an awesome innings". "He looked class from the time he went to the crease. In the context of the game, it was a brilliant knock, especially compared to what the others did."

His contribution to the series was by no means over. After a double-failure in the second test, which New Zealand lost, he made 71 and 42 not out to steer New Zealand to victory in the low-scoring third test at Perth. It was a euphoric time for the New Zealanders, none more so than Crowe.

The test season continued in New Zealand soon after when Border's Australians played three further tests. This was not the honed test side of the 1990s and Border was far from the confident skipper he became. During this tour he wondered at two press conferences if it was worth carrying on trying to lead such a poorly performed side. The Australian ranks included Ritchie, Matthews, Phillips, Bright, Gilbert, Zoehrer and Davis, all of whom were about to have their test careers curtailed. Some of them were not good enough, while others did not meet new coach Bobby Simpson's approved standards of discipline.

The batting hero of the home series was Coney, who had two 90s and a century in three innings, and averaged 146 for the series. Crowe played one substantial innings – 137 at Christchurch. It was a testing innings in more ways than one. Replying to Australia's 364, New Zealand were not going well at 48-4. Crowe and Coney were performing their usual salvage operation when Crowe, on 51, was hit on the chin by a no ball from Bruce Reid. He was fractionally early with his attempted hook shot and was hit flush on the jaw. He pitched sideways to the ground, rolled over twice and was taken from the field with a bloodstained towel covering a gash on his jaw. At hospital an x-ray showed no break or damage to his teeth. The wound took eight stitches, then Crowe returned to the park.

Glenn Turner, the New Zealand coach, had a delicate balancing operation. "Obviously he had to come off, but when you've been conked on the nut, it's best to get back out there batting as soon as possible. The less time you sit there and dwell, the better.

"Martin was cleaned up and x-rayed, to make sure there was no major damage, then I urged him to continue batting. He was initially reluctant, but when Smithy was out and we were six down, he went back out and he batted very well. It was an important innings."

Crowe said that evening the encouragement of Turner and John Wright had got him batting again – he resumed his innings two hours and

20 minutes after being hit. "I felt not too bad. Then John Wright came up to me and said, 'Listen, mate, go back out there. The pitch is playing well, the bowlers are getting tired. Go out there and do your stuff.' For the first 15 or 20 minutes I was shaking. I didn't know what to do. Then I had a couple of wafts at Matthews [both of which went for fours] and that seemed to settle me down."

The 1986 tour of England was really the culmination of the golden age of New Zealand cricket. A few of the key members of the era – Howarth, Reid, Cairns – had either retired or been dropped. But with Turner coaching and Coney as captain the New Zealand team performed above themselves. The key figures were Hadlee, Crowe, Coney and Bracewell, but the beauty of this team was that everyone contributed when needed. Thus Bruce Edgar made a plucky 83 in the first test and Evan Gray a valuable 50 at Trent Bridge to help win the second test.

For the first time, New Zealand won a test series in England. Mike Gatting ungraciously described playing against this New Zealand team as "facing the World XI at one end and the Ilford Second XI at the other". Of course, Gatting overlooked the spirit, the camaraderie and the support the New Zealanders gave one another. England had individual stars like Gower, Gooch, Gatting, Lamb, Botham (when he returned from a suspension for smoking marijuana), Edmonds and Emburey, but they couldn't match New Zealand as a team.

Crowe had a splendid tour with 787 runs at 65.58. He did not play the single most outstanding innings of the tour – that belonged to Ken Rutherford, with his scarcely believable 317 against D. B. Close's XI – but he did reserve his best innings, appropriately, for the Lord's test. England made 307 and then had New Zealand at 5-2. At that point Edgar and Crowe came together in a third-wicket record stand of 210 in five and a half hours. Crowe's fifth test century came in 299 minutes and his innings of 106 contained 11 boundaries. Edgar recalls: "He batted so well. He was timing it better than I was. I struggled. It was overcast and the ball was moving around. I hung in there, but Martin batted really well."

Edgar says one of the things he most enjoyed about batting with Crowe was his speed between the wickets. "Martin used to do a lot of training and his speed and athleticism showed out. He was such a fast runner between the wickets that things used to keep moving in the middle."

There was another reason Edgar and Crowe clicked. They shared an interest in the psychological side of sport. Edgar: "By 1985 or '86, Martin had moved into the mind business. I'd bought some books about sports psychology and found them very helpful. It was not an area that was even touched on in the New Zealand team till then. In fact, there was a sort of macho image, where you weren't able to express yourself, let emotions show through.

"Martin was always able to express himself. I guess he was a sensitive new age guy. He was ahead of his time in that regard. It made people feel uncomfortable. Martin was always quick to try out new ideas, looking for an edge. He was always trend-conscious, the first to get a walkman, a discman, a computer, that sort of thing. But people shouldn't knock that. He taught a lot of us how to present ourselves better because of his dress sense.

"When Martin found I had an interest in the psychological side of sport, he was very happy to discuss it. Until 1985, the New Zealand team didn't even have a coach. There was the captain, the chairman of selectors and the manager, but there was a glaring hole. There weren't the people you could turn to for advice."

The psychology of sport has always intrigued Crowe. Some of his teammates say he has become too immersed in it. "It has sometimes badly affected my game," he conceded to brother Jeff in the TV programme *Crowe on Crowe* in 1992. "But sometimes you come across things and they intrigue you. Sports psychology interests me because it's all about getting the edge. I guess the older you get the more experienced you get and you start to simplify things. I probably don't use it so deliberately now. There was a time when I had to do my visualisation and it used to work for me. There were times when I didn't enjoy cricket so much because I became too mechanical, too deliberate in my thinking. The key is to think positively and use your imagination."

Crowe took this psychological side of cricket far beyond the level of most New Zealand players. Bruce Edgar recalls the time Wellington were playing Central Districts at Levin, when Crowe was the CD captain: "He had them sitting on the ground in front of the stand while he stood and gave a team talk. It was like he was talking in tongues. He was addressing the psychological dimension, discussing focusing, visualisation and so on. Around him these guys from Motueka or out in the country were looking at him as if he was from Mars. It was Martin sharing his knowledge, but it's a question of whether others are ready to absorb it."

During the late 1980s, Crowe often spoke of how he would like to become a sports psychologist when he finished with cricket. One who saw how absorbed Crowe was on the subject was top tennis player Brett Steven. The pair trained together for a time when both were in Auckland recovering from injuries. "I found Martin very friendly and good company," says Steven. "But he was intense when he talked about his career and sport. He got me to go along to a course being run by John Kehoe. He was a Canadian motivator/psychologist who was offering advice on how to organise your life and get conditioned to perform as well as possible. It was mostly commonsense, but it was quite good. I think the course ran over four evenings.

"I listened, and felt it was useful, sort of confirmation for what I already felt. But I wasn't a disciple. Martin, on the other hand, got right into it. He got books out and read all he could on the subject. He is a lot more analytical about that sort of thing than me. His goals were very specific."

Within the New Zealand cricket team of the 1980s, talk of psychology, or any undue talk of emotion, tended to be frowned upon. John Bracewell feels it was a weakness in the structure of the New Zealand team in those days. "At team meetings Martin would attempt to contribute. But it was a status thing: if you were young, then you were expected to speak only when you were spoken to. Martin can be direct and honest. There's a lot of passion there. He does get emotionally confused sometimes. He was unfortunate to come into the team when the leadership did not look at a player's emotions. I like people who are emotional and passionate. It was a matter of people knowing how to deal with Martin, rather than just saying he was in one of his moods and walking away from him."

And what was he like as a teammate in these middling years, before he began to gather more publicity than the rest of the team put together?

Bracewell: "Everyone respected his genius. He wasn't more or less popular in the side than anyone else. The side got on and did the business. We went through a phase where players were individuals. The walkman and tracksuit days. Not much team socialising. There were splinter groups. Martin was just one of the team."

Jeremy Coney says it was fortunate Glenn Turner was the team coach. "Turner was one person who Crowe respected. In a way, Glenn seemed to answer the questions before Martin came up with them. Glenn read him well. He dealt with our better players, such as Crowe and Richard Hadlee, very well.

"Martin was never a problem player when I was in the side. However, he did push things. I wouldn't have used the word tolerant for Martin. Basically, Martin did what Martin wanted. If he wanted to turn up the music – it was Dire Straits in those days – very loud, he would, until he was told to pull his head in. He had an approach to life where he pushed things – clothing, cars, restaurants.

"He always formed his own opinions. He was reasonably intelligent. He questioned things and would challenge established opinions. I thought he did very well to overcome that bad start to his test career. The fact that he has worked his average up from that situation means he has worked hard."

Crowe could be extremely sensitive, sometimes surprisingly so. He sometimes caught Turner by surprise by his admission during pre-test team talks that he lacked confidence or doubted his ability.

Once, in Australia, Turner and Coney confronted Crowe about his daily habits. Crowe had been getting up late on match day, developing a routine which the senior team members felt was too sloppy. So Turner and Coney confronted him, speaking about maturity, the need to organise himself better. They were surprised at Crowe's response. He got quite distressed by the rev-up, but took the advice on board.

Ian Smith, Crowe's roommate for much of the 1980s, says one thing a person had to get used to when sharing a room with Martin was an ever-expanding array of clothes. "Martin was never a tidy roommate. He had so many clothes that by the end of the match the room was generally split one-third/two-thirds. His clothes seemed to expand as the match wore on. He was a great sleeper. He could sleep anywhere, any time. I was quite envious. He liked his music. There was always a lot of the walkman. He wasn't a great reader, but liked to watch the odd movie.

"Before a test he'd get fairly worked up, but only the usual pre-test tension. No-one is particularly good company at times like that, and he got nervous, like anyone else."

Smith recalls Crowe's youth and natural enthusiasm when he first made the test side. "He had a real drive to play early on. As you keep going, this is replaced by routines and habits."

By the end of 1986 Crowe had hauled his test batting average up to a respectable 38.44 while at first class level he was only a whisker under the statistically important average of 50 an innings.

Chapter Six

COUNTY PRO

FRANK KEATING:

"All Somerset, devoted almost in idolatry to Richards, thought they had bought a pup. Well, they had. But a gritty one... It will be intriguing to see how long it takes the bonny young prince to totally quell the rebellion."

A surprising number of New Zealand cricketers have strutted their stuff on the county circuit, but none of them had to endure the pressure Crowe did while playing county cricket. Through a set of freak circumstances, Crowe found himself in conflict with three of the game's all-time greats, and representing a county in which a sizeable proportion of the membership did not want him. To his credit, he maintained his dignity in an awkward situation and, what's more, batted so well that he gave the doubters no latitude to criticise.

The first New Zealanders to be involved in English cricket were Daniel Reese and Arthur Sims, way back before the First World War. Reese, a leading batsman, useful spin bowler and brilliant fieldsman, played eight matches for Essex as an amateur, as well as appearing alongside the immortal W. G. Grace for the London County team. His good friend Sims played for London County between 1907 and '13 and enjoyed several partnerships with the famous bearded doctor.

Between the two world wars, some of New Zealand's greatest players, including Bill Merritt, Stewie Dempster, Ken James and Ces Dacre, played county cricket. Others, such as Roger Blunt and Giff Vivian, represented Nottinghamshire furniture magnate Sir Julien Cahn's team. Ian Cromb, the Canterbury all-rounder, had a spell of league cricket in 1933 and Tom Lowry, the W. G. Grace of New Zealand cricket, represented Cambridge University, the Gentlemen of England and Somerset during the early 1920s. Legend has it that he chose Somerset because, he said, he was born close to Wellington. The English didn't realise by Wellington he meant the New Zealand capital, not the English town.

Generally the New Zealanders acquitted themselves well in England. Dempster, a beautifully balanced opening batsman, moved to England at Cahn's invitation, but stayed and qualified for Leicestershire, captaining the county for a couple of seasons. In six straight English seasons he averaged 40 or more – three times over 50 – putting himself alongside Hammond, Hutton and Hardstaff in the averages. From 1935 to '39 he played 108 matches for the county, scoring 4659 runs at 49.04, with 18 centuries. He represented Warwickshire briefly after the war, then returned to Wellington.

James, one of the best three wicketkeepers in the world in his prime, threw in his lot with Northamptonshire in 1935. Northants at the time were one of the lowliest counties and James was an outstanding figure in the club. He scored 88 run out on his debut against Lancashire and by 1939 had claimed 220 victims, as well as scoring 3500 runs for the county. In 1938 he snared 49 victims, including the incomparable Don Bradman, and scored more than 1000 runs.

Merritt, the brilliant leg-spinner of the 1927 and '31 touring teams, played in the Lancashire league for Rishton for two years, for East Lancashire for a further five and then for Dudley in the Birmingham league from 1940 to '55. He also had three seasons of county cricket for Northamptonshire, where he resumed his lethal combination with wicketkeeper James.

Dacre, a smashing, dashing batsman and a national sporting hero in his prime, qualified for Gloucestershire in the early 1930s and, batting alongside the great Walter Hammond, achieved some prodigious feats, once scoring 223 against Worcester (with 25 fours and five sixes) and another time 119 and 125 not out against the same county. In six successive seasons he topped 1000 runs and Hammond described him as "a splendid forcing batsman who could hit the ball really hard". Dacre revealed his intentions early when he smashed the first ball he received in county cricket onto the pavilion roof.

In the years after the Second World War, there were quite a few New Zealanders playing county cricket, most of them for the accommodating Warwickshire club. Martin Donnelly, regarded for a time as the best left-handed batsman in the world, was the pick of them. After an outstanding sports career at Oxford University – during which he represented England at rugby – he played for Warwickshire from 1948 to '50 and was ever productive. Donnelly, of course, is still remembered in England as one of only two people – the other was Percy Chapman – to score centuries at Lord's in a test, the University match and for Gentlemen v Players. He added one for the Dominions against England for good measure. Other New Zealanders who campaigned for Warwickshire in these years, or soon afterwards, were pace bowler Tom Pritchard, opening batsman Don Taylor and Ray Hitchcock.

Of this trio, Pritchard was by far the most prominent. He was the first New Zealander to play county cricket for an extended period as a professional and was so good the English test selectors would dearly have loved him in their team. Tom Dollery, his Warwickshire captain, said that he was faster than any English bowler of his time and not much slower than Larwood. Pritchard represented Warwickshire from 1946 to '55, being granted a benefit season in 1952. He had a dozen games for Kent as an amateur and then played league cricket for a further six or seven seasons.

Strangely, from the mid-1950s no New Zealanders had a real crack at county cricket until the young Glenn Turner, with encouragement from Billy Ibadulla, dipped his toe in the water in the late 1960s. Many, of whom the most prominent was John Reid, played in the leagues, but none played county cricket for an extended period.

Turner inquired initially at Warwickshire, then from 1967 settled with Worcestershire, where Tom Graveney's batting greatness and the admirable cool and commonsense of the sagacious Basil D'Oliveira rubbed off on him. Turner became a pivotal figure for New Zealanders, a forerunner to pros like Geoff Howarth, David O'Sullivan, John Parker, John Wright, Richard Hadlee and Crowe, and later Chris Cairns and Danny Morrison.

In a very short time, Turner developed from a frail-looking teenager who struggled to hit the ball off the square into a world class player, a beautiful striker of the ball who became a one-day wizard. As early as 1970, he created a Worcester record by hitting 10 centuries in a season. In 1977 against Gloucester, he scored 141 not out of Worcester's total of 169, a record 83.4 per cent. Throughout the 1970s, he scored a pile of runs, averaging above the magic 50 runs an innings mark. In fact, he scored more first class runs than any other player in the 1970s.

Turner closed his county career in 1982, the season he reached his 100 hundreds with a superlative innings of 311 not out against Warwickshire.

It was Turner who battled the New Zealand cricket administration, steeped in the amateur ethos, pointing out the rights of a professional player. He made himself unpopular, but stuck to his guns and certainly made life easier for the New Zealand professionals who followed him. Howarth (at Surrey), John Wright (Derby) and Richard Hadlee (Notts) took to the county game with relish.

So by the mid-1980s, it wasn't rare for New Zealanders to be appearing on the county scene and, what's more, through the deeds of Turner, Hadlee and Wright, they had established a formidable reputation. County cricket clearly figured in the thinking of the emerging Martin Crowe. It loomed as a challenge, and for a young man who had not established an outside career and had no tertiary qualifications, it was an especially appealing career option.

It so happened that, as the 1984 English season approached, Somerset, a pleasant county in England's south-west, had a vacancy for an overseas pro. The West Indies were touring England that season, so their two overseas stars, Richards and Garner, were out of commission.

Somerset's cricket chiefs put their heads together. They needed a stop-gap measure, a player who would perform well and preferably one who would add fresh life to a county team which was in decline.

Ian Botham, the Somerset captain, had been impressed by what he'd seen of Crowe – his batting expertise and his enthusiastic approach to the game – in England the previous season with the New Zealand side. When he mentioned Crowe to Michael Hill, the Somerset club chairman, Crowe was duly offered a contract, which he accepted.

Things didn't go too well initially for Crowe. He began with a century against the gentle Oxford University attack, but for a while afterwards didn't have much to show for his efforts. A scratchy 77 against Leicestershire was the only relief from a series of failures which ran 1, 10, 1, 0, 3, 5, 3. He was struggling to adapt to the demands of playing cricket every day of the week. He stayed at Botham's flat briefly, before establishing his own accommodation when he discovered that Botham's pacy lifestyle did not suit his own desire for order and organisation.

Crowe turned things around during Bath Festival week. On June 11 against Middlesex, whose potent attack included Cowans, Daniel, Emburey and Edmonds, he cracked a beautiful 126 that launched him on a run blitz of four centuries in successive matches – 113 and 54 against Lancashire, 152 not out against Warwickshire, 70 not out and 190 against Leicestershire. His fine form in June – 993 runs at 66.20 – won him the Cricketer of the Month award of two magnums of champagne and a silver salver from the *London Evening Standard.*

He finished the season with 1870 runs at 53.42 in first class matches (seventh in the batting averages), plus some outstanding all-round efforts in the assorted one-day competitions.

Wisden noted prophetically: "He virtually filled the huge gap left by Richards, and his mature influence and general deportment rounded off his wonderful introduction to the county."

John Arlott was spot on when he wrote: "He would be welcomed back in Somerset or, if not, in any worthwhile corner of the cricket world."

Yet when he looked back on the season, there were as many troughs as peaks. He described May as one of the darkest periods in his life, the month when he couldn't get anything working. And he broke down later in the season as well, not because of lack of success, but because he couldn't handle the pace of what was happening.

"I lost all confidence in May," he told *Sunday News* sports editor Richard Becht on his return to New Zealand. "I was working hard, but I was away from home and just didn't feel relaxed. There was a lot of talk from various people about the fact that I was replacing Viv Richards. When I was getting low scores, I could hear people in the crowd telling me to go back to New Zealand, or they'd be mumbling and groaning. But I knew I had five months; I just had to sort it out myself."

Sort it out he did, with that magic sequence in June. "Then," he recalled, "I had an emotional breakdown in July. I was going so well, but I broke down mentally. I'd just had enough. The computer had gone haywire. I think I experienced all there was to experience emotionally in one season of county cricket. By the end of the county season, I could cope. I learned how to pace things. But a season of county cricket was much harder than I'd ever imagined it would be. I hadn't counted on so many distractions like travelling, Sunday league cricket and the other one-day competitions. At one stage, I played 18 days in a row."

Crowe's batting was a revelation. Scyld Berry wrote in the *London Observer:* "Already this 21-year-old challenges David Gower, Graham Gooch and the Australian Allan Border for the unofficial title of the best white batsman in the world today (admittedly a runners-up award).

"Not only has Crowe made as many runs as Richards was wont to score, but has also taken as many championship wickets as Joel Garner would in an average season, delivering aggressive full-length inswingers like a part-time strike bowler...

"What is instructive is the way Crowe has batted. With him there is none of that twitching outside the off stump, or running the ball through the slips, or playing across the front pad and working it through mid-wicket, which bedevils English batsmanship nowadays. When Crowe bats, the umpire is forever knocking the bowler's stumps back in, following straight drive after straight drive, and even when he hits in the air – as when he went down the pitch to Andy Roberts while contributing 190 to a record Somerset third-wicket stand – he was still hitting the ball back over Roberts' head.

"The comparison is frequently made with Greg Chappell, but Crowe, although he was vastly impressed by a Chappell century when he was picked as a schoolboy protege against Australia, says he is unaware of any conscious imitation. Besides which, he has outstripped what Chappell did in his two seasons with Somerset, 1969 and 1970 (2349 runs at 29 and 70 wickets)."

Peter Roebuck, then a senior member of the county side, recalls how the two Bath Festival matches provided Crowe with his first major county successes. These festival weeks are a feature of English cricket, and the two matches in the historic town of Bath provided Crowe with runs at a desperate time for him. "It was a big week for Martin," says Roebuck. "He made a lot of runs, and as I recall he met a girl there in a jazz club and fell for her. Anyway, after that, he never looked back.

"Not only did he score runs consistently, but he forged the younger players into a group with the idea that they would seek their own excellence. When he started, he was conscious of being the overseas star, but he fitted in well. The young players looked up to him, morale was good – far better than it had been the previous year – and we finished in the middle of the championship, a good result given our team personnel that year."

Ironically, in view of the friendship that was to develop, Roebuck and Crowe did not especially hit it off initially. Roebuck: "We were certainly not bosom pals. I think he regarded me as a stiff and distant figure. I was fed up with some of the strife at the club and looked at Martin as a young fellow who had just rocked up from New Zealand and didn't warm to him at first."

Their friendship blossomed when they put on more than 300 against Leicester, Crowe's share of 190 being his career best at the time.

All in all, Crowe did extremely well that first season. He handled the travel (about 16,000km on the county circuit), the variety of pitches and the professionalism of the opposition well. He hit six centuries and, in addition, his attacking medium-pace bowling brought him 44 wickets. Somerset awarded him a county cap in mid-season. Wisden named him as one of its five cricketers of the year.

It was a significant year for New Zealanders in county cricket. Richard Hadlee became the first player since Fred Titmus in 1967 to perform the double of 1000 runs and 100 wickets, and John Wright averaged more than 60 an innings for Derby.

While his cricket had the stamp of class, Crowe impressed Somerset officials with his ability to draw together the team's younger players. The group, all uncapped, became known as the Young Naggers because of their frequent meetings at the Nag's Head, a local watering-hole. Crowe often stressed to them the importance of pride and hard work.

Richards and Garner returned to Somerset the following season, but it was obvious to those in the club that things were not going well. Somerset's successes of the late 1970s and early '80s – they won the Gillette Cup (later the Natwest Trophy) in 1979 and '83 and were runners-up in 1978, and won the Benson and Hedges Cup in 1981 and '82 – had been built not just on the back of the batting of Richards, the bowling of Garner and the all-round ability of Botham. Rather, the team had been built by Brian Close in the 1970s and included a number of excellent county players; not stars but consistently productive performers. By the mid-1980s those players, such as Rose, Denning, Taylor and Moseley were either retired or on the wane. Somerset was not a major county and had limited back-up strength, so results were poor. In addition, the club management was old-fashioned, lacking in flair.

In 1985 Somerset finished 17th – last – in the county table. There was a lot of strife, the sort of internal bickering that had plagued Yorkshire for a decade. Eventually Botham quit the captaincy, only hours, it was said, before it was to be removed. Roebuck, a solid batsman and a clear, precise thinker, was made captain.

"It was hard to turn it around," says Roebuck. "In 1986 we were 16th and there was strife again, a great deal of it. The team was not happy, and the club as a whole was not running well. Membership was falling, our supporters were not happy. The club, and the county team, were in decline. Really, the trouble had been brewing since 1983, but we'd won a trophy that year, which had disguised the problems. We'd got away with it.

"By 1986 it was obvious something had to be done. The young players were not up to the standard of their predecessors, so more was needed of the major players just when they were easing back.

"Various solutions were suggested. Then they remembered Martin Crowe. There was a long debate about whether we needed a batsman or a bowler. In the end they went for a batsman, reasoning that at least we'd be strong in one department. And with Martin, and the way he'd played in 1984, it was felt he would bring a fresh approach. He was obviously a fellow who was dedicated to the task. He'd returned for a few weeks in 1985, played a match or two and worked hard with the youngsters. At the time this was very much resented by Viv and Botham, less so by Joel."

In one of those ironies which makes sport so intriguing, it was Allan Border who set the whole deal in motion. Border had in 1986 signed a two-year contract with Essex, but informed them midway through the first season that he would not be returning for his second year. He was finding it difficult to spend enough time with his family when so committed to cricket and was under pressure from the Australian selectors to take a break and so be fresh to lead the Australian test side.

Essex, suddenly discovering they were to be without their overseas batting star for 1987, asked Crowe if he was interested in signing with them. At the time Somerset had Crowe on their books, so Crowe approached the Somerset officials, laying out the situation.

Somerset, knowing something had to be done to turn the club around (they were losing 500 members a season), took a deep breath and decided to sack Richards and Garner, two of the all-time greats, and replace them with the 24-year-old New Zealander. Knowing of Botham's friendship with Richards (particularly) and Garner, they realised there was a possibility he would leave the club.

"Getting rid of Viv and Joel had more to do with bringing the club and team together than with making a cricketing judgment," says Roebuck. "Things had gone sour where they'd used to be sweet."

No sooner had news of the sacking of the two West Indian stars broken, than Botham, in his extravagant manner, duly announced he too was leaving the club, out of loyalty to his West Indian mates. In his autobiography, published in 1994, Botham described "most despicable behind-the-scenes machinations" at Somerset. And the man he blamed was Roebuck. In fact, Botham confessed to pinning a Judas note on Roebuck's dressing room peg after the sackings. "He was a traitor to the people who thought they were his friends," wrote Botham. "Roebuck planted the seeds of the coup for nigh on 18 months. It was very well planned. We had all heard how Crowe was going to come out and do this and that."

Botham said Richards was forever being compared to Martin Crowe, "the blue-eyed boy who had arrived to become flavour of the month. This in a way was very unfair on Crowe, because it made the rest of us draw instant conclusions as far as he was concerned: either you liked him because he was going to be the saviour of Somerset cricket, or you disliked him driving this wedge through the county".

For the last third of the 1986 season there was a poison atmosphere at Somerset. Botham and Crowe met during the third test at the Oval that year, the test in which Botham was returning to international cricket after his marijuana suspension. "When I went into the England dressing-room for a drink after the match," Crowe told Eric Young of the *Auckland Star*, "I said hello to Botham and he just shrugged. I ran into Viv straight after the test. I shook hands with him and we talked for a while."

Many club supporters were angry over the decision and a special meeting was finally held in November. There the club received a surprisingly strong vote of confidence: the decision was endorsed 1828-798; very strong really, considering that in meetings like that it's usually the unhappy members who make a point of attending.

But things were very uncomfortable within the Somerset team. Botham was vehement in his public condemnation of Somerset as a club and Roebuck as a person. Various mini-coups were planned. It was a similar situation to what had happened in Yorkshire when that great county had torn itself apart during the Boycott Affair.

As Roebuck says: "People felt very passionately about the issue. Some people think in names, and a lot remains hidden about the whole thing.

Many of the members sensed that things were wrong – hence the strong vote – but to outsiders it must have seemed puzzling that we would sack Viv and Joel and risk Ian Botham departing. There was a highly emotional and orchestrated group, very vocal about the decision."

Crowe was in New Zealand while much of the debate raged, but waded in with a column in the *Sunday Star* headed: "This is a mess I can do without". In it he spoke of how, if the members' vote had gone against the committee, he would have turned his back on English cricket. "It would be a shame to see it [his county cricket career] ruined by people who I feel don't have the best interests of the game at heart."

Crowe strode into this melting pot of controversy at the beginning of the 1987 season. He'd rushed to England when the New Zealand tour of Sri Lanka was halted after a terrorist bomb killed more than 100 people in Colombo, where the New Zealanders were staying.

Frank Keating, the much-admired sports columnist for the *Guardian* and *Punch*, put things into perspective: "As a performing crowd-puller, he has a daunting job on his hands. Not only Watchet, Wedmore and Westonzoyland are watching: the whole cricket world will be keen to see how he copes. I fancy he will rout the doubters. In his one season for Somerset, in 1984, when he stood in for Richards, the 21-year-old displayed considerable mettle and courage – as well as an upright, clean-shaven, Boy-Scout manner that endeared him to the county establishment... All Somerset, devoted almost in idolatry to Richards, thought they had bought a pup. Well, they had. But a gritty one... It will be intriguing to see how long it takes the bonny young prince to totally quell the rebellion."

In *The Crowe Style*, Crowe describes his first match that season: "It was very important to me. I was so nervous. I felt my stomach turning over, and for the first 10 minutes my feet wouldn't move at all. It was a relief to be accorded a warm welcome from the crowd, for up to then I could only guess at their feelings. I was encouraged to make 65 and then produced a satisfying 148 and 52 against Surrey in the second championship match."

Crowe was then signed by the *Daily Express* as a columnist. His first column was not exactly designed to appease the aggrieved at Somerset. He wrote that he admired Botham for his ability, but as people the two of them were quite different. "I'm low-key. I like to keep a balance and that's why I'll never become what Ian says is a great player. I'm always working at my game, trying to perfect it, instead of just going out and blasting.

"I see myself trying to contribute rather than dominate, and that is important. Ian and Viv Richards and Joel Garner did dominate the team, but we've got to get away from all that. We've got to have all eleven contributing. When I'm batting for Somerset and I'm out, it's not as if the world has come to an end. I think when Botham and Richards were out, the side packed up. Richards may look great, but there's no point if all the others are getting noughts… I believe cricket is not about individuals; it's about a team."

Despite Keating's confidence, the rebellion could never totally be quelled. Battle lines had become too entrenched for that. Nevertheless, Crowe was the first player that season to reach his 1000 runs, which he achieved on July 1 at Edgbaston during a superb innings of 206 not out off 283 balls.

One who had good cause to remember that innings was South African fast bowler Allan Donald, then in the embryonic stages of what was to become a fine career. "Crowe was incredible to bowl to," Donald recalls, "though he was nice to watch from slip. The first ball I bowled, he played and missed. That was the last time that happened for five hours. For the first 50 or 60 he just played away quietly and that was that. It was a green seamer and he was being pretty careful. But the next day he made another 150 or so and was just awesome. He had such a lot of time to play his shots, it was difficult to know how to even worry him."

Crowe went on to play 18 first class matches that season and scored 1627 runs at 67.70, with six centuries. He topped the English batting averages, and contributed well in the one-dayers. Roebuck recalls a record third-wicket partnership of 263 with Crowe against Hampshire. Crowe blazed away for 155 not out, his best one-day score. "We seemed to bat well together," says Roebuck. "He was terrific to bat with. You raised your game when you were out there with him. He was an excellent runner between the wickets. Also he was the best technical coach I've had. I was older and his captain, but he helped my batting a great deal. I doubt Martin played better in his life than in 1987. He had trepidation when he started, but played extremely well, which helped the situation."

Perhaps his best innings of the season was an unbeaten 102 against Middlesex on a sticky wicket at Bath when he handled test spinners John Emburey and Phil Edmonds with great skill. John Woodcock, *The Times'* veteran cricket writer, described it as a "well-nigh perfect exhibition of batting, like Barry Richards at his best – utterly sound technically".

By contrast the low point of the season was the clash between Somerset and Worcestershire in July. Botham, now playing for Worcester, had vowed to rub Somerset's noses in the dirt, and indeed he did score an unbeaten 126 in a rain-affected drawn match. Afterwards, Crowe attacked both Botham and his own captain, Roebuck, saying: "My feeling was that I wished Botham and Peter Roebuck and the media had taken their pathetic fun and games to another planet because it really felt as though the rest of us were just standing doing nothing. We were totally irrelevant to what was happening. It was the most uninspiring first class match I have ever played. The feeling throughout was that Botham was there to back his famous words and Roebuck tried to stop him with some pretty irresponsible tactics in a way that made the game a joke."

It was a generally happy period for Crowe, despite the turmoil at the start of the season. He settled into a cottage in a small village aptly named Crowcombe, and he had the good fortune to have for company his schoolmate and Central Districts teammate Mark Greatbatch, who spent the season playing with some success for the Somerset seconds. Various people, including golfer Greg Turner, stayed with him and he presented a happy picture. So settled did he seem that there was speculation that he would soon be the ideal person to captain the Somerset side.

Despite Crowe's productive batting, Somerset struggled in 1987. Roebuck, who hit four centuries early on, hurt his thumb, and the team rather lost their way when he was absent. They lost to Northants in the quarter-finals of the Benson and Hedges competition. It was an unhappy match for Crowe, who bowled 11 overs and hurt his back in the process, and was out for a second ball blob. Worse was to follow in the Natwest Trophy when Somerset suffered the humiliation of losing to the local minor counties team at High Wycombe, in Buckinghamshire. The defeat, by six runs, to a team the Somerset seconds had demolished just a week earlier, was the upset of the season.

But so well did Crowe bat that he seemed on target for 2000 runs until a Clive Rice rising delivery broke his thumb in the match against Nottinghamshire. Not only did the delivery curtail Crowe's county season, but it prevented him playing for a World XI against an England XI in the MCC bicentenary match at Lord's.

Roebuck says one of Crowe's best contributions was his continuing work with the county team's younger players. "He spent a lot of time in the evenings with them, as a group. Someone had to do it. Viv by that stage was not so interested in that, though in his earlier days he was outstanding in that area.

"Martin seemed to really enjoy it. He likes instructing young people, and being a mentor, a guru, a demagogue almost. He likes to have people looking up to him. It's a simple life with the young: they don't judge, they listen. He's generally found communication easier with younger players than with his contemporaries."

Crowe returned for another season in 1988, but played just five matches before a back injury and general ill-health (it was discovered later that he was suffering from salmonella) meant he had to curtail his season, and, as it transpired, his county career. It was a pity because he had been in outstanding form, scoring 487 runs at 60.87 with two centuries.

"Martin seemed tired to me," Roebuck says. "We didn't know about the salmonella then, but he had the flu and seemed to be struggling with his health. And there was always the back thing. Before that he'd been a very useful bowler. He'd scored more than 4000 runs in 1987, under colossal pressure much of the time. I think he needed a rest. And the Somerset Affair didn't help. It rumbled on and that made things unpleasant for him."

As a matter of interest, Chris and Lance Cairns, Mark Greatbatch, John Wright and Kassem Ibadulla all played first class cricket in England that season. Crowe's place was taken by Steve Waugh, who was spectacularly successful, scoring nearly 1300 runs at an average of more than 80.

Of course, Crowe's departure delighted Botham and his backers. Even in 1994, when the Somerset Affair should have been ancient history, Botham wrote in *Botham: My Autobiography*: "We had all heard how Crowe was going to come out and do this and that, but some of us had our doubts, and as it turned out, we were proved right: he played one full season then four championship matches the following year before a back injury forced him out, and that was the last seen of him in Taunton. I can turn round now and say 'I told you so', but what would that achieve?"

Chapter Seven

TOP OF THE MOUNTAIN

RICHARD HADLEE:

> *"Crowe is totally dominant at the moment. I can't see his record for most runs in a New Zealand season ever being broken. He hasn't just scored hundreds, he's got big ones. His batting says much for his dedication, determination and consistency."*

One of the curiosities of watching sport is that you can never be sure when you are witnessing the peak of a person's career. Who could have imagined, when watching Allison Roe run so effortlessly to victory in the 1981 Boston and New York marathons, that she would never run as well again? Or, watching in awe while Rodney Redmond hit a century and a half-century on his test debut, against Pakistan in 1973, that he would never play another test?

In hindsight, and these things can only be judged with the benefit of hindsight, 1987 was the highpoint of Martin Crowe's career. He has played many splendid innings since then, including his 299 against Sri Lanka and that magic sequence in the 1992 World Cup.

But for assurance and poise, quality combined with quantity, his batting throughout 1987 was of mind-boggling brilliance. He proved himself in the domestic competition, when he piled on so many runs that he set a New Zealand record which may never be beaten. He took on the might of the West Indies pace attack and scored two centuries and an eighty in the three tests. He batted consistently well under all sorts of conditions during the English county season. And he finished off the calendar year by showing his mastery over the Australians. In addition, he squeezed in one test in Sri Lanka and in November played a central role in New Zealand's World Cup campaign.

In his mid-20s, fit and eager, he was a formidable obstacle for any bowler, good enough that year to rank alongside virtually any of the great names in cricket history.

Indeed, that's what he did because through 1987 Crowe joined an elite band of immortals who have scored more than 4000 runs in a calendar year.

The list reads like this:

	Year	I	NO	Runs	HS	Ave	100s
Denis Compton	1947	69	11	4962	246	85.55	22
Walter Hammond	1933	69	7	4445	336*	71.69	16
Don Bradman	1930	52	7	4368	452*	97.07	14
Herbert Sutcliffe	1932	62	8	4340	313	80.37	16
Len Hutton	1948	69	9	4167	176*	69.45	15
Bill Edrich	1947	69	9	4103	267*	68.38	12
Martin Crowe	1987	60	9	4045	206*	79.31	17

Besides his number of centuries, which only Compton of the 4000-plus club has exceeded, Crowe made 16 scores of between 50 and 100. Eight of his centuries were in New Zealand, six for Somerset and three on the Australian tour.

He scored 1676 runs in New Zealand, 27 on the aborted tour of Sri Lanka, 1627 in England and 715 in Australia (the latter figure also a record for a New Zealander on tour in Australia, beating John Parker's 627 in 1973/74).Crowe's form during the 1987 New Zealand summer was breathtaking.

His sequence was:

Opponent	Runs	Min	Balls	6s	4s
Northern Districts	56	47	39	2	8
	29	49	41	0	4
Wellington	160	310	254	1	25
	73	112	111	2	10
Otago	73	106	106	0	12
	66	106	92	0	8

Auckland	154*	245	230	1	20
	45	102	101	0	3
Canterbury	175*	274	230	5	22
	50	98	102	1	5
Otago	13	30	32	0	2
	8	29	26	0	1
Northern Districts	151	238	194	1	22
Canterbury	144	189	175	3	21
	151	205	155	3	18
West Indies (1st test)	3	50	37	0	0
	119	385	308	0	15
West Indies (2nd test)	10	48	36	0	1
	104	382	264	1	8
West Indies (3rd test)	83	213	154	0	13
	9*	39	17	0	0
	1676	**3257**	**2704**	**20**	**218**

He scored his runs at a rate of 62 per 100 balls faced and averaged 93.11 an innings.

Before Crowe's onslaught, Glenn Turner had held the record, set during the 1975/76 season, when he scored 1244 runs at 77.75. Graeme Hick was in stupendous form during the 1988/89 season and scored 1228 runs at 94.96. Other than these three, only Jeff Crowe (1063 at 62.52 in 1991/92), Bert Vance (1037 at 64.81 in 1988/89) and John Wright (1019 at 53.63 in 1986/87) have exceeded 1000 runs.

Obviously it was Crowe's batting in the test matches which deserves most credit, but his astounding run in the Shell Trophy cannot be overlooked.

Before the season began, he spoke of how keen he was to have a full season playing for Central Districts. It was his fourth season with the province and in the previous three, because of heavy international commitments, he'd been available for a total of only 10 first class matches. "At least there'll be some continuity this time and I'll be able to play regularly in the side," he said.

Richard Hadlee, playing for Canterbury, was on the receiving end of three centuries and a fifty and said after Crowe had scored centuries in both innings against Canterbury at Pukekura Park: "Crowe is totally dominant at the moment. I can't see his record for most runs in a New

Zealand season ever being broken. He hasn't just scored hundreds, he's got big ones. His batting says much for his dedication, determination and consistency."

With Crowe in sublime form, Central Districts, not a particularly strong combination on paper, won the Shell Trophy for the first time. The last time they'd been the No 1 first class side in the country was way back in 1971 when they won the Plunket Shield.

The West Indies series had a lot of needle. As well as the Somerset wrangle overhanging the principal performers, Richards and Crowe, the West Indies had vivid and sour memories of their previous tour of New Zealand, in 1980. They'd lost that series and been involved in a number of ugly incidents, the most serious of which was Colin Croft's barging of umpire Fred Goodall.

New Zealand were defending a record of not having lost a series at home since 1979, but knew they would be up against it in taking on the unofficial world champions. So the series was awaited with relish.

There was another challenge for Crowe personally: he always measured himself against the best batsman in the opposing team. On this occasion it was Richards. Was it to be a passing of the baton?

New Zealand soon found themselves in trouble during the first test, at the Basin Reserve, and were bowled out for 228. Except for John Wright, the New Zealanders offered little. Crowe batted nearly an hour for three runs. The West Indies replied with 345 and very quickly New Zealand were staring at a heavy defeat, especially when they sagged to 20-2 in their second innings.

Then Crowe and Wright came together. They defied the West Indies attack – Marshall, Garner, Walsh, Holding and Richards – for more than six hours and added 241. Wright won tremendous praise for his 582-minute vigil which brought him 138 runs. But Crowe, who scored 119, played a far more elegant and attractive innings. He hit 15 boundaries and nothing the West Indies pacemen – all of them great bowlers in their own right – threw his way unsettled him. Even Richards commented at the end of the match: "They did a wonderful job. New Zealand should be proud of them."

It was Round One to Crowe.

Off they moved to Auckland, where the West Indies scored a 10-wicket victory late on the final day. Only one New Zealander managed a fifty – Crowe, who in the second innings (after a first innings score of 10) batted another six hours-plus for 104. It was his seventh test century, equalling the New Zealand record he was soon to make his own. The West Indies won the match comprehensively, but in the battle of the batting supremos, it was Round Two to Crowe.

The third test was played in Christchurch, where Crowe again led the New Zealand effort. In the New Zealand first innings – after the West Indies had been bowled out for 100 – Crowe hit 13 fours in his 83. His scoring rate was slow for him, but only because the West Indies speedsters took so long to get through their overs. When Crowe batted, he looked immensely secure and poised. At Christchurch he was assisted by his brother Jeff and John Bracewell, who also scored half-centuries.

When the West Indies were dismissed for 264 in their second innings, New Zealand were left needing just 33 to win. Losing five wickets in the process, they were grateful for the calming influence of Crowe, whose nine not out righted a wobbling ship.

So during the test series Crowe scored 328 runs at 65.60. Gordon Greenidge led the West Indies figures with 344 (including one score of 213) at 68.80. And Richards? His 77 runs at 19.20 left no doubt about the winner of the heavyweight contest.

Because of the circumstances at the time, and the quality of the opposing bowlers, Crowe's performances in this series are widely regarded as the best of his career.

John Wright watched Crowe with awe, often from the other end. "Geez, he batted well in that series. It was a big challenge for him and I know he trained really, really hard for it. It was a personal confrontation between Viv Richards and Martin, and Martin won. It was an outstanding effort. They bowled bloody quick on wickets doing something. But he didn't just survive; he played shots."

Don Neely emphasises the style with which Crowe batted. "He gutsed it out. He proved himself against the quickest and best attack in the world. He was fighting the whole way, yet he got his runs in style."

The West Indians felt that but for Crowe, they would have cleaned up the series comfortably, instead of having a 1-1 draw. Courtney Walsh says Crowe was clearly the best batsman in the New Zealand side. "We tried and tried to get him out. But we could never manage it twice in a match, or not cheaply anyway. He had a good technique against the fast bowlers, a different sort of stance with an upright approach. He won the Christchurch test for them and all season he seemed to be getting in our way."

At about this time, Crowe was named in a World team, selected by a panel of 10 well-known international cricket writers and commentators. The team was Gordon Greenidge, Graham Gooch, Sunil Gavaskar, Javed Miandad, Martin Crowe, Allan Border, Viv Richards, Imran Khan, Richard Hadlee, Jeffrey Dujon, Malcolm Marshall, Abdul Qadir. Four players – Border, Marshall, Richards and Khan – were unanimous choices. Hadlee polled eight votes and Crowe five. By the end of 1987, Crowe would certainly have moved into the automatic selection category.

Before Crowe headed for Somerset to attempt to quell the doubters there, he had the little business of a hastily arranged New Zealand tour of Sri Lanka. He wasn't keen to tour and initially made himself unavailable, but was leaned on to go. So, under his brother Jeff's captaincy, he headed for Sri Lanka. It was to be a short, grisly visit.

Crowe stood down for the tour opener, against a President's XI, but came in for the first test at Colombo, the match in which Andrew Jones made his test debut.

For once, he had to fill a minor role to brother Jeff, who played an almost interminable innings of 120, in 609 minutes. Not that batting conditions were easy – it took Richard Hadlee 406 minutes to make 151. Hadlee's century was the 100th in tests for New Zealand.

Martin's contribution was a relatively minor 27. Doubtless he steeled himself to do better in the following test. But there was no second test. Shortly after the Colombo match finished, a bomb exploded in the Sri Lankan capital, killing more than 100 people. In view of the civil unrest, the tour was abandoned.

So Crowe hot-footed it to England, where he settled in for a productive county season, even if it was ended prematurely by the Clive Rice delivery which cracked his thumb. As detailed in the chapter on his county career, he scored 1627 runs at 67.69 in England.

By the time he arrived back in New Zealand, his year's tally in first class matches was 3330 runs at 77.44.

This is disregarding all the one-day matches he'd played, in New Zealand and England. Even more demanding was the 1987 World Cup in India and Pakistan. New Zealand didn't have a great time of it, but Crowe finished second to Ken Rutherford in the averages with 222 runs at 37.00 an innings.

The New Zealanders arrived back just in time for their tour of Australia. Far from being stale because of all the cricket he'd played and the runs he'd scored, Crowe seemed fresh and eager. He obviously enjoyed playing under his brother's captaincy – he rated Jeff the best test captain he played for – and he certainly seemed to try even harder to help his brother. Jeff, though he proved a popular captain, struggled desperately for runs and was eventually dropped in the series that followed, against England. Martin could see his brother struggling and tried to compensate. As Jeff told me: "Martin knew I was hurting, that my form was becoming a burden. He tried extra hard and he had a tremendous series. You could say he would bat that well anyway, being such a key batsman. But I know part of his determination came from wanting to help out his brother."

Martin was in superlative form throughout the Australian tour. He opened the first class matches with 119 against Western Australia and followed that with 144 and 56 not out against South Australia. Then came the three tests, which brought him scores of 67, 23, 137, 8, 82 and 79. For the tour he scored 715 runs at a shade under 90 an innings. In the tests his 396 runs were scored at an average of 66.

The third test finished on December 30. When Crowe went to the crease, history beckoned. He had scored 3966 runs in the calendar year. As ever, he proved equal to the task, and his 79 lifted his year's tally to 4045. He was the first person to top 4000 in a year since Len Hutton in 1948.

Yet it is an interesting insight to his character that he finished the test, which was drawn with Australia nine wickets down in their second innings, less than happy with his batting. This at once reveals the perfectionist nature which has made him the batsman he is, and the intensity which has at times caused him anguish.

Ron Palenski wrote an excellent story about it in *The Dominion Sunday Times*, during which he pointed out that while cricket was abuzz with the gripping finish to the test and the record-breaking feat of Crowe, the man himself was one of the last to leave the Melbourne Cricket Ground that evening.

"The reason he was away late," Palenski wrote, "was that he had spent a considerable time in the New Zealand dressing room staring at a wall and analysing his 'failure'...

"Crowe's name went up on a runs honours board under names like Denis Compton, Walter Hammond, Don Bradman, Herbert Sutcliffe, Len Hutton and Bill Edrich. There have been many renowned batsmen – Gary Sobers, Greg Chappell, Viv Richards – who don't rate on that particular honours board, but Crowe does. Yet he had seen failure. He was disappointed, disconsolate.

"Crowe has touched greatness, but doesn't acknowledge it. 'My name is now among the greats of yesteryear, but I'm not among the greats of today,' he said.

"He was pleased, of course, to have reached such a milestone and said it was a pleasant surprise when he heard over the MCG loudspeaker that he had passed the 4000-run mark. It had been a back of the mind goal, he said, but not one of paramount importance. Of more importance to him, and the reason for the disappointment when all about him was celebration of a shining talent, was his inability yet again to play the perfect innings...

"'There's something missing and I don't know why,' he said. 'I don't know why I can get so far, hitting the ball bloody well, and not score big innings.' "

That's as good a way as any I know of describing the enigma that is Crowe: always striving for perfection in a game where perfection is impossible, and therefore being doomed always to disappointment.

Don Neely stresses Crowe's perfectionist nature. "It's the John McEnroe aspect of him. It's not enough to score a century. He wants it to be a classic innings, a perfect innings. He's one of the very few batsmen you could imagine scoring a test century and being unhappy with his innings."

When Don Bradman was bowled second ball by Eric Hollies for a duck in the Oval test in 1948, it left him with a career test average of 99.94, just shy of the statistical perfection of an average of 100. It was as if the fates were flexing their muscle: not even Bradman could leave test cricket having achieved perfection.

Cricket is the great game it is because the margin between success and failure can be so slight. The fates don't let even the greatest away with perfection, as Crowe discovered during the year of his greatest batting.

Chapter Eight

SIMPLY THE BEST

JOHN BRACEWELL:
> *"Teaching was never a problem for Martin. He wanted to help.*
> *But unfortunately, if the player offered an opinion and it was*
> *contrary, Martin became quite dismissive."*

Martin batted only moderately as New Zealand comfortably qualified for the 1988 World Series finals in Australia, eliminating Sri Lanka from the three-way contest. In the finals, New Zealand were soundly beaten by Australia 2-0 and Martin played second fiddle to Andrew Jones, whose one-day record at about this time was outstanding.

Back home, New Zealand hosted a big tour by Mike Gatting's England team in which the key performers were batsmen Martyn Moxon and Chris Broad and pace bowler Graham Dilley. By this point New Zealand skipper Jeff Crowe was in dire need of some runs to justify a middle-order position in the test side.

Jeff's horror run with the bat continued though, as he scored 28, 0, 11 and 1 before being replaced by Bert Vance in the batting line-up and by John Wright as skipper. Crowe was honest enough to concede he'd have dropped himself.

Meanwhile, Martin had his own problems. He had 5 and 6 in the first test, 36 and 26 in the second. After a visit to his former Auckland Grammar headmaster John Graham, and some advice from Englishman

Geoff Boycott, he came right in the third test, at the Basin Reserve, with a 402-minute innings of 143. "John Graham gave me a bit of a dressing down, and rightly so. He told me that in my batting and about the field I was just going through the motions. He told me to play straight and to work hard."

The advice obviously worked. With Ken Rutherford also scoring a century, and John Bracewell and Mark Greatbatch making half-centuries, New Zealand were able to declare at 512-6, a dream start for Wright as captain. However, rain washed out much of the proceedings after that and England were left at 183-2. All three tests in a rather tedious series were drawn.

Crowe failed to fire in the subsequent one-day series and made himself unavailable for the tournament afterwards in Sharjah.

Then followed his frustrating English county season, cut short after just six matches because of recurring back problems. While recuperating from the back injury, Crowe was diagnosed as having salmonella, evidently picked up during the 1984 tour of Sri Lanka.

And that was it for the year for Martin. He returned home to rest and ready himself for New Zealand's rugged tour of India at the end of the year. But his recovery took much longer than he'd hoped. He pulled out of the Young New Zealand team's tour of Zimbabwe and then had to miss the tour of India.

Though he wasn't playing cricket, Crowe continued to contribute to various media outlets, one being his *Dominion Sunday Times* column. In one rather strange column, in December 1988, he used John Bracewell as an example of one problem New Zealand cricket apparently faced: over-modesty.

Bracewell bowled New Zealand to victory in the second test at Bombay, taking 6-51 in the second innings. When he failed to take a wicket in the next test, at Hyderabad, Crowe, from a distance of several thousand kilometres, deduced that it was because Bracewell had been too modest. He felt Bracewell had belittled his match-winning performance and that therefore he did not believe in himself as he might have when the next test began. Of course, this was all vastly amusing to the other New Zealand players who knew how combative and belligerent a player Bracewell was. If anyone suffered from a lack of belief in himself, it was not Bracewell.

In the course of the same column, Crowe mentioned how he too had suffered from his own over-modest behaviour. He mentioned his feat in 1987 of scoring 4000 runs in a calendar year. "I think that milestone was worthy of a Sportsman of the Year nomination, in the same bracket as Glenn Turner getting 1000 runs before the end of May in 1973, and that won him the award. But because I played it down, it didn't have the impact it should have."

By this stage of his career, Crowe was sometimes seeking out coaching advice from Harold Whitcombe, a stalwart of the Cornwall club and an Auckland coach. Whitcombe, now in his 60s, has at various times coached Jeff Crowe, Mark Greatbatch, Adam Parore, Gary Troup and a host of other Aucklanders. He'd first spotted Martin Crowe when Martin was just a youngster. "He always had the technique. That came from his dad and he has to take a lot of credit for that. By the time he got to Auckland Grammar, he looked a terrific bat. He appeared older than the other boys; that was the mana he had."

Whitcombe first offered coaching to Crowe after Crowe's successful county season in 1987, and has worked with him semi-regularly since. "He rang me up when he got back from England and asked me to see if anything was wrong, if any faults had crept in. We got a bowling machine and I helped him... just little things. I noticed his right arm was starting to float and got that back in by his side.

"He's terrific to coach because once he believes what you say is right, he really works at it. You're not doing any major overhaul; his technique is pretty sound. I imagine it's like David Leadbetter with the golfers – he just fine tunes them. Sometimes Martin gets a bit lazy with his feet and takes only half-steps."

One of Crowe's greatest attributes, says Whitcombe, is that he's generally not content merely to occupy the crease. "He likes to dominate. That makes him so much harder to bowl to. In that last test he played, against South Africa, he tried to occupy the crease in the first innings and didn't look half as good. You don't often make hundreds just by occupying the crease."

Whitcombe says one area he generally steers clear of is psychological advice. "I don't talk about the mental side. It's very overrated. Can you really believe a guy of Martin's ability and love of his country needs a motivator, a head-shrinker? Martin might believe that, but I feel you should simply go out there and enjoy the game."

I asked Whitcombe for a technical assessment of Crowe. "He is one of the best in the world because he has so much time and power. He has got his technique right. Over the years he has had more practice against pace than spin, so is probably more comfortable against the faster bowlers. But I wouldn't say he's weak against spin. You don't find his opposition whipping on their spinners as Martin walks out to bat."

By the time Pakistan toured New Zealand in early 1989, Crowe had been out of the national team nearly a year. He announced his return in the most emphatic manner, scoring a magnificent century in the second test, at Wellington (after rain had wiped out the first test in Dunedin).

John Wright says the innings came at a crucial time for Crowe. "We'd been through a hard tour of India which made us a pretty tight unit, so Martin had to get back into the swing and become part of the team again. It was a technically superb innings."

Crowe came out with a typical Croweism at the press conference afterwards while discussing why he had missed out on a test double century: "I didn't really make a conscious note of saying 'I want 200.' I've learnt that you can get too carried away with setting those specific goals. They can hold you back. I never thought about playing any particular shot, and I never thought consciously I had to get after the bowling. So if I'm to blame anything, I'm going to have to blame my subconscious."

He never looked back after that, scoring 78 in the third test, and having a good one-day series. But Andrew Jones claimed the Redpath Cup as the best batsman of the season in first class cricket. It was the first time since 1985 that Crowe had been overlooked for the award, an indication of how much he had become the backbone of the New Zealand effort.

During the New Zealand winter Crowe captained a star-studded World XI in England, the focal point being the match against the MCC at Scarborough, in which Crowe scored a blazing 130 not out. Also in his side was Mark Greatbatch. As well as his big innings at Scarborough, Crowe had a good day against Glamorgan, hitting 44. Greatbatch also did well, getting 52.

While in England, Crowe, looking for some cricket to keep him honed, played for the MCC, had a few matches for the Somerset Second XI and did some coaching.

Crowe was chosen as John Wright's vice-captain when New Zealand had a short tour of Australia before Christmas and battled to a gritty draw in the one test, at Perth. The match, and the tour, are recalled for Greatbatch's magnificent batting in the test, when he scored 76 and 146 not out and was at the crease a total of 876 minutes (14½ hours). It was Greatbatch's defiant second innings century – well supported by several others – which saved a test that had seemed irretrievably lost after New Zealand followed on 290 behind and were 11-2 in their second innings. Don Neely rightly said most great test batsmen would have swapped two or three of their centuries to play an innings of the character Greatbatch displayed in Perth.

Crowe didn't have a bad test either. After warming up with 87 against Western Australia and a century against South Australia, he had a double of 62 and 30 in the test.

By this stage of his career, Crowe seemed able to make big scores at domestic first class level almost at will. As Don Neely says: "Over the past few years, Martin has become almost exclusively a test batsman." He is far too good for most provincial attacks, but, even by his standards, the occasional innings stands out. One such was his score of 242 for Central Districts against Otago at Pukekura Park (one of his happiest hunting grounds) in January 1990. Crowe smashed 39 fours and three sixes in his 286-ball innings. His score, which equalled his personal best at the time, was a record for Central Districts and left spectators staggered by its brilliance.

Taranaki Cricket Association president Laurie Denton described the innings as "virtually out of this world". "Mark Greatbatch started it with his 86, but Crowe really let rip and it became embarrassing for Otago. A lot of players here with first class experience who were among the spectators were bewildered by it. It was unbelievable."

India toured New Zealand in early 1990 and the three-test series turned into a batting bonanza. Crowe scored one century – 113 at Auckland – and averaged 53.66 for the series. Yet this placed him only sixth in the averages. Andrew Jones averaged 122.50 and still had to take second place to John Wright.

The New Zealand Cricket Council tried something a little adventurous with a triangular one-day series, involving India and Australia. Unfortunately, rain interfered and the council lost money on the venture.

For Crowe, who scored a century and an unbeaten 51, the series was significant because he played as an opening batsman. His century came at Carisbrook, but was marred by a clash with Indian opening bowler Manoj Prabhakar. Crowe was struck with what he alleged was a deliberate bean ball. He slumped to the ground after the ball had struck his gloves and crashed into the collar bone. There was a heated exchange betwen the pair, and umpire Steve Dunne asked Crowe to apologise for "a very offensive, racist remark". The pair had another exchange after Prabhakar bowled Crowe two overs later. Crowe later apologised to Prabhakar.

He injured his leg in the one-dayer at Auckland, and so missed the series final against Australia, which Australia won embarrassingly easily, and the test that followed at the Basin. New Zealand won the test, due largely to the brilliant bowling of John Bracewell and a blazing last-afternoon century by John Wright.

At the end of the season Crowe set a record he was less proud of when he was fined a New Zealand record amount of $750 for his criticism of umpire Steve Woodward in his Sunday newspaper column. It followed a less than satisfactory final match for Central Districts for Crowe, who had just bought a house in Wellington where he was to play his cricket the following season. In the Shell Cup final against Auckland at Napier, umpire Steve Woodward gave him out lbw to Willie Watson for 11 when his side were chasing 198 for victory.

While the Auckland players gathered to congratulate Watson, Crowe remained near the crease and Woodward had to raise his finger again before Crowe departed, obviously not happy. "I whacked the cover off the ball. It was a staggering decision," he later explained. He said he'd not bothered to look at the umpire because he had hit the ball.

Crowe then lowered his sights on Tony Blain (17 off 44 balls), blaming him for Central's eventual 22-run loss. He said Central had been on target to win going into the last 20 overs, but had lost momentum. "Tony Blain can take a lot of responsibility for not keeping the score moving. He played abysmally. In the end result, that was the crucial stage."

In spite of the sourness of his last game for Central, Crowe left the province with very good memories. Blair Furlong, the association's executive director, says Crowe was invariably professional, excellent to deal with. "He did what you asked, or told you why not. And he played magnificently. We couldn't have asked for more. I suppose his disappointment was that CD never won anything after the Shell Trophy victory, but he went with our best wishes. He had one more year to run on his contract when he asked to be released because he'd bought the house in Wellington."

Furlong says that Crowe shone on promotional tours. "I remember touring with him after he'd come back from Sri Lanka and was sick. He was marvellous. He wasn't the sort to go down to the pub for a beer, but at our house he'd talk cricket all night, and was very relaxed."

The legendary Viv Richards – replaced by 24-year-old Crowe at Somerset.

Sean Neely

Allan Donald – on the receiving end of a double century at Edgbaston in 1987.

Joseph Romanos Collection

Don Neely collection

Peter Roebuck – Somerset's beleaguered captain.

Ian Botham – sour grapes, right to the end.

A master batsman, bristling aggression.

Drinks break for Martin and Jeff Crowe against the West Indies.

Ian Smith – strong supporter of Crowe as captain.

Simone and Martin Crowe on their wedding day, with best man Mark Greatbatch.

New Zealand Woman's Weekly

J.G. Blackwell

A day at the cricket for Simone Crowe.

Plenty to discuss for the Crowe brothers
during a worrying home series against
England in 1988.

Dear Hog!

Great stuff! But be there at tea

We can do this. The whole of the NZ
boys need you to do it. Don't
throw it away now.

Brace is playing superbly for you
(and us).

God speed.

"Cones"

P.S. I like to, to, to, ... (poetic justice)

You're good enough to save this, if you want
AS

This note, hidden in a batting glove, helped
Crowe maintain his concentration during
his century in the second test against the
West Indies. Crowe had just been dropped
and was starting to tire when Jeremy Coney
decided it was time to offer some
encouragement. He had Stephen Boock
run onto the field 20 minutes before tea and
offer Crowe some new batting gloves.
"Thanks for the encouragement, and I'll
keep the gloves as well," Crowe responded.

"Now Martin, how will you do it next year
when you're captain?" New Zealand skipper
John Wright discusses matters with his
deputy, Crowe, in 1990.

110

Still able to muster considerable pace when aroused.

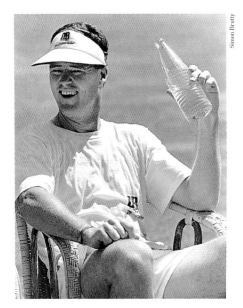

John Bracewell – too modest? Lacking in belief? So Crowe suggested in one column.

Mark Priest – "I wasn't prepared to suck up to him and I've paid for it."

Shane Thomson – initial problems with Crowe.

John Wiltshire also watched with satisfaction Crowe's performances for Central Districts. In fact, Wiltshire was the Central captain when Crowe signed to play for the association and was one of the factors which lured Crowe there. "When Martin arrived at Hastings he tutored at Lindisfarne College. He'd do some cricket coaching, help with the roster and do other duties to help out the masters. He became part of the school family until the first class season started. He was very well received.

"After that he turned to playing and promotional work, and it was a very satisfactory arrangement. There were no injuries in those days and the kids in particular really enjoyed his coaching."

Crowe was involved in a curious episode at the end of March 1990, when he travelled to Brisbane, ostensibly to watch New Zealand play Australia in a Davis Cup tie. The New Zealand team included Brett Steven, with whom he'd become friendly while training in Auckland.

While in Brisbane, Crowe had a short meeting with Queensland cricket officials. There was talk of Crowe possibly representing Queensland in the Sheffield Shield. Crowe performed the intricate balancing act of rubbishing such suggestions while at the same time fanning the flames of speculation. "I just had a 10-minute chat with the Queensland chairman," Crowe explained to Don Cameron of the *New Zealand Herald*. "I learned a few facts about cricket in Queensland, and checked out a few things. There was never any formal suggestion that I would play there. However, that is something I would like to look at in the future. I am always interested in developing my game... and a couple of years in Sheffield Shield cricket might help me develop further."

However, he told Dianna Leslie of *The Press*: "It is early days yet. I was just gathering information. The Sheffield Shield starts in November and goes through to March and games are spread out over that time. There is no real opportunity to slip away and play for New Zealand. It is fair to say that I will have to make a decision one way or the other. I am keen to give it a go. It is a great challenge for me. Offers to play Sheffield and county cricket don't come along that often."

He finally put an end to all the rumours, fuelled mainly by himself, by calling a press conference in early April and stating: "I'm pleased to announce I will be playing cricket in Wellington next season and continuing my test career for New Zealand. In the end I decided I'm very patriotic toward my country and I don't want to miss out on the opportunities that are there in representing New Zealand at test level."

The 1990 tour of England was very much a changing of the guard occasion. John Wright led the team, Bob Cunis was coach and Richard Hadlee, John Bracewell and Martin Snedden were key bowlers. Trevor Franklin, Wright, Andrew Jones and Martin Crowe led the batting. It proved to be a farewell to international cricket for Hadlee, Bracewell and Snedden. Cunis stood down from his job following the tour, to be replaced by Lees. And Wright was unavailable for the next tour, to Pakistan, and therefore relinquished the captaincy – for good as it turned out – to Crowe, who was vice-captain in England.

That England tour is recalled with mixed memories. Hadlee was knighted during the tour, a significant honour, especially while his playing career was not quite finished. With true Hadlee class, he finished his test and first class careers with a wicket with his final ball. Bracewell completed both his 1000 runs and 100 wickets in test cricket, lifting him into exalted all-rounder territory not trodden even by John Reid, and Trevor Franklin, a popular member of the party, made a century in the Lord's test.

Wright recalls the tour with much fondness, marred, he says, by defeat in the third test. "That was extremely disappointing. I blamed myself because I won the toss and bowled. I could tell after about two balls it was the wrong decision. They made 435 and we were always struggling."

Another factor marring the tour was excessive talk about who would be the next New Zealand captain.

"I wasn't going to be available for the next tour, to Pakistan," says Wright. "In fact, I thought that might be my lot. I believed then that you don't retire until the start of the next season, but I did wonder if I was near the end of my test career. Martin was obviously the heir apparent. I felt he should be next captain, so was happy enough when he was named vice-captain, even though Martin Snedden had done a very good job in that department previously.

"But from my point of view, I didn't manage things very well. I learnt a lot about captaincy on that tour. The only trouble was, I was just finishing as captain! Looking back, a new regime was setting up. Ian Taylor was manager, Martin was going to be captain, Smithy was there as the most experienced player. There was quite a lot of talk about the next captain. I really didn't get very involved. I was concentrating on the tour of England. But Martin prepared a plan for how he saw the future of New Zealand cricket, and there was a meeting in London with Martin and one or two cricket officials. Looking back, it would have been better to concentrate totally on the tour under way, but when you're caught up in things, you sometimes don't see where people's focus might be wandering."

Crowe seemed, at least on the surface, to struggle with his commitment during the tour. Though his first class figures were excellent, he had a poor test series with one score of 59 and three failures.

He was involved in an unsavoury incident in the third test at Birmingham when he was given out leg before by umpire Barrie Meyer. Crowe looked away as Meyer raised his finger and then waited several seconds before leaving the crease. Former England captain Tony Lewis wrote in the *Sunday Telegraph*: "It is simply good manners to look at the umpire who is responding to an appeal. He can hardly claim he was unaware he was given out because the reaction of the crowd was suitably loud and spontaneous. One may think poker-faced acting clearly is one of the skills required by young men who wish to emulate some of the best players. That would be a pity because he is a terrific player to watch and for schoolboys to copy." Crowe subsequently apologised to Meyer.

Besides the Meyer incident, Crowe fell out further with Bracewell, with whom he'd had an uneasy relationship previously, and had skirmishes with all-rounders Shane Thomson and Mark Priest.

Thomson began the tour with something of a golden boy reputation, almost like a young Martin Crowe. But during the tour he drifted. "Shane couldn't bat in the top six," says Wright. "He'd been picked primarily as a bowler, but was injured and, anyway, didn't seem terribly keen on bowling. He was very young. I talked to him a bit and said that he had to go away and decide what he wanted to do in cricket. If he wanted to be a bowler, he had to do a lot of work.

"Mark Priest was okay. He was going to be picked for the third test, but in the match before, against Essex, he'd been smashed around by Gooch, who scored a century. He should still have been picked.

"I wasn't really aware of the problems between Martin and one or two of the players. Perhaps I should have kept my eyes open more, but on a long tour there are always going to be the odd dramas, and I tried to ignore them where possible. Otherwise the danger is that you blow up things that would just pass over in a very short time."

Crowe and Thomson had a big blow-up during the Somerset match, in which Wright didn't play. Things became so heated that when Wright and Bob Cunis returned later in the day they found Crowe had threatened to send Thomson home. Thomson, suffering from a leg injury, had been required to bowl 17 overs of medium-pace. He went for 104 runs. Crowe was not impressed with his attitude, and Thomson was not impressed with his captain's understanding of the situation. Manager Ian Taylor was involved by then and it required a lot of calming before order was restored.

Oddly enough, Crowe had been very supportive of Thomson initially, and went out of his way to help. They've since sorted out their relationship and get along quite well. Crowe is unabashed about his dealings with Thomson: "I didn't think he was ready for test cricket at that point, and he had to decide what he wanted to do with his game. I'm proud of his development." There is an interesting logic about this: Thomson had gone on to prove himself at top level, and Crowe claims some credit. Priest has not, so Crowe justifies his negative reaction towards Priest by saying he was right all along about him. Crowe thus finds himself in a win-win situation.

Thomson says stories of him being threatened with dismissal from the 1990 tour have become exaggerated in the retelling. "There was a chance that I might have been sent home, but not so much because of a falling out with Hogan as because of my injury. I'd been picked as a third or fourth seam bowler, and because I had hurt my leg, I wasn't able to bowl as much or as well as I should have. So I suppose a decision to send me home would have been fair enough. As it was, Chris Pringle, who was not in the side, ended up playing a game for us as cover."

He says his relationship with Crowe has advanced a long way since 1990. "That was such a long time ago. A lot of things have happened in the meantime to change the way both of us are. In the five years since, I've had a lot of opportunity to express myself on the field. I got dropped from the New Zealand team for a couple of years, and was able to play more as I wanted for Northern Districts, so that when I got back into the New Zealand side, I was more confident and in control of things. When I got back, I managed to put a few decent scores on the board and perceptions of me changed a bit.

"Martin has changed too. He's much more at ease with the guys now. He's still a hard competitor, but is a lot more approachable. When you're captain, you have to be a bit aloof, keep a distance. As a player you can simply be the guys' mate, and I think that's what has happened. Martin has helped me with my cricket. He is very good on the technical side. I always welcome his advice. Obviously his methods don't suit everyone, but I've certainly benefited."

Unlike one or two others, Thomson does not feel that his falling-out with Crowe in 1990 was the reason he failed to make the New Zealand team for some time. "I doubt that. I'd hope not. You'd like to think New Zealand Cricket is more organised than that and that no-one is that powerful. It's a scary thought that anyone would wield that power. A player who feels like that should concentrate on performing in the middle. When he produces the goods, he'll get back into the side."

The Thomson and Priest cases highlight a problem Crowe has faced for several years. John Bracewell sums it up: "Teaching was never a problem for Martin. He wanted to help. But unfortunately, if the player offered an opinion back, and it was contrary, Martin became quite dismissive. "Another test teammate of Crowe's, who asked not to be named, says: "Martin is a complex sort of guy who pours a lot of energy into people he thinks are deserving of it. Then when he decides you aren't deserving, he will walk away. He is a little obsessive about it. He decided Thommo wasn't dedicated enough. The same with Priest. He wrote me off. He pushed and encouraged me, then turned away. It was a problem with his captaincy. He was too moody. Guys have to know where they stand. You can't have someone who is your pal one day, but not the next."

In hindsight, these rumblings with fellow players were an interesting preview of problems Crowe would run into as captain. Wright: "Martin had definite ideas on players' ability and attitude and there's nothing wrong with that, but it's a learning process as a leader. You learn that people have different buttons you have to push to get the best out of them. Some of our team annoyed Martin because they were far more laid-back than him. Martin's intense, a perfectionist, and he gets irritated by that. But people are people – sometimes you have to take the good with the bad."

Cunis says Crowe was reasonably supportive during the 1990 tour. "He took part in the selection meetings, and involved himself. Martin saw the game a different way to us, but he was quite content to go along with us, and we didn't have any big hassles. I found him very enthusiastic as far as being involved with helping the younger players to practise and not sit around. I admired him for that.

"We did come to grief over one or two little things. Two days before a test, I used to make us go out as a unit. Most of the team liked this. We'd go out and have a couple of beers, whether we were in England, Wellington, wherever. Sometimes it might go a little longer than a couple of beers. Martin had a lot of trouble coping with this. He had other things he wanted to do – social functions, golf etcetera. So it really annoyed him. He wanted them wiped. But Wrighty, Braces, Hadlee, Martin Snedden… they all liked them."

By this stage of his career, the word "intense" was being used increasingly to describe Crowe. Often writers used it in a critical manner, as if there was something wrong with a cricketer applying himself to his job with all the dedication he could muster. Crowe's teammates are almost unanimous in support of him in this regard.

Lance Cairns: "I've always had a lot of time for Martin as a player. As a person, he has a totally different style to myself; he's a high-flyer. He has tended to stick to himself a lot. That's good. If a guy is going to be one of the boys, he's never going to stand out. Martin had the will and organisation to do what he needed to achieve his goals.

"Occasionally he got criticised for being too much of an individual. There were questions about his team spirit. But how good is the team spirit if you're not winning? I'd rather have eleven Martins in a team. Martin was a good contributor at team talks. He thought a lot about the game. He was analytical.

"But there's no denying his intensity. It's all to do with ability and the way he plays. He's very similar to Richard Hadlee in that regard. They worked on goals to keep motivated. Outside things didn't matter. They didn't care about it. Success at cricket comes before anything else. You can always put up with these sort of people; in fact you love to have them. They're the big achievers."

Cairns says he sees a similarity between his son Christopher, and Martin. "Christopher has the ability, which he hasn't produced consistently. They are quite similar in their aims and goals, though I don't think Christopher is quite so single-minded as Martin. He plays more for the team.

"Martin has had problems over the years taking the good with the bad. When someone has been critical of him, he goes straight onto the attack. He will not lie down and take it. He takes it very personally. Once, in his early days, a left-arm spinner had him out lbw. Martin sat down in the dressing room and drew diagrams and wrote a letter to the umpire to show how he could never have been out to that delivery. It takes a unique sort of person to think that way. But Martin is unique. Overall we've been very lucky to have had him in our test team."

Ian Smith: "I don't think Martin was ever too intense about his cricket.

He was and is more intense than most, and for longer, but look at his results."

John Bracewell: "As a player, as a technician, his work ethic was extremely high. He was professional and ruthless and he set about achieving his goals."

Richard Hadlee: "I think intensity is a good trait, because it means you are thinking about what you have to do. Martin is very single-minded about his cricket. It's something others could learn from. I'm not sure why the word intensity is used in a derogatory manner; it can be a very positive thing."

What was going to be interesting, as the new era dawned, was how that intensity would manifest itself in Crowe the captain. Few doubted his cricketing knowledge. But what sort of a captain would he be off the field? Did he have the man-management skills of, say, his brother Jeff, or would there be further ructions and fallings-out with teammates?

Chapter Nine

*C*APTAIN *AT* *L*AST

MARTIN CROWE:

> *"I like to be involved and in control. When I'm not, I find it hard to*
> *score runs. I've wanted to do it [captain New Zealand] ever since I*
> *can remember."*

It's doubtful if New Zealand has ever fielded a more tactically astute captain than Martin Crowe. Equally, has the test team ever been led by a person who struggled as much to get alongside some of his players?

With Crowe's batting, there are no caveats. He was an outstanding schoolboy cricketer, quickly established himself at first class level and has become one of the world's great test and one-day batsmen. He can score runs spectacularly quickly, as he did in the 1992 World Cup; he can defend grimly as he did in Sri Lanka in 1984 and Perth in 1993. He is a complete batsman.

But the same cannot be said of his captaincy. His cricket future is in doubt because of his various ailments, particularly his dodgy knee. Perhaps he will again captain the test side. He is certainly young enough. At the end of the 1995 New Zealand summer, he was still just 32. Tom Lowry, Walter Hadlee, Graham Dowling, Bevan Congdon, Geoff Howarth, Jeremy Coney, John Wright and others skippered the test team well beyond that age. It is questionable, though, whether Crowe and the New Zealand selectors should feel secure enough about his fitness to name him captain for more than a one-off situation.

So for now he must be judged as a captain on how he handled the job from 1990 to '93. In hindsight, he was a mixed bag.

Here is how Crowe compares statistically with other New Zealand captains who have led the test side in five or more matches or the national team in seven or more one-day internationals:

Test matches

	Tenure	P	W	L	D
John Reid	1956-65	34	3	18	13
Geoff Howarth	1980-85	30	11	7	12
Graham Dowling	1968-72	19	4	7	8
Ken Rutherford	1992-95	18	2	11	5
Bevan Congdon	1972-75	17	1	7	9
Martin Crowe	1990-93	16	2	7	7
Jeremy Coney	1984-87	15	5	4	6
John Wright	1988-90	14	3	3	8
Glenn Turner	1975-77	10	1	6	3
Mark Burgess	1978-79	10	1	6	3
Harry Cave	1955-56	9	0	5	4
Walter Hadlee	1946-51	8	0	2	6
Tom Lowry	1930-31	7	0	2	5
Curly Page	1932-37	7	0	3	4
Jeff Crowe	1987-88	6	0	1	5
Geoff Rabone	1953-55	5	0	4	1

One-day internationals

	M	W	L	NR	T
Geoff Howarth	60	31	26	3	0
Martin Crowe	44	21	22	1	0
Ken Rutherford	37	10	24	2	1
John Wright	31	16	15	0	0
Jeremy Coney	25	8	16	1	0
Jeff Crowe	16	4	12	0	0
Glenn Turner	8	5	2	1	0
Mark Burgess	8	2	6	0	0
Bevan Congdon	7	2	3	2	0

These then are the bald figures, and clearly Geoff Howarth emerges with colours flying. Yet strangely, two men widely regarded as among New Zealand's best test captains, Tom Lowry and Walter Hadlee – so different in personality and style – have mediocre records.

Lowry, a giant of a figure in the pioneering days of New Zealand test cricket, led the country in its first series, at home to what was virtually an England B team in 1930, and then through three tests on the 1931 tour of England. Not only did Lowry have no coach to assist him on that tour, but he managed the side as well as leading it! He had some wonderful players in his side, including Stewie Dempster, Jack Mills, Roger Blunt, Ken James, Bill Merritt, Curly Page and Giff Vivian. Against that, though, New Zealand were novices to test cricket and found themselves up against all-time greats like Herbert Sutcliffe, Les Ames, Frank Woolley and Walter Hammond.

In the circumstances, Lowry's side did surprisingly well, making a fine comeback in the first test at Lord's to force a draw with England on the back foot. Lowry, an innovative, unpredictable captain, certainly had a flair for captaincy, "a man more given to command than to obey" it was said. He showed his imaginative talents in the match against MCC in 1931, when he opened his bowling with leg-spinner Merritt on the last afternoon. Merritt responded by taking 7-28 off nine overs, the MCC were humbled for 48 and New Zealand won by an innings and 122 runs. As the MCC team included well-known players such as Jardine, Hearne, Chapman, Robins and White, this was a significant milestone in New Zealand's cricket history.

Hadlee was a different sort of captain altogether. An accountant by profession, he planned meticulously, like a commander going into a battle. He had a thorough grounding in the basics of cricket, and applied logic to extract the best from his team. Hadlee had an inglorious start to his test captaincy career when Australia caught a young New Zealand team on a wet Basin Reserve wicket in 1946, and bowled them out for 42 and 54 to win by an innings and 103 runs.

But he showed himself to be a top-flight captain during the arduous tour of England in 1949. He had at his command an array of gifted attacking batsmen, including Sutcliffe, Donnelly, Wallace, Reid, Smith and Hadlee himself. His bowling resources were more limited, for he had to rely on an ageing Jack Cowie, the accuracy of left-arm spinner Tom Burtt and Geoff Rabone's mixture of spin and pace. New Zealand played attractive cricket that summer, drawing the four-test series 0-0 and winning 13 first class matches and losing just one. Hadlee must take much of the credit for these results. He invariably strove for a result, and if the tests that summer had been of four or five days' duration, he would almost certainly have been New Zealand's first winning test captain.

With his precise field placing and selflessness, Hadlee won much praise from the England critics and certainly deserves a lofty ranking among New Zealand's test captains.

John Reid has led New Zealand in the most tests, and to him fell the honour of achieving the first victory, over the West Indies at Eden Park in 1956. He also led New Zealand to a 2-2 draw in South Africa in 1961/62, so certainly enjoyed great moments.

It must be stressed, too, that often his teams were appallingly weak in batting, the 1958 side to England being a case in point.

However, despite his longevity and his dominant personality, Reid was not regarded as an overly astute captain. He led from the front, by example, and may have lacked some of the subtler skills of test cricket's greatest leaders.

Howarth was the man who led New Zealand through its golden era in the early 1980s. It is often said a captain is only as good as his players, and Howarth was fortunate that in his sides were two champions in Richard Hadlee and Martin Crowe, and other world-class players like John Wright, Bruce Edgar, John Reid, Jeremy Coney, Ian Smith, Lance Cairns, Ewen Chatfield and John Bracewell.

That said, it was Howarth who instilled in the New Zealand team a tremendous sense of belief – they beat the acknowledged world champion West Indies in Howarth's first series as captain and took on a fine Australian side with heads held high. Howarth's team never lost a series at home.

Television commentator and 1960s Australian skipper Bill Lawry ranks Howarth the best New Zealand captain he has seen and among his own players Howarth also scores well. Ian Smith, who played under five test captains, named Howarth to lead his all-time best New Zealand side (which also contained Wright, Martin Crowe and Coney) and scored Howarth very highly in areas such as field placing and bowling changes. Richard Hadlee, who played under a vast array of test captains, named Howarth as the best. John Wright is another who speaks glowingly of Howarth's ability on the park.

Yet few captains have every base covered. For instance, teammates who discuss Howarth's captaincy refer also to his problems off the field with sloppy training habits and a tendency to over-socialise.

Crowe scores as high as any New Zealand captain who has gone before him in areas like tactical know-how and innovation. But he does not deal particularly well with some of his fellow players. This is strange because his brother Jeff, though he eventually lost the captaincy when he could not score enough runs to justify his place in the side, was an extremely popular captain. As Martin said on *Crowe on Crowe*: "You're the nice guy and I'm a sort of Darth Vader. I always seem to upset people…"

Jeff put it this way in a *Metro* article about Martin early in 1995: "He sees me as more of a people person than he's ever been. I wanted to bat like him; he's wanted to be able to shake hands and meet and mix like me."

Geoff Howarth, who watched Martin develop from a teenage test hopeful to a player of immense stature, feels he never came to terms with the interpersonal side of captaincy. "Martin was technically an excellent captain, but, by his own admission, he's not a great man-management captain, not so good at the one-on-one. From my discussions with him, and we had quite a few over the time I was coach, he is enjoying his cricket without the captaincy."

Besides struggling with his interpersonal skills, Crowe has a question mark over another aspect of his leadership. His teammates say his captaincy was at its best when he was playing well himself. If he felt positive and successful, then he captained superbly. If he'd failed, and was moody or grouchy or low, then anything could happen. Walter Hadlee often says: "The captain must regard himself as the least important member of the team." He is not referring to the captain's batting or bowling, but to his outlook. The captain must be utterly selfless.

John Graham is well-placed to talk about this, as he was a successful All Black captain, then ran a large and significant school for many years, and has become a leader in the business world. "The skipper of an international side, especially in a game like cricket which takes a long time to play, must be liked by his team," he says. "It's a personal thing. There should be a certain modesty there. A captain has no need to push his own performance. The skipper has to be a man for all seasons, so to speak. The status should come simply from having the job. That should be enough to satisfy his ego."

Crowe falls down in this area, failing to treat those old imposters, triumph and disaster, just the same. Graham: "He could not see outside himself. By the time he got the New Zealand captaincy, he was into that introspective period when it had to all centre around him. There's no warmth there. Many of his teammates didn't like him. It's interesting that in the World Cup when he captained the team superbly, he was the star player. It is an intriguing question: how would Martin have been if New Zealand had done equally well in the World Cup, but he had had a succession of low scores? I guess that's the test. Those who know Martin will have their own views on that one."

This is a point which Andrew Jones picks up. "When things were going well for Martin, he was a very good captain and when things did not go well . . . I'll leave it at that. On the field, Martin could be very, very good at times – the World Cup was a good indication.

"But Martin was incredibly dependent on Wally Lees. Martin had a difficult personality for him to be captain. He recognised that and felt that Wally Lees was the guy who could bridge that. The question is how far should Wally have gone in complying with Martin. As it was, wherever Wally went, Martin went, and vice versa. It was an I'll-scratch-your-back-and-you-scratch-mine sort of thing."

Crowe was always destined to captain New Zealand. Jeremy Coney feels it may have been a return to the "John Reid days" when the best player was automatically the captain. Even so, it was obvious when John Wright took the New Zealand team to England in 1990 that there would soon be a change in captain. Wright, about as popular as a player can be, had waited a long time to be captain, and made a good fist of the job when he got it. But he was not available for the tour to Pakistan later in the year. In the circumstances, the choice for replacement was likely to fall on Crowe, with Ian Smith the only other candidate.

Says Smith: "Ian Taylor asked me quite early in that tour of England if I thought Martin would be a good choice as the next test captain. I thought he'd be excellent, but stressed that it was important for him to have a coach he could work with."

Crowe was duly appointed captain, and long-serving Otago captain and wicketkeeper Warren Lees was brought in as coach to take over from Bob Cunis.

It was an incredibly difficult time to take over the captaincy. New Zealand cricket followers had become used to their side winning a lot more than it lost. They had been spoilt by the glories of the 1980s. Crowe conceded he had been ambitious for the job and set about planning for it as well as possible. He made a bad start when he fell out with a key player, off-spinner John Bracewell, who says: "For some reason, Martin and I always had a fierce sort of rivalry from when I arrived in Auckland. We didn't get on as teammates. It was to do with our socio-economic bracketing or a perception of class. Or there might have been two conflicting egos wanting dominance of a team. It's extended all the way and I'd say we're not the greatest of mates today.

"He struck me as a joker who knew he would be captain because he was the best player. It was his dream, his ambition since his Hogan's Heroes days in his back yard. Martin did say that, the moment he became captain, I would no longer be in his side. It was one of about 10 factors for me retiring, not a main one. At the time it appeared Martin was picking the team. His attitude wouldn't have dictated my decision. It was incredible timing on my behalf that, just prior to him taking over, I achieved some test goals [1000 runs, 100 wickets]."

To have an argument was one thing, but Crowe made the mistake of following it up with a letter to Bracewell, reiterating that his days in the New Zealand team were over once he (Crowe) became captain. Bracewell used that letter as motivation for his Auckland team that season.

He says he no longer has it. "I threw it away. I thought it was a nonsense."

When I questioned Crowe about that letter, he was anything but reticent. I pointed out he had taken personal difficulties and escalated them to a cricket level by questioning Bracewell's role in the team. "He [Bracewell] told me if I was going to captain New Zealand in future, we were going to be in bad shape. I said to him if he had a problem, that was his choice, and I followed it up with a personal letter. It was a waste of a 45-cent stamp."

Besides getting offside with New Zealand's best spinner, Crowe had to face the Pakistan tour, always a torrid experience, without Richard Hadlee, Martin Snedden, Ewen Chatfield, John Wright and Andrew Jones, all leading test players until at least the year before.

As John Wright points out: "You have to have bowlers who can bowl sides out to win matches, and we'd lost many of our leading bowlers."

Nevertheless, Crowe attacked his new job with commendable gusto. He called a press conference for September 3, 1990, to introduce what he called a new time, a new era of New Zealand cricket. He announced the New Zealand team would play attractive cricket. "This is something that has not happened in the last couple of years. Perhaps a couple of us old blokes were a bit greedy with our own approaches to the game and probably have not moulded into a side attractive to the public."

Far from being daunted by the understrength side he had inherited, he said it would be a great challenge. "In fact, it is a great situation, a chance to get the side together and mould it. We will have small objectives. We will not be setting our goals too high, but something we can reach out for." He mentioned a one-day victory in Pakistan, perhaps even a test victory, "something to put us on the board".

He pointed out the comparative inexperience of the bowling. "We now have Danny Morrison as our senior bowler in terms of test wickets. The second bowler to Danny is me."

Before leaving for Pakistan, Crowe spoke again of the challenge, this time to the *Evening Post's* Lynn McConnell. "I like to be involved and in control. When I'm not, I find it hard to score runs," he said. "I've wanted to do it [captain New Zealand] ever since I can remember. Managing the efforts of all 11 players in the team is a challenge. Every one of those players is different with different needs and understanding their goals and motivations is part of it. I would like to develop a strong line of communication and develop trust, loyalty and confidence with them." He spoke of wanting to develop the spirit that Jeff Crowe had in his team. "Jeff led by example, but he was unselfish."

In *Sunday* magazine, Crowe told Steven O'Meagher that he wanted the captaincy so much "I sometimes think I'd give up all the runs, all the test centuries I've scored, to be in charge".

Crowe wasted little time in making his mark. A four-day camp for building team morale was held at the Devonport naval base in mid-September. He talked to his vice-captain (Smith), coach (Lees) and manager (Ian Taylor) to discuss guidelines and vision, spelling out specific targets he wanted the team to achieve. He brought together the key sports journalists in Wellington and Auckland to outline his plans for the future, and to bury any hatchets.

When O'Meagher asked him to comment on what had gone wrong with New Zealand cricket, Crowe said he was not interested in "shit-bagging individuals". How could his plea to let bygones be bygones be taken seriously, he asked, if he started slinging off at current or former teammates in public?

So Crowe took his side to Pakistan. Smith, Rutherford, Greatbatch and Morrison were there, but all the other big names of the 1980s were missing. Crowe himself was magnificent. He averaged 59.33 for the tour and 61.00 in the three tests. He headed the tour, test and one-day averages. Though New Zealand lost all three tests and all three one-dayers, Crowe generally led the team with understanding and energy. His own performances were better than ever and his captaincy was excellent in trying circumstances.

Perhaps the only concern about the Pakistan trip was the way he was unable to communicate with one or two players. He clearly did not rate Canterbury spin bowler Mark Priest very highly. Priest played no tests and just two first class matches on the tour. He scored no runs and took only three expensive wickets. Today Priest has very bitter memories of the tour.

"The training camp at Devonport was good, and Martin obviously had a lot of ideas and energy, but the tour of Pakistan was bloody awful, at least for me. It didn't help the situation that I wasn't getting played. There was no reason why. We were getting dorked anyway.

"With Martin there seemed to be just one way of doing things – his way. He expected everyone to prepare the way he did. It's okay for him. He's a very intense person. But with some people, that makes them too nervous and they can't play well. We had a discussion one day and I told him that what's best for him doesn't necessarily suit everyone else. He came back by telling me I wasn't getting picked because I wasn't mentally prepared to play tests. I said that was absolute bullshit, and that he had no right to make that comment because he hardly even knew me.

"Well, that was the end of me. He got rid of me after that tour. He had a very big say in picking the team. Since then, I've felt that to get back into the test team I would have to take 10 wickets in every match, and that even then I would struggle. I've outperformed every spin bowler in domestic New Zealand cricket, yet they've picked spinners almost from high school, like Haslam and Hart. And look what's happened to them. It was inevitable."

Priest feels one of Crowe's major failings as a captain is that he is too moody. "One day he's matey, the next it's like a bomb went off. Warren Lees' main job in Pakistan was just making sure Martin was happy. I had no idea what would happen after Pakistan. Others have gone along with him and kept on his good side and kept getting picked. But I wasn't prepared to suck up to him, and I've paid for it.

"The other thing that made it hard for a bowler was that he wanted to have the total say. We'd argue over my field-placing. But I was the bowler, they were my figures. It put so much pressure on because if you got hit for a four he'd pack a sad. It got to the stage where you didn't want to look around."

Even though Priest was recalled to the New Zealand team briefly to cover for the injured Hart in South Africa in December 1994 (his Canterbury teammates chided him by saying, "Will Martin be meeting you at the airport?") he had very little to do with Crowe. "I was taken over for the one-dayers, which wasn't really ideal anyway, but what can you do – say no when you're picked for New Zealand? I didn't really talk to Martin. He's just not my cup of tea. Since that Pakistan tour, I've just ignored him. He's not worth the hassle."

Crowe is unabashed about his dealings with Priest. "He proved in South Africa he's not up to international class," Crowe told me. "And besides, Dipak Patel has been the obvious choice since 1990."

Andrew Jones says he has some sympathy for Priest's position. "He's the best left-arm spinner in the country, so he has a right to feel sore about not being in the test team. There is no doubt that while he was captain Martin had a great deal of sway in the selection of the teams. If Martin rated you, you were on your way. But it worked the other way too, as a few players have found out. He has demanded a high input into team selection, and on the very rare occasions when he hasn't got his own way, he has kicked up a fuss. Shane Thomson was another example. For some years, Martin didn't have a lot of time for him, and it was hard for Shane to get into the team."

Crowe defends himself against charges like these. "Yes, when I was captain I did influence team selection," he told me. "I'd give my opinion in the most professional way I could. What's wrong with that?"

Immediately after the Pakistan tour came the World Series Cricket triangular affair in Australia when New Zealand performed above themselves to shade England for second spot. Though they lost the finals 2-0, it was still a commendable effort with a rather ordinary-looking attack. Even though Wright came back into the team for the one-day series, Crowe held on to the captaincy.

Back home, Crowe was a key figure in Wellington's victorious Shell Cup run. His opening partnerships with the equally attacking Richard Reid captured the imagination of the Wellington public, who flocked back to domestic cricket. Crowe and Reid scored their runs so fast that often a match was all but decided after 20 overs of the Wellington innings. In the Cup semi-final against Auckland, Crowe made a match-winning century. In the final, against Central Districts, Crowe hit 33 and Reid 47 to lead a Wellington charge to 214-8 to which CD could manage only 140 in reply.

Sri Lanka toured during the 1990/91 summer and by the time they arrived Crowe was really buzzing.

His stocks rose further still when in the first test, at the Basin Reserve, he and Andrew Jones added 467 for the third wicket to not only save the match, but to set a world test and first class record. Crowe's 299 was the highest test score by a New Zealander. New Zealand were bowled out for 174 in the first innings, then Sri Lanka plundered 497, due almost entirely to a fabulous innings of 267 by Aravinda de Silva.

Wright and Franklin opened the second innings well for New Zealand, but when Jones and Crowe came together not long before lunch on the fourth day, the score was 148-2 and New Zealand still trailed by 175 runs. By stumps Crowe was 126 not out and Jones 82 not out and New Zealand were 369-2. On and on they went on the fifth day, establishing all sorts of records. They set a third-wicket test record for New Zealand when their stand reached 242. Later they passed the all-time New Zealand test record of 387, set by Jarvis and Turner in the West Indies in 1972. Then Crowe achieved his maiden test double century, in 431 minutes. New Zealand marched past their previous test highest score of 553-7, against Australia in 1985.

By tea they were just one short of the biggest ever test partnership of 451, a record held jointly by Bradman-Ponsford, and Miandad-Mudassar. Four balls after the interval, Crowe took a quick single to mid-wicket and the record was theirs. It had taken them 525 minutes.

The test by now was, of course, destined to be drawn, but there was intrigue in how long Jones and Crowe could go on for. With the total 615-2, they had taken New Zealand to the highest score in a test by a side with only two wickets down. When Crowe was on 258, the partnership was broken – Jones was dismissed for 186. The stand was worth 467, the highest in New Zealand first class cricket and the world record for a third-wicket stand in any first class cricket.

Still Crowe raced on. He passed Glenn Turner's New Zealand test record of 259. Only two milestones remained. A triple-century (which would make him test cricket's 13th triple century-scorer) and, less probably, Gary Sobers' world test record of 365.

But on 299, Crowe attempted to run a ball through the slips, edged it and was caught behind by Tillakaratne. Crowe had batted 610 minutes and faced 523 balls. He had hit 29 fours and three sixes. Even the bowler, Arjuna Ranatunga, confessed to a little embarrassment: "Really, it was just an ordinary ball, and I was trying to stop him getting that last single. Now I am a bit uncomfortable about it. He deserved to get 300. He was very unlucky; that was one of the few bad shots he played."

Crowe, initially angry at his dismissal, described it later as "like climbing Mt Everest and pulling a hamstring on the last stride".

His effort was stupendous, as was the Crowe-Jones partnership. Jones and Crowe made the finalists in the team category for the Sportsman of the Year and Crowe was named Sportsman of the Year. He went within a whisker of winning the overall title, which was won by world champion rower Philippa Baker. At the end of the year, Crowe was awarded an MBE.

Crowe said afterwards he doubted he would get another chance to score a test triple-century. "Every dog has his day, and I might have had mine, even if I know I have to keep on striving for better innings. You might have a chance if you bowled the other side out cheaply, batted two and a half days to get the triple, declared and then bowled them out again. Otherwise you might have to bat to save the match and run out of time, as happened with this game."

He said Sobers' world record had not entered his mind: "It was just too far away."

Jones and Crowe said they got very nervous on learning about the looming world record at the tea interval. Crowe: "We had not aimed for any world record. It was just batting, batting, batting, with no real plans except to bat for sessions. We were working together, not trying to dominate, just concentrating on simple batting. It became important that we had targets to aim for, knowing that every half-hour or 45 minutes there was some target ahead."

Crowe admitted he did allow himself a little record-chasing after lunch when it was obvious New Zealand were clear of danger. He hit Aravinda's off-spin for 4, 6, 6, 4 and then got a two when Arjuna Ranatunga dropped a skier at mid-wicket. "I was a bit interested in getting 24 off an over for a record, as I remembered Ian Smith had done that last season. When I was dropped, I realised the other aims were more important."

Jones said: "We just had a job to do and really I am not sure how I kept on going. I did give away my hook shot early in my innings, because

I wasn't batting very well, so it was very satisfying to stick in there. The only disappointment was not going on to get a double-century. I might not get another chance."

Looking back on that record stand, Jones says it means more to him now than at the time. "You get caught up with things at the time. We were losing the test, and had to bat for a very long time on a good, flat Basin wicket. It was one of those situations where you could score as many as you wanted, but you had to concentrate. In hindsight, with the drama of saving the game, and then all the congratulations having died away, it does mean a lot to me. You can't plan for a record like that, and there aren't many opportunities for it to happen. Martin and I didn't say a lot during our partnership. We never had to communicate a lot while we were batting. We'd talk a few times, but generally we just enjoyed the opportunity to get on with the job."

In the second test, Crowe turned an ankle while fielding and limped out of the match and the series, Ian Smith taking over the captaincy for the third test. Smith thus became New Zealand's 21st test captain and the first wicketkeeper to have the job.

It was a series of absurd averages. Crowe averaged 121.66 and Jones, who hit three successive centuries, 102.60. For Sri Lanka, de Silva finished with an average of 98.60.

The season finished with three one-day internationals against England, New Zealand winning two of them. Though Crowe didn't bat particularly well, the New Zealand performances were excellent and the crowds flocked to see the new-look national team in action.

So Crowe had good reason to be happy with his first season at the helm. New Zealand had maintained their unbeaten record at home, which stretched back to 1980, and some young players had hinted that they might soon develop into substantial test players.

The *Cricket Almanack* commented that Crowe's efforts in moulding together a young side had been outstanding and hoped for more of the same the following season, in which the focal point would be the World Cup.

In hindsight, this was really the last time Crowe seemed entirely comfortable with the captaincy.

Chapter Ten

WORLD CUP WONDERS

ANDREW JONES:

> *"Captaincy is an honour, and some people don't respect that. They become captain and then think it's their right. When you become captain things either go well or you have to go. We have had people leading New Zealand teams who think it's their divine right."*

The story of New Zealand's triumphant run through the 1992 World Cup – one of the most glorious passages in our cricket history – really begins at 6.20pm on Sunday, February 9, 1992, when Martin Crowe walked into a meeting at the Basin Reserve with the three national cricket selectors, Don Neely, Ross Dykes and Bruce Taylor.

It was that meeting, less than a fortnight before the World Cup began, that provided the impetus for a most remarkable turnaround in Crowe's, and New Zealand's, cricket fortunes.

It hadn't been a happy season for the national side, rather outrageously billed as the Young Guns. Many, including Wright, Jones, Patel, Latham and Smith, weren't young, and the team certainly weren't playing as guns. Unfortunately, some of them appeared to be believing their own publicity, leading to John Bracewell – now a forthright *Sunday News* columnist – branding them a team of "Gucci cricketers".

England toured that summer. It was a useful England side, boasting Gooch, Hick, Smith, Stewart, Lamb, a rather rotund Botham, DeFreitas and Lewis as the principal performers. But it wasn't a fearsome combination, and the bowling attack was definitely ordinary. When New Zealand toured England in 1994, the New Zealand bowling was labelled a cafeteria attack – help yourself. England's in 1992 wasn't that bad, but it was by no means devastating.

Yet England won all three one-day internationals, two by embarrassing margins. Worse, in the tests, they comprehensively outplayed New Zealand. The first test at Christchurch was notable for a pre-match controversy over the inclusion of the out-of-form Greatbatch at the expense of the in-form Rutherford. New Zealand Cricket boss Peter McDermott waded in by mentioning that Rutherford was being excluded for factors other than run-scoring. Words like "maturity" and "discipline" were mentioned. Rutherford evidently didn't have them. Rutherford naturally took umbrage at such suggestions, as did a goodly portion of the cricket public.

Eventually national cricket panel convener Don Neely was forced to go public, explaining that Rutherford had missed out entirely on cricket grounds. Neely pointed out in some statistical detail that while Rutherford had batted productively for Otago over the past few seasons, his test average in that time was under 20. By omitting Rutherford, the selectors were showing a certain consistency, for the Otago skipper had already been omitted from the early-season team-building jaunt to South Australia.

With or without Rutherford, New Zealand were never in the hunt against England at Christchurch. England made 580. Stewart made a big hundred, and four others scored half-centuries. New Zealand replied with 312 and 264 and lost by an innings and four runs.

Oddly enough, they were within a whisker of forcing a draw. When Tufnell began his 47th over of the second innings, New Zealand were 264-9, with Crowe facing and Chris Pringle the non-striker. If New Zealand could survive 10 more minutes they would eke out a draw. Or, if they could score four more runs and so force England to bat again, the match would be drawn because there would not be time for an innings change.

Crowe took strike and holed out to wide mid-off where Derek Pringle held the catch that won the match. Predictably, Crowe was subjected to much ill-informed scorn. Interestingly, former great Bert Sutcliffe chimed in with: "It's easy to be critical from the comfort of your La-Z-Boy rocker with a beer in your hand."

Ian Smith summed up the situation well: "He backed his ability to score, rather than the other guy's to defend. I don't think anyone in the side blamed him for the shot, but he copped a lot of flak elsewhere."

The furore over the end of the match did not deflect attention from a poor New Zealand performance. Except for Wright, who scored 28 and 99, and Patel, who made 99 in the first innings, there wasn't much to enthuse over. New Zealand, 81-1 at the start of the fifth day, played badly and batted without sufficient grit. As Smith says: "We crumbled on the last afternoon."

Crowe himself was hampered by injury problems. He'd damaged an already suspect knee on the pre-season trip to South Australia and required an operation. Then he injured his left hand at practice during the match.

"I wasn't happy with our performance at Christchurch," he said. "I rang Wally [Lees] after the game and said we had to sort out our roles and that I had to lead more from the front. Wally agreed with that, but wondered if he might then be surplus to requirements. Then John Wright slotted in and made our group more complete; he has the special ability to touch the hearts of everyone."

Rutherford came into the side for the second test, his selection vehemently opposed by Crowe, who threatened to stand down if that happened, offering the selectors a "him or me" ultimatum. Rutherford, never a great harvester of runs at test level, was an extremely popular personality, a bloke everyone related to. And he'd been scoring a packet of runs in the Shell matches. People close to the team felt Crowe did not respect Rutherford professionally, and that he also resented Rutherford's folk hero status. However, the following day Crowe told selection panel convener Don Neely that he would accept Rutherford and suggested they room together.

New Zealand played only marginally better, losing by 168 runs early on the fifth morning. Crowe made 45 and 56 and Rutherford chipped in with 26 and 32; otherwise there wasn't much else. Cairns had a hostile spell in the first England innings, and returned figures of 6-52, but these were scattered moments of joy in a depressing test for New Zealand.

English commentator Henry ("my dear old thing") Blofeld waded into the picture with a scathing attack on Crowe in *The Independent*. "It is questionable whether New Zealand will ever achieve significant success under their present captain," he wrote. Blofeld said it appeared Crowe felt success was his by divine right, said Crowe played too little cricket, that he was a muddled thinker about the game and not as good a captain as his brother Jeff or John Wright. He said that New Zealand, at a time when rebuilding was not going too well, were also having to come to terms with "an extraordinary enigma".

"When Martin Crowe succeeded John Wright as captain, it looked as if the Crown Prince had moved to his rightful position. Yet it has not worked out that way. He has been captaining the side like a man whose interest is half-hearted. He is not a great tactician, but neither is Graham Gooch. Unlike Gooch, he does not seem to have the side behind him . . . The powers-that-be would be better to make Wright captain for the World Cup."

Even critics of Crowe's captaincy – and they were a growing number by this time – felt Blofeld's criticism was a little over the top. The Englishman was right about Crowe struggling to get the team behind him, not playing enough (because of injury), and perhaps even being half-hearted in the test series. Crowe himself said later his focus during the season was on the World Cup. But to call Crowe a muddled thinker on cricket and to suggest he did not work hard enough at his game was palpably wrong.

Besides his knee problem, which seemed to be worsening, Crowe was having other health problems at this time. Twice during the test series he had dizzy spells, and a poisoned finger after the second test prevented him holding a bat in the build-up to the third test at the Basin.

Going into the Basin Reserve test, England were buoyant with the series in the bag, New Zealand desperately trying to get their game together with the World Cup looming.

New Zealand played better, and centuries by Wright and Jones helped them to a first innings lead. But it was still not a convincing performance. There was continuing media speculation about Crowe's fitness and health, and criticism of the test side's poor results.

So, on the evening of the fourth day, came the fateful meeting with the selectors. Crowe's version, as he told his brother Jeff on the television programme *Crowe on Crowe*, was that the selectors wanted to take the captaincy off him. "The people that were putting me in the position of being captain were about to take it away from me." Wife Simone was more blunt on the same programme: "The day before the team was announced a couple of the selectors asked Martin to resign."

Not true, says selection convener Don Neely. "I know exactly what was said. When I have something important to say, I always write it down and read it, so there can't be any misunderstandings."

The public weren't aware at the time that some officials were suggesting that Crowe had got too big for the game and "had to go". Team manager Ian Taylor, coach Wally Lees and chairman Peter McDermott entered the fray. Finally the selectors met with Crowe.

Neely: "I said to Martin we were unanimous that he was the best on-field captain in New Zealand, but that things like his injuries and illness, and the media pressure, seemed to be affecting him. We wondered, if he was just a batsman, would he be better able to play to his own high standards. That was the background.

"I said, 'If we were to recommend someone other than you to be captain, would you be available to play in the World Cup?' Twice he said very strongly he wasn't prepared to play under anyone else."

For Crowe, it was all a huge shock. As he told brother Jeff on the controversial TV programme: "I thought they were going to ask me what the World Cup side was going to be, which was going to be announced in 24 hours' time. That wasn't what the meeting was about. They were asking me about the captaincy. How I was enjoying it, how the season was going.

"Basically it got very tricky because my captaincy was in question. I walked out of that meeting not knowing what was going to happen in 24 or 48 hours' time. I didn't know whether I was going to be playing myself. I guess every player still has that little feeling when they wait upon the announcement of a side to be playing a game. I had that feeling that I might not be named to go into the World Cup . . . a tough 48 hours."

That evening Crowe drove home to Eastbourne with Andrew Jones, who recalls: "He was pretty upset. He hardly talked about it, but was very down. He realised the selectors had genuine doubts about whether he should take the team to the World Cup. But I thought the selectors were well within their rights to question Martin's leadership at that point. The thing about captaincy is that it's an honour, and some people don't respect that. They become captain, then think it's their right. When you become captain, things either go well, or you have to go. We have had people leading the New Zealand team who think it's their divine right."

Crowe called it "the worst two days of my life". In a sense he had called the selectors' bluff. He knew that if he was willing to play as a batsman, he would of course be chosen. But he had stipulated that he had to be captain. Would the selectors agree?

Martin and Jeff Crowe spent a lot of time on the phone that night, Martin vowing that he would not back down, that he would "stick it right back up to them" and Jeff advising Martin to back off. "I dreamed of it for 18 months and I'd be letting the team down by resigning and passing the captaincy over," Martin reasoned. "Shit no, I'd gone through too much to let it go, so that was it, almost like right, this is where I'm going to get into it."

Smith, who was the team vice-captain during the test series (though Wright took over the job during the World Cup), knew of the meeting the next morning. "Martin said something odd like, 'Good luck in the World Cup.' I said, 'Why? What do you mean?' He answered that he wasn't sure he'd be there. He genuinely thought that he would lose the captaincy and that therefore he would not be picked."

But there had been further behind-the-scenes activity. Wright, New Zealand captain for three years until 1990 and the senior player in the side, had been asked if he would be willing to do the job, if required.

"We had a very bad test series against England before the World Cup," recalls Wright. "Martin was defending us not losing at home. You don't want to be the first and he was struggling. He'd already had to take an under-strength side to Pakistan, which was a very hard tour. Then his health problems came in. So there was a lot of drama going on.

"Before the World Cup, the wheels were really falling off. It was during the England series that there was a move afoot to replace Martin. They asked me if I'd do the job. I said I would, but I advised them very strongly not to replace him because, a, we wouldn't have him as a player, and b, we wouldn't have a chance in hell of doing any good in the World Cup without him.

"I told them I was 37, and that he was the guy. He had it ahead of him."

Andrew Jones endorses Wright's view of what went on, and says that Crowe seemed to feel particularly insecure because for some reason he got the impression Wright was agitating for his job. "I think Martin got it all wrong. Wrighty was very supportive of Martin keeping the captaincy. Wally Lees was the person who went around asking senior players who they thought should be captain. He wasn't exactly advocating a change in captain, but he was asking us what we thought. When he asked me, I told him I thought that if Martin still wanted the job, he should keep it. There was no takeover bid being engineered by John, far from it. It was an illusion on Martin's part. I'm not really sure why."

So the selectors eventually retained Crowe as captain. Smith feels things weren't as bad within the team as they might have seemed to outsiders. "Our performances leading to the World Cup weren't a slight on Martin's captaincy," he says. "Leadership is a big factor, but individuals have to do their job. No-one was playing that well. From the outside, the team looked to be struggling, so people assumed it was being badly led."

Smith feels the World Cup dominated the players' thoughts in the weeks and months beforehand. "It's a bit like rugby these days, where the All Blacks, with their proud record, are still almost willing to concede the odd test to make sure they've rebuilt for the World Cup. We still wanted to win the tests, but the World Cup was a big factor. Martin had blueprinted that from a long way out. He wanted to beat England, but his thoughts were on the World Cup, no question."

Wright had been watching the unfolding drama over the captaincy, and over Crowe generally, and been singularly unimpressed. "When we flew down to Dunedin for the one-dayer there, I sat on one side of Martin and Andrew Jones sat on the other. We had a pretty frank discussion about things he could improve. I told him if he wanted the leadership, there were things he would have to acquire quickly. The man-management side of things was falling down. I said if he didn't have that, he was courting disaster."

Jones was equally vehement. "We gave him a fearful talking to and told him as bluntly as we could that he was letting himself down the way he was handling himself and the team. By that stage of the season things were in a shambles and needed to be sorted out smartly."

Wright says after that discussion a balanced management set-up was put in place. "There was Martin; Ian Taylor, the manager; the physio, Mark Plummer; Andrew Jones; Wally Lees, the coach; Ian Smith and myself. I was the grumpy old pro. It all worked very well. Martin had gone and got his knee fixed and he was in a very positive frame of mind. The whole thing came together like magic. Wally would handle the off-the-field stuff. I would do a bit of a pep talk after the warm-up run. Wally and Martin did the team talks. There was good communication between the players. Ian Smith was heavily involved too.

"Under Martin's captaincy, we had one of the best spirits in all my time in New Zealand cricket. The guys got on. There was a pretty formalised approach, with everyone having a job to do. And Hogan was getting runs. This was important because it lifted him, and when he was fizzing the whole team fizzed."

Coach Lees felt a lot happier by the time the World Cup began. He told me he had been working hard to separate his and Crowe's roles. "It took me two years to get it so he'd leave the off-the-field stuff to me. He was great on the field, but not in handling the guys. That was my role, and by the time the World Cup began, I think he understood this."

One man missing from the management structure was Don Neely, even though as convener of selectors he was another vital cog. The relationship between Neely and Crowe was extremely frosty, and even today it is not warm. They did not talk during the World Cup and communicated only through Lees.

It is fascinating what goes on in cricket. In 1987 Jeremy Coney, the New Zealand skipper, and Richard Hadlee, the team's outstanding player, weren't on speaking terms during the Christchurch test against the West Indies and were using Wright as an intermediary. These are serious problems, yet when a team is successful, they can be hidden. It's when a team begins to lose often and badly, as New Zealand did in South Africa in 1994/95, that questions are asked and all the unpleasantness surfaces. If New Zealand had won in South Africa, would the issues of player drunkenness, dope smoking and general ill-discipline have ever been raised?

John Parker, who covered the World Cup from the radio commentary box, says he cannot praise Crowe highly enough for his batting and captaincy during the World Cup, yet feels there was an element of serendipity in how it all came together. "The fact that the selectors had contemplated dropping him focused him on the things that matter, and not the side issues, the things of fringe importance. When you get threatened with death (or, for a sportsperson, being dropped), you quickly get back to reality. The selectors did that by questioning his right to be captain, yet I am very doubtful that they planned it that way. They stumbled into a situation which turned out superbly for New Zealand cricket. I don't think the New Zealand selectors planned it like that and I don't give them any credit for it, but they did get Martin to focus on his real job."

Even with the captaincy issue sorted out, and the New Zealand team properly organised, Crowe's side were at long odds when the World Cup began. Australia, led by Allan Border, were heavy favourites, followed by England. Pakistan and the West Indies had their backers, and even India and South Africa were fancied more than struggling New Zealand.

"We needed to pick up a win early," says Smith. "Our first game was against Australia at Eden Park, and it was a real bonus for us. We went to the ground hoping for the best and came away believing. That was a huge factor in what followed. If we'd lost that day . . . It was a big crowd, but not a sellout. We had to win back the public's confidence.

"Some good thought went into our approach. Opening the bowling with Patel worked out very well. Australia were chasing a largish total and, when we opened with Dipak, they had to reassess their approach. We were able to sneak in 10 overs from him. Things fell into place and we won."

As Martin said on *Crowe on Crowe:* "I was already planning it [the World Cup] during the 1990 tour, went to camps, didn't know how it would... sometimes I felt it was all falling apart. All of a sudden the day arrives, good atmosphere at Eden Park..."

Crowe led the way against Australia with 100 not out off 134 balls. Throughout the innings he reminded himself to "show some guts" and have "soft hands". He said Simone had told him he had to have courage. He wanted to have soft hands, to let his instincts flow. From there he went from strength to strength. "Before I knew it, I'd played quite well and I was on about 40. The Australians were starting to bowl shorter. That was the innings that started to change the game."

It was a dream game for New Zealand. Rutherford made a good 57, Patel got through 10 overs for 36 runs and Larsen 10 overs for a mere 30. Cairns, who was expected to be a bowling spearhead, bowled just four overs. Chris Harris effected a crucial run out by hitting one stump from halfway to the boundary. The ground fielding was superb.

"After that," says Smith, "things fell into place. We began opening the batting with Mark Greatbatch. That was a fluke, fate really. Wrighty got injured, so Greatbatch came in as opener and he really came off. The draw worked well because after Australia we had Sri Lanka. And we'd worked out we had to win only four or five to make the semis.

"The team spirit was great. There's a lot of unity in a World Cup squad. It's like a mini-tour; it's easier to build feeling because you know you're there for a month, and that it'll be the same squad throughout. It was the most impressionable month of cricket I played in. The brand of cricket we played, and the way we were received, made it a real pleasure to be in the team.

"Martin captained the team brilliantly. Once the captaincy issue had been raised and squashed, he started to feel more supported and became more comfortable in the job."

Several New Zealanders played superbly as New Zealand peeled off successive wins over Australia, Sri Lanka, South Africa, Zimbabwe, the West Indies, India and England before losing to Pakistan in the last preliminary game. By then they had charged into the semi-finals and were the form team of the tournament.

Greatbatch was fantastic at the top of the order, smashing 68 against South Africa, 63 against the West Indies, 73 against India, 35 against England and 42 against Pakistan. He charged the quickest bowlers in the game, including Akram, DeFreitas, Dev, Ambrose, Marshall, Cummins, Benjamin and Donald and got New Zealand away to some flying starts. Rutherford and Jones scored consistently quickly. Patel was the most economical bowler in the competition, with Larsen not far behind. Chris Harris picked up 16 wickets, second only to Akram. Others chipped in as required. Smith behind the stumps recovered from a confidence crisis earlier in the season and was back to his best.

But make no mistake; the man responsible for sweeping New Zealand into the semis was Crowe. His on-field leadership was a revelation. A lifetime of studying cricket, thinking and talking about it, paid dividends that month. Every bowling change seemed to work, his field placing was imaginative and astute. He gambled on attack whenever the chance arose, and was rewarded for his courage. Until the World Cup, New Zealand's best captains were regarded as Tom Lowry, Walter Hadlee and Geoff Howarth. Crowe was at least their equal during this tournament.

And then there was his batting. The statistics tell part of the story: 100 not out, 5, 3 not out, 74 not out, 81 not out, 26 (run out), 73 not out, 3 and 91 – 456 runs at an average of 114. Named Player of the Tournament, Crowe also earned this accolade from Imran Khan: "New Zealand had the most fabulous run during the World Cup, and owed it all to one man."

Crowe scored the most runs in the tournament, had the highest average (next was Miandad's 62.43) and hit the most fours. It is impossible to imagine better batting. Jeremy Coney, while paying tribute to his bravery and skill against the West Indies speedsters in 1987, says that World Cup batting marked the high water mark of Crowe's career.

Parker says: "I've never seen any batsman play better. I put him up there with Greg Chappell, a wonderful player. Some of those pull shots at Eden Park were executed so swiftly, and his straight drives off the fastest bowlers went right past the bowler. It's easy to deflect or drop kick off a

National selectors Bruce Taylor (left), Don Neely and Ross Dykes caused Crowe anguish by inquiring if he'd be willing to play under another captain in the World Cup in 1992.

On his way to a century against Australia – the perfect opening to the 1992 World Cup.

The strain shows as Crowe conducts a press conference in Colombo the day after the suicide bomber threw the tour of Sri Lanka into disarray.

Lance Cairns – called for Rutherford to replace Crowe as captain.

ENGLAND v. NEW ZEALAND

THURSDAY, FRIDAY, SATURDAY, SUNDAY & MONDAY, JUNE 16, 17, 18, 19 & 20, 1994
(5-day Match)

CORNHILL Insurance

Test Series

NEW ZEALAND	First Innings		Second Innings
1 B. A. Young ...Northern Districts	lb w b Fraser	0	
2 B. A. Pocock...Northern Districts	c Smith b Such	10	
†3 K. R. Rutherford..............Otago	c Stewart b DeFreitas.	37	
4 M. D. Crowe ....Wellington	c Smith b DeFreitas ...142		
5 S. P. Fleming ....Canterbury	lb w b Fraser	41	
6 S. A. Thomson ....N. Districts	run out	69	
*7 A. C. Parore ....Auckland	c Rhodes b Taylor	40	
8 M. N. Hart ...Northern Districts	b Such	25	
9 D. J. Nash ....Otago	b White	56	
10 C. Pringle....................Auckland	c Hick b DeFreitas	14	
11 M. B. Owens ....Canterbury	not out	2	
	B 3, l-b 15, w 1, n-b 21,	40	B , l-b , w , n-b ,
	Total 476		Total ....

FALL OF THE WICKETS

1—0 2—39 3—67 4—138 5—318 6—350 7—391 8—397 9—434 10—476
1— 2— 3— 4— 5— 6— 7— 8— 9— 10—

ANALYSIS OF BOWLING   1st Innings   2nd Innings

Name	O.	M.	R.	W.	Wd.	N-b	O.	M.	R.	W.	Wd.	N-b
Fraser	36	9	102	2	...	9	...	...	...	...	...	...
DeFreitas	35	8	102	3	...	6	...	...	...	...	...	...
Taylor	20	4	64	1	...	6	...	...	...	...	...	...
Such	30	8	84	2	...		...	...	...	...	...	...
White	21.1	5	84	1	1	...	...	...	...	...	...	...
Gooch	5	1	13	0	...	...	...	...	...	...	...	...
Hick	2	0	9	0	...	...	...	...	...	...	...	...

ENGLAND	First Innings	Second Innings
†1 M. A. Atherton ....Lancashire		
2 A. J. Stewart ....Surrey	c Parore b Nash 45	
4 G. A. Gooch ....Essex		
3 R. A. Smith ....Hampshire		
5 G. A. Hick ....Worcestershire		
6 C. White ....Yorkshire		
*7 S. J. Rhodes....Worcestershire		
8 P. A. J. DeFreitas......Derbyshire		
9 A. R. C. Fraser ....Middlesex		
10 J. P. Taylor...Northamptonshire		
11 P. M. Such ....Essex		
	B , l-b , w , n-b ,	B , l-b , w , n-b ,
	Total	Total ....

FALL OF THE WICKETS

1—65 2— 3— 4— 5— 6— 7— 8— 9— 10—
1— 2— 3— 4— 5— 6— 7— 8— 9— 10—

ANALYSIS OF BOWLING   1st Innings   2nd Innings

Name	O.	M.	R.	W.	Wd.	N-b	O.	M.	R.	W.	Wd.	N-b

Umpires—N. T. Plews & S. U. Bucknor   Scorers—E Solomon & M. Jones
† Captain   * Wicket-keeper

Play begins each day at 11.00   Luncheon Interval 1.00—1.40
Tea Interval 3.40—4.00 (may be varied according to state of game)

Stumps drawn 1st, 2nd, 3rd & 4th days at 6.00, or after 90 overs have been bowled, whichever is the later - 5th day at 6.00, or after a minimum of 75 overs for playing time other than the last hour, when Law of Cricket 17.6 and 17.7 shall apply (except a minimum of 15 overs). Except in the last hour of the match, in the event of play being suspended for any reason other than normal intervals or one or more changes of innings, the playing time on that day shall be extended by the amount of time lost up to a maximum of one hour. The captains may agree to stop play at 5.30 on the 5th day if there is no prospect of a result.

New Zealand won the toss

FORTHCOMING M.C.C. AND OTHER NON-COUNTY MATCHES

Tuesday 28 June ETON v. HARROW (1 day)
Wednesday 29 June OXFORD v. CAMBRIDGE (3 days)
Tuesday 12 July M.C.C. v M.C.C. SCHOOLS (1 day)
Wednesday 13 July M.C.C. SCHOOLS v. N.A.Y.C. (1 day)
Thursday 14 July N.C.A. YOUNG CRICKETERS v. COMBINED SERVICES (1 day)
Wednesday 17 August M.C.C. v. SCOTLAND (2 days)
Wednesday 24 August M.C.C. TROPHY (MINOR COUNTIES) C.A. KNOCK-OUT FINAL) (1 day)
Friday 26 August ABBOT ALE CLUB CRICKET CHAMPIONSHIP – FINAL (1 day)
Sunday 28 August NATIONAL VILLAGE CRICKET CHAMPIONSHIP – FINAL (1 day)
Tuesday 6 September M.C.C. v. HOLDERS HILL C.C., BARBADOS (1 day)

T.C.C.B. Official Statement: **The good behaviour of all spectators adds to the enjoyment of a day's cricket. DON'T LET YOUR SIDE DOWN.**

MICHAEL ATHERTON
(Born Failsworth, Manchester,
March 23rd 1968)

It is less than a year since Atherton succeeded Graham Gooch as England captain, but he has already experienced the full range of emotions. There was the joy, in only his second Test in charge, of leading the team to a long overdue victory against Australia. Then, in quick succession last winter, came the agony of 46 all out in Trinidad and the ecstasy of beating the West Indies in Barbados. But if England's form has fluctuated wildly, Atherton has gone from strength to strength – both as opening batsman and captain.

KEN RUTHERFORD
(Born Dunedin, October 26th 1965)

Given his poor start (a 'pair' on debut and just 12 runs in all from seven Test innings during New Zealand's 1985 tour of West Indies), Rutherford's rise has been remarkable. Thrust into power last year by Martin Crowe's chronic knee injury, he is now not only a key member of the batting line-up but also a popular captain. Rutherford will be particularly keen to show a Lord's audience what he can do, having been on the M.C.C. Young Cricketers' Staff during the summer of 1984.

A memento of a wonderful innings, autographed by Martin Crowe and sent by his father to the author.

Ken Rutherford – things were touchy in England in 1994.

Murray Deaker – "He had more talent than anyone I've seen in my life."

John Graham – "The lad either hasn't taken advice or has got beyond taking advice."

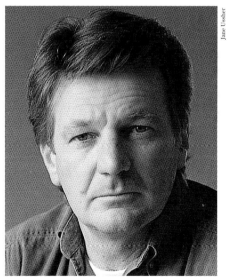

Trevor McKewen – on the receiving end of Crowe outburst.

Geoff Howarth – "Martin is doing the fighting, not me."

Previous opening: Even going under a bouncer, Crowe never loses his poise or the sense of having time to spare.

151

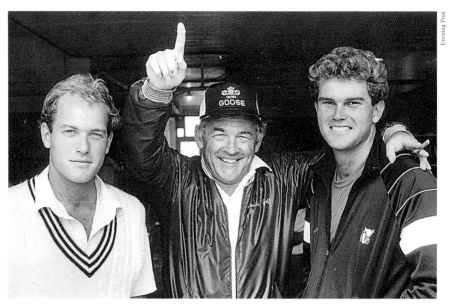

Proud father Dave Crowe, flanked by sons Jeff (left) and Martin. The picture was taken at the end of the 1984 series against England when both Jeff and Martin scored their maiden test centuries.

All White Ricki Herbert (left), Martin Crowe, Darryl Sambell and trainer-driver Peter Davis with Sharvid Miandad, the horse the four men owned.

fast bowler, and the ball flies over the turf and looks great. But Martin was driving straight past the bowler. It was unbelievable."

The *New Zealand Cricket Annual* was spot on when it noted: "Within 10 days, the transformation from a man with the weight of the nation on his shoulders to an inspirational hero was so complete as to defy description. A century, brilliantly executed against Australia in the opening game, became the forerunner to some of the most audacious strokeplay under controlled conditions seen from a New Zealand batsman in recent generations. No bowler, no situation, no field seemed capable of containing him and as the momentum developed, so Crowe's class dominated."

Crowe himself rates his 81 not out against the West Indies as the best innings of his career. He was asked by Jack Bannister, who was compiling a book called *The Innings of My Life,* to single out his best innings and said: "It was a fascinating exercise to pick my best, because there are so many factors to take into account. I decided it had to be a match in which I influenced the result, and it had to be against a top bowling attack. That is the real satisfaction for me – to perform against the best when they are in top form, which is why I have gone for the World Cup innings against the West Indies in Auckland. I didn't miss a ball and I was at my best." The West Indies made 203-7 and New Zealand were finely balanced at 100-3 when Crowe settled down to play a superb innings. Though Rutherford and Harris departed, he never allowed his attack to flag, scoring his 81 out of 109 while he was at the crease. He hit 12 boundaries and New Zealand won by five wickets with nine balls to spare.

And yet, from this story of utter triumph, Crowe closed out the World Cup on a discordant note. It's something he has made a habit of during his career. When he should have been revelling in national hero status, he'd started the talkback callers and letter-to-editor writers off again. First, he emerged from the semi-final defeat by Pakistan with less than total grace, and then he involved himself in *Crowe on Crowe,* an ill-judged and crass programme which seemed little more than a thinly veiled attack on the national selectors and reeked of "I told you so" childishness.

New Zealand were desperately unlucky to lose the semi-final. With Crowe leading the way, they reached 262-7, which might easily have been a winning total. Even then they were unfortunate. Crowe was taking the Pakistani bowlers apart when he tore a hamstring. He was forced to bat with a runner and the momentum seeped away until he was run out for 91 after a mix-up between his runner, Greatbatch, and Ian Smith.

It still seemed New Zealand had compiled a winning total when Pakistan began their chase. Wright captained New Zealand in Crowe's absence. At the 30-over mark, Pakistan still needed 140 runs at seven an over. In a situation like that, the batting team would fall short at least 95 per cent of the time. Then Imran and Malik departed in quick succession and it appeared only a miracle could stop the New Zealand charge.

Unbelievably, a miracle man arrived in the form of Inzamam-Ul-Haq, who cut loose with the most furious onslaught imaginable, scoring 60 off just 37 balls. He smashed seven fours and a six, and there was nothing Wright or his bowlers could do. Miandad worked steadily through to 57 not out and Moin Khan came in near the end to belt 20 from 11 deliveries.

New Zealand had snatched defeat from the jaws of victory. Imagine how the injured Crowe felt on the sideline. It must have been terribly frustrating. Later he said New Zealand had panicked. "It started to slip away in the 40th over. You could see it in our players' body language, and the Pakistanis started to climb back. We threw away our chance of playing in the final. We'd done everything right till the last hour."

This was widely seen as a swipe at Wright's leadership. "The implication was there for all to see," says Wright. "Fair enough, I take the rap. If there's one thing you'd change, it's getting Inzamam or Miandad out. I'd back myself to defend that total against any team.

"People said we should have done this and that. Hell, I'd like to have had four Gavin Larsens to bowl to Inzamam. We bowled as well as we could and he batted amazingly. At the time I found Martin's comment pretty gut-wrenching, especially given the issue at the start of the tour when I'd been vehemently in his camp over the captaincy thing.

"But Martin is Martin. I look back and I understand his position, his feelings. He's a very emotional person and he had done so much during the World Cup."

After that match the New Zealanders did a lap of Eden Park to salute the crowd. They hadn't even reached the final, and they were doing a victory lap. Normally this would be ridiculous. But they deserved that moment in the spotlight. They had won back the New Zealand public. They were playing again in front of sellout crowds, and they were winning. At the start of the tournament, when the New Zealand anthem was played, Crowe was obviously very emotional. Now, during the victory lap, he struggled to hold back the tears. Others felt similarly. Ian Smith, who was retiring, was terribly worked up. And players like Latham, Larsen, Patel and Watson, who'd been around for some years, must have wondered if they'd ever know such a moment again in their cricket careers.

Pakistan – "fight like cornered tigers," Imran had advised them when they looked to have lost all chance of qualifying for the semis – duly won the final over England. It was just the way the dice rolled; New Zealand could easily have been the World Cup champions and everyone knew it.

For Crowe, the World Cup also emphasised how his attitude to one-day cricket had changed. He had been brought up believing traditional cricket – test and first class matches – to be the core of the game and it took him many years to warm to the one-day version.

Typically, when he did apply himself to one-day cricket, he proved brilliant at it. "I had been looking at it selfishly. I didn't look at the overall aspect of the game, and what it meant to New Zealand. We had to play it well and have the attitude it was as important as test cricket, so get on with it and enjoy it. I decided I would open the batting [which he did for New Zealand in 1990], which was different for me, a new motivation. That set me on my way to loving the one-day game, while still thinking that test cricket was the ultimate. I looked at the 15-over rule and thought I'd try to utilise the first 15 overs by opening the batting and getting stuck in."

So it seemed a season of incredible turmoil and controversy had ended gloriously for Crowe. Shortly afterwards, he was named New Zealand Cricket's Personality of the Year and awarded the Walter Hadlee Trophy for one-day batting. A *Dominion* headline "Crowe's rescurrection like a fairytale" was repeated in similar sentiments throughout the country. But he was lauded not only in New Zealand. "Crowe was perfection," former England captain Tony Lewis wrote in the *Sunday Telegraph*. "He is upright and technically a model. Yet elegance merges almost imperceptibly with savagery as the final wristwork goes into a cut or a drive." In the *Sunday Times*, Robin Marlar wrote: "It was impossible not to feel huge sympathy for Crowe. Truly he had played the innings of the tournament [his 91], an exhibition of controlled flair in which runs ticked up with no apparent hurry or brutality."

Patrick Smithers of the Melbourne *Age*, picking a World Cup team at the end of the tournament, included four New Zealanders – Crowe, Patel, Greatbatch and Larsen. "For the brain," he wrote, "we can't go past Martin Crowe, the man who helped change the way people think about one-day cricket, brazenly opening the bowling with Dipak Patel and the batting with Mark Greatbatch. A small portion of his cerebral organ will be removed, the section that is obsessed with 'desire' and 'focus' and other buzzwords, and replaced with a portion of the grey matter belonging to Warren Lees who helped cook up his madcap scheme."

Former England spinner Vic Marks, a Somerset teammate of Crowe's years earlier, looked beyond the innings to his position in New Zealand cricket. "This World Cup campaign has secured his position, not only as one of the world's top three batsmen, but, which is increasingly important to him, as New Zealand's undisputed leader."

But instead of heading off into winter with warm fuzzy memories of blazing boundaries and matches won in splendid fashion, Martin Crowe was back in the news again, and once more it wasn't because of his batting.

New Zealand bowed out of the World Cup on March 21. On March 23, *Crowe on Crowe* screened. During the programme, Martin and his wife Simone lashed out. Emotions which had been pent up during the World Cup were expressed.

Some examples:

Simone: "There are aspects surrounding cricket that I dislike intensely and there are certain people who have shown a lack of faith in Martin and I think it's really disappointing. People are fickle. When times are down, then you find out your real friends."

Martin: "There were heaps of doubts in my mind because the people that were putting me in the position of being captain were about to take it away from me."

Simone again: "The day before the team was announced, a couple of the selectors asked Martin to resign. I hope they're eating their words."

Purely in television terms, it was a muddled programme. As reviewer Rowan Dodds wrote in the *New Zealand Herald:* "*Crowe on Crowe,* at least judging by its time-slot, was aimed at the general viewing public rather than the die-hard cricket fan. Someone should have told Martin and Jeff. The hour-long special was peppered with obscure references to incidents and innings most of us knew nothing of . . . It was confusing with half-asked questions leading to rambling replies . . .

"Quibbles aside, it was an interesting and at times candid glimpse of a man we know little about, despite his profile. Now we know a little more – and it was clear an obsession to better his big brother has driven the younger Crowe to the sporting heights. We also got the picture of a stubborn, strong-willed individual who plays cricket with his mind as much as his body. And he's not very modest either."

While people like Dodds struggled to understand the under-currents of cricket politics, fulltime cricket writers were only too aware of what was going on. *Dominion* sports editor Peter Bidwell, in a column headed "Crowes put pre-election pressure on selectors", pointed out the revelations in the programme would make life more difficult for the national selectors when their jobs came up for re-election the following month.

But Bidwell was at pains to stress how unfair this would be. "It was easy for Crowe and his wife to point the stick at Neely and [Bruce] Taylor in the light of Crowe's subsequent brilliant batting and innovative captaincy," he wrote. "But at the time Neely and Taylor placed the acid on Crowe, they were trying to settle on a cup squad in trying circumstances. By his own admission, Crowe's fitness was marginal and it was badly affecting his batting. He was not sure whether his troublesome right knee would get him through the cup, and there had been dizzy spells, the classic symptoms of stress.

"The New Zealand team had not been performing and, as captain, Crowe had to shoulder most of the responsibility for that. Crowe conceded that on the eve of the World Cup the New Zealand team was in danger of falling apart, a situation that was quite evident. Neely and Taylor did only what any responsible selectors would have done . . .

"Crowe, a highly complex and often insecure individual, is not easy to deal with. When he is doing well the New Zealand team tends to. Immediately he is not, or his attitude seems a little out of tune, it is reflected in the team's performance."

So for days, just after one of the greatest chapters in New Zealand cricket history, and before the World Cup final had even been played, the headlines were dominated by the spat – which the Crowes had elected to make public – between the country's test cricket captain and the selectors.

Doubtless, Crowe felt aggrieved. Since he was a kid in shorts at school, Martin Crowe had been the star of every team bar one in which he played. The notable exception was his first series in test cricket, when he was reduced to bit-part status and became very resentful and indignant about his treatment. Now the selectors had questioned his right to be there. As Don Neely says, "I have no doubt he was shattered. He was really annoyed." More importantly for New Zealand cricket though, did the selectors by their action consciously (or accidentally, as John Parker suggests) inspire Crowe to pull himself out of the mire?

"Perhaps what we did was a spur to him," says Neely. "Perhaps when he was out there he thought he was hammering us [selectors] each time he scored a run. Or perhaps he'd have done it anyway. Who can say?"

The mature response would have been to have acknowledged that the selectors' action had added to his resolve to make a triumph of the World Cup, a resolve that had been building since 1990. But that is not the Crowe way.

Chapter Eleven

MISERY AND ABDICATION

MARTIN CROWE:

"There are lies being written and a lot of innuendoes that affect me personally – my marriage and all that sort of thing. I really do wonder if it's all worthwhile."

Rather than setting up Martin Crowe for an Allan Border-like reign as his country's test captain, the 1992 World Cup proved little more than one golden month in an ever-increasing storm of controversy. After initial problems, Border settled into the Australian captaincy so well that his position was taken for granted. He became ever more successful as his team gained in experience and by the time he retired, in 1994, he was regarded as an Aussie treasure. That dream-like scenario stretched out ahead of Martin after the World Cup, when it seemed he had silenced the doubters once and for all with the quality of his batting and captaincy.

He headed off to Italy, where he coached the Italian national team, as it attemped to become an associate member of the International Cricket Council. He was recruited during the World Cup by the Italian cricket star of the 1980s, and president of the Italian association, Simon Gambino. Conditions in Italy were in stark contrast to the hype and drama of the World Cup. Crowe discovered there were just eight teams in Italy. Every Sunday they played 80-over games. Some of the teams had to travel for up to five hours to take part. And there were no cricket grounds, so teams had to make do with an open ground in a park or paddock.

His sojourn in Italy gave Martin and Simone Crowe an ideal chance to take a holiday well away from the New Zealand spotlight. The couple had hoped to be married in Florence, but had decided against it because of the difficulties that would have posed for their relatives. Instead they decided to spend their first anniversary there. There was good news for Crowe on his return when he was made New Zealand Cricket's first fulltime contracted player in a 10-month-a-year deal stretching over three and a half years. The deal was said to be worth $300,000-plus. In another major business development, Crowe ended his long association with the Duncan Fearnley equipment company and signed for Gunn and Moore. The Gunn and Moore and New Zealand Cricket contracts, negotiated by Martin's new manager, brother Jeff, and announced in August and September 1992, were about the last good news Crowe got for some time.

He returned from the inaugural Hong Kong sixes tournament suffering from a viral complaint later diagnosed as a mild form of glandular fever. Initially it threw his availability for the tour of Zimbabwe and Sri Lanka in doubt, but he eventually travelled to Zimbabwe with his team, though he could not play for the first week.

New Zealand won both one-dayers, won one test and drew the other in Zimbabwe. Crowe gathered another test century in the second test, which New Zealand won by 177 runs. It was Crowe's first win as a test captain, in his ninth match, and naturally he was delighted to have shaken off that bogey. However, he knew that Zimbabwe were easy pickings at international level, and all the New Zealand batsmen used the two tests to boost their averages.

The more testing part of the tour was to take place in Sri Lanka. As it transpired it was testing in more ways than one. No sooner had the team arrived in Colombo and begun preparations for their first match than a suicide bomber chose the outside of the team's hotel to make his grisly protest. The explosion occurred while the tourists were at breakfast. Some, who raced outside to see what had happened, were shocked and appalled to see human body parts scattered around the immediate vicinity. Some were physically ill with what they'd witnessed. No amount of walking on the beach alongside the hotel could remove memories of human carnage.

Though it would have been the last thing on his mind, the bomber's action had major repercussions for New Zealand cricket as well as for the internal politics of Sri Lanka.

Experienced Radio New Zealand cricket commentator Bryan Waddle, surveying the mess that was New Zealand cricket during the 1994/95 season, says virtually everything could be traced back to that bomb in Sri Lanka: "Things were going well until then. There'd been the World Cup the season before, which was great. The New Zealanders had played well in Zimbabwe. But after that bomb went off in Sri Lanka, the wheels fell off. Lees was dropped as coach, when most people near the team felt he was doing a good job. And, partly because of that, Martin Crowe came under more pressure as captain. The whole thing has just unwound since then."

The Sri Lankan tour was a disaster. After the bombing, the team met to discuss whether they should continue, or return home. Crowe, already on antibiotics as he struggled to get over a relapse of the viral attack that hit him before he'd left for Zimbabwe (by now he had two leg injuries as well), reported that there had been too much of a negative vote for the tour to continue. Appearing on the *Holmes* television show, he was clearly unwell, and looked weighed down with responsibility and worry as he explained why the tour should not continue: "I as captain need a team that is unanimous about staying, unanimous about playing their best cricket over the next six weeks. So, in a lot of ways, we've no choice but to head home."

A cancelled tour would have been a financial disaster for New Zealand Cricket and chairman Peter McDermott rushed to Sri Lanka to try to save the tour. Rushing through Auckland airport, he said, with admirable candour: "I'm in a hell of a panic – I'm going to try to save the tour."

And save it he did. He leaned very hard on every player and persuaded enough of them to stay that the tour could continue. He could not stop the ones who were set on returning home from leaving. So Mark Greatbatch, Gavin Larsen, Rod Latham, Dipak Patel and Willie Watson returned. So too, crucially, did coach Lees. They were replaced by Grant Bradburn, Michael Owens, Justin Vaughan and John Wright, and Crowe took over the coaching duties as well.

The tour became totally unsatisfactory. Ken Rutherford said he was staying only because of the money. Greatbatch complained that too much pressure had been applied on the players who wished to leave. In some quarters New Zealand Cricket was branded cavalier in disregarding the players' safety. In others, the returning players were labelled wimps. The captain of three decades earlier, John Reid, felt the tour should not be abandoned and offered his services free of charge as a replacement coach.

Cricket seemed the last thing on anyone's mind. Not surprisingly, New Zealand lost the series 1-0 with one drawn, and lost both one-dayers. Crowe, after scores of 19, 11 and 0, scored 107 in the second innings of the second test (which was eventually lost) and rated it as perhaps his best test innings.

He explained to Jack Bannister in *The Innings of My Life*: "I was proud of my performance for several reasons. It was a difficult tour after the four deaths caused by a bomb strapped to a suicide motorcyclist, and six players went home. The team had been split right down the middle about going home or staying, and I was pretty down . . .

"When I went in to bat for the second time, we had followed on early on the third day, 292 behind and we were 30-2. The pitch was a real turner, and their spinners were a handful. I got 107 and played as well as I could. My only problem came when I was 39. I was given out caught bat-pad on the off-side, but I asked Gurusinha if he had caught it. When he said no, I stood my ground, and I managed to hit a hundred which gave me a great deal of personal satisfaction."

Despite Crowe's century, Sri Lanka duly completed their third test victory, their first against New Zealand. The tour is best forgotten.

Worse was to follow. Everyone who returned home was assured their decision would have no bearing on how they were regarded in future. Yet Lees, despite another fairly successful season, was dumped as coach. He was replaced by Geoff Howarth, which did not suit Crowe at all.

And Crowe, instead of returning from Zimbabwe and Sri Lanka on a high, was a weary, worried person on his arrival at Auckland airport. He was to be a lot more weary and worried before the end of the season.

The Pakistanis arrived at almost the same time as the New Zealanders. They split the two one-dayers, then the teams travelled to Hamilton for a one-off test. Here Crowe was plunged into controversy again when he withdrew from the test late in the piece because of a bruised finger. Rutherford took over the captaincy, and did a splendid job. It appeared he would begin his captaincy career with a victory, until Wasim and Waqar bowled out New Zealand on the last day for 93 to earn their team an unlikely victory by 33 runs.

The spirit in the New Zealand camp was good and it was noticeable how relaxed Rutherford appeared. The players responded well to him and there was a positive air about the side. Australia arrived in February for three tests and four one-day internationals. But the talk was about far more than the actual games. Crowe's captaincy was under public question again, from all sorts of quarters.

The first test at Christchurch was a shocker for New Zealand, who lost by an innings and 60 runs. Only Rutherford, with 57 and 102, profited at all against McDermott, Hughes and Warne. Crowe failed twice and seemed ill at ease.

After the Christchurch test, Crowe stated publicly that he was not getting sufficient support from the senior members of the side. Says John Wright: "I read that and I was pretty shocked. There were really only two older players he could be talking about, Andrew Jones and me. It was the first I'd heard that there might be a problem and to raise it through the media was an unusual way of going about it."

Though he was hurt by the criticism, as he had been by Crowe's outburst when the World Cup semi-final had been lost, Wright understood the pressure Crowe was under. "Martin had high expectations of taking over the leadership role and very strong ideas about how New Zealand cricket should develop. But when he got control, it wasn't a strong team. It's difficult when you are captain and the team isn't playing well and you aren't getting the results you want. It becomes a personal thing, like you've got ownership of it. That can be tough. You can't do it all yourself in a team.

"I felt the public understood the situation, but Martin is very intense. It got to him personally, just as it did to me when we didn't win. Captaincy is a funny thing. Everyone wants it, but it's one of the hardest jobs in sport."

Wright feels Crowe was very similar to Geoff Howarth as a leader, though it's doubtful it's a comparison either would enjoy. "Both were tactically very good, but not strong on their consistency of communication; and in the New Zealand team you need that skill. Geoff was lucky he had a reasonable side. Martin was unlucky. And he had these injury things. It was important when Martin was captain that he did well with the bat, important for Martin and the team. He could get down and sometimes it would be hard to get a 'good morning' out of him. He's a complex character and needs a strong structure to supplement his skills as captain.

"Wally Lees worked well with him. Martin felt comfortable, and Wally knew how to get the best out of Martin. With Geoff Howarth, it was never going to work. You can say they're both professionals and they have to make it work, but it really wasn't on. There was too much history between the two, and their strengths and weaknesses didn't gel. I've always felt

Martin is happiest as a great batsman. As a captain, the disillusionment of being in a side where results didn't come made things difficult for him."

There was a lot of talk about Crowe in the days immediately after the Christchurch test. Doug Golightly in *New Zealand Truth* pushed for Rutherford (the newspaper's columnist) to take over the captaincy. "I wrote a back page story saying the team was not functioning well with Martin Crowe at the helm. I mentioned a lunch during the Christchurch test in which the players had eaten at different tables. The lunch was symptomatic of what was going on with the team. I wrote that Ken Rutherford would make the better captain. It wasn't a negative story. I offered Rutherford as captain. Ironically, history has proved me out."

Crowe suggested to the selectors they consider taking the captaincy off him for the tests. "It was just an idea, something which might shake up the team, get them to realise their responsibilities. The idea was not followed through, but instead of that being the end of it, it was made public." Crowe complained on the *Fraser* TV programme that a confidence had been breached by his suggestion being made public. Certainly, once news of his idea surfaced he was obliged to explain the reasons for suggesting he be stood down from the captaincy, and said, "It's not working at the moment and I am prepared for anything. All the insecurity around the side needs to be cleaned up. Guys have been a bit scared to say anything at our meetings. Something indefinable is missing. I've got an awful record in tests and if they want to bring back John Wright as captain for the two remaining tests I would accept it. But I'd want to come back into the job for the one-dayers.

"In the 13 tests I've been captain I've not had the Richard Hadlees in the side, but in Christchurch we were quite dreadful and a bit of self-doubt does creep in."

Don Neely quickly scotched Crowe's suggestion. "As far as we are concerned, Martin is the best man for the job and we stand behind him and the team," said Neely. "It was a courageous move of Martin's to offer such a drastic solution and it shows he is thinking more of his team than himself. It took great courage to make such a statement because he has always publicly aspired to be captain of New Zealand. The players will look at what he has said and realise how serious he is about getting things back on track. He was prepared to make a huge personal sacrifice."

On the Friday night of the Wellington test a TV3 sports show panel debated Crowe's captaincy. Opinions were divided, but both Murray

Deaker and Trevor McKewen spoke strongly against the high profile Simone Crowe had within the New Zealand camp.

McKewen: "The pot was stirred during the *Sinbin* sports segment. The question was asked: should Martin retain the captaincy? I said he was a great batsman, but was unsuited to captaincy, just as great players like Botham and Gower had been. I said the side's performances relied on his mood swings. Then I drew a comparison with the Aussies and them in their No 1s [blazer and ties] and us wearing tracksuits and T-shirts and Martin and Simone first off the plane. Murray Deaker chimed in by saying, 'If you're asking me if Simone Crowe should be sacked from the captaincy of the New Zealand team, I'd say, "Yes, right now." ' There was more discussion, then Murray, who supported Crowe as captain, ended with, 'Martin stays, Simone goes.' "

Simone herself had been far from quiet. She'd done a provocative interview with Radio Pacific defending her husband against all the rumours, which she proceeded to detail. These included Martin being homosexual, having Aids, and their marriage being in trouble. Just before the Christchurch test, she was interviewed by Tony Potter of *Sunday News* for a front page article, posing for the accompanying photo for freelance photographer John McCombe at Lancaster Park on the Saturday of the test.

In Potter's story she again complained about all the vicious rumours, listing them again. McKewen, the paper's sports editor, was surprised to see the story the next day, but certainly had no problems with it. "I didn't know we were running it, but I read it and thought it was a good story. I mean, if Allan Border's wife complains that he's into sado-masochism, it's a story."

By the time the second test at the Basin got under way, Crowe looked like a man under siege, which indeed he was. The talkback callers were feasting on him.

New Zealand held their own at the Basin and on the Saturday Crowe made 98 before being bowled by McDermott. That evening he gave one of the most remarkable New Zealand sporting press conferences in memory.

He came in and began by saying: "Righto, I'm going to ask some questions. Trevor, do you think I'm a homosexual?"

McKewen, once he got over his shock at this turn of events, replied: "Of course not, Martin."

Crowe: "Well, how come you keep inferring it in your paper?"

McKewen defended himself, saying he had never done that.

Crowe then turned his sights on Golightly, asking him about the story about the team eating apart. He wanted to know Golightly's source. Golightly refused to say. Crowe then said, "Whoever told you that is a liar."

Golightly said: "I stand by the story."

Crowe then asked: "Is it a professional or a personal attack?"

Golightly: "It's purely professional."

Then Crowe complained about the "lies and innuendos" which, he said, were affecting his marriage and making him question his desire to lead his country. He said he felt victimised by persistent rumours about his personal life. He was also deeply upset by the TV3 discussion.

"It just doesn't seem to stop," said Crowe. "It seems every day there is something. My wife is demoralised by the whole thing – and justified too after last night [the TV3 programme]. It's very, very sad to see that in a country that you love and in a situation where you love playing for millions of people. It's only a minority that stuff it up and it's that minority that you have to deal with every day.

"Professionally, I am accountable for my results. That's fine – everyone is entitled to write about what I do as a batsman or captain. But there are lies being written and a lot of innuendos that affect me personally – my marriage and all that sort of thing. I really do wonder if it's all worthwhile; why I decided to take on the job and give it 100 per cent."

At this point Don Cameron, the *New Zealand Herald's* veteran cricket writer, raised the question of whether these comments were on or off the record. Richard Hadlee, the BNZ cricket ambassador, who was running the press conference, attempted to smooth things over and have the comments go unreported. But the stunned Australian journalists, sensing a good story, kept returning to the subject. For a time it was agreed no-one would report Crowe's comments. But then an Australian asked: "Do you feel persecuted by your own press?"

Crowe replied that he did, and unleashed another barrage. At the end of the conference Hadlee stated that all the comments about the media were off the record, but the Australians disagreed and Cameron said that as Crowe had revisited the subject, his comments had to be on the record.

Hadlee recalls that conference well. "I had no prior warning of what Martin was going to do. If I had, I might have had a quiet word with him, suggested he think about it a bit more. He was obviously very emotional;

he felt sad and depressed and felt that confronting the journalists would be the best way of handling the situation: to attack. It was a sad conference in that what it really achieved was that it gave the media another story. Perhaps he wonders now if it was the best way of handling the situation, or perhaps he was just pleased to get it off his chest."

Crowe's outburst certainly shocked the Australian journalists. Robert Craddock, an experienced Queensland cricket writer whose material is run in various News International outlets, describes it as "memorable".

"I can't recall a press conference where the captain has been more emotional. My first reaction was sympathy that he'd been reduced to criticising the media. I must say I felt that Crowe's private life was subject to undue scrutiny. But I was impressed with the way Trevor McKewen and Doug Golightly stood their ground. I've never seen a more coolheaded performance than Doug's from a journalist defending his story.

"What stunned me was that it seemed so incongruous with other aspects of New Zealand society, which is so laid-back.

"The great mistake Martin and his wife made was in opening their mouths too much. They had to learn to shut their mouths. But he was clearly deeply offended and frustrated. The whole thing took us by surprise. You aren't used to seeing a star doing that. Kim Hughes had a very emotional press conference when he quit as Australian captain. But that was a cricketing thing; Martin's was his private life."

The following day, Crowe took a break from captaining the side with Rutherford assuming control for half an hour after lunch. Lees explained Crowe had been fielding under the helmet all morning and had had little sleep the previous night. "Obviously things have been worrying him and eating away."

Hadlee was right about one thing. Crowe's outburst merely gave the media another story. Crowe might have felt better for having vented his spleen, but his outburst did little to shore up his position.

Jeff Crowe stepped into the controversy in an extended interview published in the *Sunday Times* on March 14. "I totally endorse everything Martin has done," said Jeff. "People say the best way to handle media of this type is to shut up and say nothing. I'm not sure if they understand what it's like when you get personally abused . . . you just can't shut up.

"Martin is very capable of handling it all himself. He is not going to be the nice humble person or the all-round good guy that everyone wants. He is a hell of a nice person. But how would you handle Merv Hughes being humble and the all-round good guy? That's my point. They can't fault him [Martin] as a player because he's too bloody good to criticise."

Even Allan Border chimed in. Having watched and listened to the raging debate about Crowe's captaincy, he said: "You have expectations and when things don't happen you start to question if you are the right fellow for the job. Personally, I think he is the right person."

After all this fuss, New Zealand went to Auckland for the third test and confounded the form book, winning by five wickets after a gripping match in which Danny Morrison and Dipak Patel were the bowling heroes and Rutherford top-scored in both innings.

The one-day series that followed was a cracker. Australia won it 3-2, winning the final match, at Eden Park, off the last ball. With Jeff Wilson brought into the one-day side and Tony Blain contributing wonderfully on the park and off, it was an excellent way to finish one of the most tempestuous seasons in memory.

But in case Crowe was tempted to sit back and reflect that the worst was over, the next bit of news from the New Zealand Cricket boardroom was that Warren Lees has been sacked as coach, replaced by Howarth. It was not a thought that filled Crowe with joy. He had built up a fine rapport with Lees and did not relate nearly as well to Howarth.

Lees has to be considered unlucky in that he had been told if he returned early from Sri Lanka it would not be held against him. Clearly it was. The season was reasonably successful as far as results went, so there could be no other rationale. My view was that Lees should be free to leave Sri Lanka, but that in doing so he forfeited his right to be coach. Further, he did not seem to be the sort of person to stand up to Crowe. I would have preferred Glenn Turner to be coaching the team, but at the time that idea was apparently an untenable situation in the view of New Zealand Cricket.

No doubt Crowe was a lot less settled when he returned to Italy during the 1993 New Zealand winter than he had been the previous year. He would have realised, more than most, how difficult he was going to find working with Howarth. They could hardly be more different in their attitudes to cricket. Crowe is incredibly focused and demanding of himself. He is driven. Howarth...well, he isn't. He plays the percentage game more, like the English county pros who know there's always going to be another game next week, so don't get too worked up about things. As Howarth says: "Martin does put a lot of pressure on himself – his expectations and the way he prepares are tough. But it's brought him a lot of success. I'd never put myself through that sort of regime. The game is too much to be enjoyed for that."

During the winter Martin and Simone moved from Eastbourne in Wellington to the Millbrook Resort near Arrowtown. Martin had been considering buying in Auckland, but was taken with the Arrowtown area when he and Jeff walked the Milford Track. "It'll be his winter retreat . . . somewhere to get away from the hustle and bustle," brother Jeff explained.

The 1993/94 season loomed as an exciting one for New Zealand cricket, with a big tour of Australia, including involvement in the World Series, then tours of New Zealand by Pakistan and India. For Crowe, though, it was a season of utter disappointment and frustration. A lot was written about Crowe, as ever, but almost none of it was to do with his batting. Rather, there was week after week of speculation about his fitness after he'd had to leave the Australian tour early. And the longer Crowe was away from the game, the more talk there was that Rutherford should be given the captaincy fulltime, rather than merely as Crowe's stand-in.

Eventually, at the end of the season, Crowe called a press conference at Hamilton and, in an emotional speech, explained that he was standing down from the captaincy. He was available to tour England the following winter as a player, but not as captain or vice-captain.

It was the end of a three and a half year roller-coaster ride for Crowe the captain. There'd been the odd glorious moment, some shattering defeats, the horror of the bombing in Sri Lanka, endless talk about his ability to do the job, and finally concern over whether his damaged knee would ever be sound enough to enable him to captain the team again.

"There was as much written about Martin as there had been previously," says Ian Smith, "but less of it concerned cricket."

The omens didn't look good for the tour of Australia when, in the first match, against a Chairman's XI at Perth, New Zealand suffered an embarrassing defeat. Old-timers Lillee, Thomson and Hadlee bowled out New Zealand for 189. And if Marsh and Zoehrer hadn't bowled for the Chairman's team and fed Willie Watson a gift half-century, the score would have been substantially less. The makeshift Australian team had no trouble knocking off the runs to win by six wickets with seven overs to spare.

Next up was an innings defeat by Western Australia. If that was bad, defeat by 110 runs in a one-dayer against the Australian Cricket Academy XI was worse.

It seemed New Zealand might have turned the corner when they eked out a three-wicket win over New South Wales, in spite of being bowled out for 163 in the first innings. A brilliant spell by Danny Morrison (6-54) ripped the heart out of the New South Wales second innings and set up New Zealand for a victory which good batting by Tony Blain ensured.

Tasmania had the better of a drawn game at Launceston when the bright point was a return to form by Crowe, who plundered a rapid century.

After this none-too-convincing build-up, it was into the first test at Perth. The New Zealanders played above themselves to force an honourable draw. Australia made 398 and New Zealand, with Andrew Jones playing the dominant role with a fighting 143, replied with 419-9 declared. Australia smashed 323-1 declared in their second innings and looked to their leg-spinning wizard, Shane Warne, to bowl them to victory.

He probably would have, too, but for the defiance of Crowe. Though by now he was batting on one leg, after his knee troubles had flared up again, a mainly defensive Crowe took most of Warne's bowling. For two hours he held up one end to finish with 31 not out. Rutherford and Jones scored more runs in quickfire innings, but Crowe's was the innings which saved the test. It was all the more commendable as he was unable to use any footwork to speak of and had to rely on a cool head and a straight bat.

Though he didn't know it then, that was the last time for at least two years that Crowe was to lead the New Zealand team, unless he was deputising for someone else.

He returned home, leaving Rutherford in charge of a struggling New Zealand side. Within a couple of days he'd had more knee surgery by Aucklander Barry Tietjens and was recuperating at his Millbrook home. Instead of leading New Zealand, Crowe was stuck at home, having four weeks of physiotherapy, followed by, hopefully, a build-up for a return to cricket. He was aiming, he reported, to return to cricket in time for a Wellington-Otago Shell Trophy game on January 18 and for the home series against Pakistan.

It never happened. And in a bizarre sort of way, Rutherford became ever more popular as New Zealand skipper, in spite of his team recording appalling results. Australia won the second test by an innings and 222 runs, New Zealand's heaviest defeat to that stage, and the third by an innings and 96 runs.

When they returned to Australia after a short break, Rutherford's men were eliminated from the World Series Cricket competition in which

Australia and South Africa qualified for the final.

At this stage it still seemed likely Crowe would be available for the Pakistan series. But should he be captain? There was a groundswell of opinion, not just from the talkback callers, but among former test cricketers, that Rutherford should keep the job. Bruce Edgar said: "Ken was on a hiding to nothing when he took over. He lost his captain, who is one of the world's leading batsmen; there were injury problems; and they were up against a very good Australian side. In the face of adversity, he moulded the team and gave them self-belief.

"The other thing is that he is a players' player. I think Martin sees the captaincy as a job. He will turn up and make directions as he goes. From an outsider's point of view, I would say Ken mixes better with the team and he's there telling the guys to believe in him. He has the ability to communicate well with his team and the public."

Lance Cairns endorsed Edgar's comments: "Ken has made some players realise they are more accountable, and has highlighted the pride needed in playing for one's country. The discipline thing may have slipped in the last couple of years. To me, Ken is more forthright while Martin tends to let things flow along. This team has learned a few things under Ken."

Ian Smith offered the counter view. "Crowe was captain during the World Cup and he did a good job. He's the accepted captain. When he's fit again, and able to play for New Zealand, he should be captain. Ken has done an admirable job, but that is no reason to make changes for change's sake."

The talk seemed endless. Crowe never did come right. He had a Shell Cup game for Wellington on January 13, another three days later, and a Shell Trophy fixture against Otago from January 18 to 21. But that was it. Even with the support of his imported $1000 titanium knee brace, his injury recurred.

He described it to the *Woman's Day's* Martine Rule as "the toughest time of my career. I've even had the odd little cry, wondering, 'Why me?' But I kept looking forward."

Crowe described how he turned to his friend Grant Fox for advice. "Grant, who had a pelvis injury, was given a hard time in 1991 and people were constantly criticising him. He told me that once he got his injury under control, he concentrated on playing good rugby and achieving personal goals. His example of finishing on top was excellent advice."

It was an unsatisfactory situation for everyone. Rutherford complained that because he kept being referred to as the temporary test captain, he was not able to impose his methods on the team as he wanted. Crowe kept being asked if he was willing to play under Rutherford. More talk about Crowe, and again not his batting.

New Zealand lost the first two tests against Pakistan and then, largely through a magnificent fighting century by Brian Young and a more blazing one from Shane Thomson, scored 324-5 in the fourth innings to win the third test at Christchurch. It was Rutherford's first test victory as captain. He and the team were elated. At last there was something to fill the cricket columns besides the state of Crowe's knee. Five one-dayers followed. Pakistan won three, New Zealand one, and one was tied.

Pakistan had an exceptionally strong bowling attack, and a reasonable batting line-up. So New Zealand's results, given the injuries to their key players, were far from disastrous.

India stopped off for a test and a one-day series. The test at Hamilton was memorable not because of any heroics on the field, but for the Crowe press conference in which he stood down from the captaincy and said he was available for the forthcoming tour of England.

Various New Zealand Cricket officials I've spoken to take credit for provoking Crowe into action. His contract allowed New Zealand Cricket to cease paying him if he stopped playing international cricket for more than three months due to injury. The threat was that when Crowe's three months elapsed, he was to be taken off the payroll.

Whatever the reason, Crowe's press conference was another dramatic twist in his career. Don Cameron in the *New Zealand Herald* wrote a story headed "Crowe's noble gesture" in which he said Crowe had played one of the greatest hands of his lustrous career. "He announced that in the interests of the touring team, which he is almost fit enough to join, he would not be available for the captaincy. Rather than hamper the team preparation, he would stand aside . . . This, said Crowe, would allow the selectors, coach and Ken Rutherford – certain now to retain the captaincy – to proceed with tour planning while Crowe could concentrate on the long, slow but most promising work which would allow him to play with a damaged knee."

Cameron pointed out how proud Crowe had been in previous years to be captain of his country. "It has been a central theme to the motivation which Crowe requires, even if it sometimes takes him on different paths from his teammates. Such is Crowe's stature he could have driven a hard bargain while trading his ability as captain against the worry about his injured knee. However, he placed the interests of the team first, and the only string he attached was a final hope that once he was fit again and scoring runs for New Zealand, he might again be considered for the leadership."

Crowe's gesture took many by surprise. He'd always cherished the captaincy so much, it was difficult to imagine him standing down voluntarily. John Bracewell had written not long previously that, knowing the Crowe psyche, he was sure Crowe would want to retain the captaincy.

Even more surprisingly, Crowe made his decision against the advice of some of his closest allies. Brother Jeff told me a few days later he had advised Martin to hang on to the captaincy. "It's all right now, but what about later when Martin feels ready to captain the side again? Then that guy out there," he said, pointing across the Basin Reserve to Ken Rutherford, "will want to hang on to it. What then?"

So the decision was made. The Martin Crowe era – a soap opera which had included more twists and dramas than any respectable fiction writer would include in one novel – was over.

Crowe was to be plain Martin Crowe, New Zealand batsman. The question now was: could Martin Crowe ever again be simply another player in the New Zealand team?

Chapter Twelve

JUST A PLAYER?

GEOFF HOWARTH:

> *"We are not good friends, but we are not enemies. His regard for New Zealand Cricket is more selfish than mine. He is an intellectual cricketer, but I am not interested in that. Martin is doing the fighting, not me."*

Martin Crowe wasted no time in letting the New Zealand public know that he was not going to slip quietly back into the role of being just another member of the test team.

Only a day or two before Ken Rutherford's team left for their 1994 England tour – the one for which Crowe had declined to be captain or vice-captain so he could concentrate on his batting – he gave Ian Fraser an interview on TV One.

During the interview Crowe:

- Spoke of the ills affecting New Zealand cricket, mentioning clashes of personality, decisions being made on personal fallouts, the need to pick the best captain, players and so on.
- Pushed for Glenn Turner as a selector. "We are missing his input. He can offer the sort of expertise we badly need."
- Stressed that an indefinable something was missing from New Zealand cricket. When pushed, he said it was the need for people to do their job in a more professional, businesslike way.

- Said New Zealand wasn't hungry enough to be the best it could be. "We are a bit shy of it. We want to be back in the pack."
- Criticised the media for "attacking my private life, the very private things I think are sacred".
- Criticised the convener of selectors (Don Neely) for a breach of confidence the previous season regarding Crowe's private offer to stand down as test captain to try to ignite the team to perform better. "I was disappointed . . . They decided to go public with it. I didn't go public with it."
- Strongly backed the work of sacked coach Warren Lees and damned new coach Geoff Howarth with faint praise. "Geoff is similar to me, a tactician and a run-scorer. So if he's doing my job, who's looking after the other guys?"

It was a lengthy interview, heavily advertised. Even if both Fraser and Crowe seemed to be revelling in being rather cerebral, things were said which were hardly supportive of New Zealand Cricket, or key officials.

This is interesting because part of the standard New Zealand players' contract reads: "The players shall at all times . . . use their best endeavours to promote the success of the tour and the image of the team and New Zealand.

"The player shall not comment adversely on fellow team members and their performance . . . The player shall avoid comments likely to cause controversy within the team and refrain from commenting on any other matter which should be regarded as confidential to the team and New Zealand Cricket."

Though Crowe had breached these conditions, there was no official censure. As had been the case for some years, New Zealand Cricket was tipping its hat to Crowe because of his dominance in a cricketing sense.

During the England tour, the rift between Crowe and Howarth grew. This became clear in various media interviews Crowe gave. He spoke to Don Cameron of the *New Zealand Herald,* to the NZPA reporter following the team, to Radio New Zealand's Bryan Waddle (a transcript of which appeared in some New Zealand newspapers), and to Michael Parkinson, writing for *The Daily Telegraph* (a story which was reproduced in New Zealand).

Immediately on the team's return he featured in a women's magazine article. There were recurring themes in his interviews – he didn't think a lot of Howarth as a coach, he had been bedevilled by all sorts of unsavoury rumours. (Crowe didn't stop after the England tour, either. He regurgitated all the rumours again for *South African Sports Illustrated,* then in a February 1995 *Metro* story, went over the rumours yet again, questioned the sort of loyalty he'd had when Ken Rutherford was his vice-captain, and painted Geoff Howarth's coaching in unflattering terms.) It would be hard to imagine any other team member publicly criticising the coach and getting no rebuke. I asked New Zealand Cricket chairman Peter McDermott about Crowe's attitude in England. "His attitude was tremendous." What about the criticism of Howarth? "We did take action, but not formal action. We chatted to people and used the gatherings at the academy after the tour. Martin was not very close to the line. There were situations within the touring party which had to be addressed."

This reaction was merely confirmation of what former players such as John Parker and John Morrison felt – that there were two rules in New Zealand cricket, one for Crowe and one for everyone else.

Parker: "Martin had been given so much space by New Zealand Cricket that he felt he was in control of every situation. That environment should never have been created. It's New Zealand Cricket's fault. Because he is such a great player they've just said, 'Yes sir, no sir, three bags full sir.' He's still testing the system to see if what he says still goes."

Morrison: "New Zealand Cricket has allowed him to run rampant. They've always shied away from addressing the whole issue of Crowe. He's a brilliant batsman, but the crap that goes with it has got to an absurd level."

Crowe's chipping away at Howarth naturally caused problems within the team. Ken Rutherford, on his first tour of England as captain, was in an awkward jam, caught between his best batsman and the coach. Asked about the public nature of Crowe's criticism, Rutherford says, "That's the standing Martin has as a cricketer. He can say it and get away with it. Things were touchy in England. I was getting snippets from home about what Martin was saying. It was counter-productive, and I was disappointed. I made the occasional snide remark to him about us keeping together as a unit. I don't think those sort of comments should have been sliding back home. They should be aired behind closed doors."

Howarth, not surprisingly, was unimpressed. "In England, there were some things he said which I could have been made aware of in a less public way. I'd have gone about it in a different way. It didn't have to be made that public, unless there was an ulterior motive." Howarth also said he felt Crowe's agenda all along was to have Warren Lees reinstated as New Zealand team coach.

Besides not fronting up to Crowe for undermining the team coach, New Zealand Cricket bosses McDermott and Graham Dowling ignored repeated warnings about the problems the management was having during the England tour. In early July, Roddy Fulton, Director of Cricket, warned McDermott (who was in London), Dowling and Cran Bull that a major rift had developed between Crowe and Howarth and stressed that the team management had been poor. McDermott's reply mentioned among the positives from the tour the fact that there were now five more young players capable of performing at test level; Crowe's attitude; Rutherford's improvement as captain; an improvement in Howarth's off-field behaviour; the image of the team.

In view of McDermott's on-the-spot assessment, the post-tour debriefing analysis must have come as a shock to McDermott, Dowling and the board members of New Zealand Cricket. Certainly the tour had been less than a success in terms of results. The test series was lost 1–0. The only county match the team won was against Glamorgan and the New Zealanders suffered two county defeats. The first one-day international resulted in an easy win to England, the second was washed out.

Crowe batted superbly in the tests, scoring 380 runs at 63.33, with two centuries. It was telling that when he had a double failure in the first test, New Zealand suffered an innings defeat. But in the next test, at Lord's, he scored a wonderful 142. He was supported by Dion Nash, who claimed 11 wickets in the match, and New Zealand went within two wickets of winning. It was the only proud result of the tour. In the third test, Crowe scored 70 and 115, his second innings a defiant match-saving effort after New Zealand had trailed by 231 runs on the first innings.

The New Zealanders were described in less than complimentary terms by the English media. Colin Bateman of the *Daily Express* said Crowe's superb batting underlined how New Zealand was a one-man team. "Martin Crowe is a world class player and, even with a suspect right knee which restricts his movement, he still stands out like a beacon in a sea of anonymity."

Scyld Berry described Crowe's 102 not out off 76 balls against Somerset as an innings of wonderful class – "by the end he was forgetting to hobble".

It was a tour in which several young players promised, but only Nash and, to a lesser extent, Parore, really delivered. Hamstrung by the most appalling run of injuries, Rutherford's team limped through the tour without ever lighting up the English summer. (The tour wasn't a total loss; the team did earn £18,000 from an advertisement for British Telecom.)

Back home, the recriminations started. McDermott put his support behind manager Mike Sandlant, said the coach had received good reports from all quarters, and rated Rutherford a captain out of the top drawer. But Fulton had each player fill in confidential questionnaires and, when these were gathered in, they told a different story.

Sandlant's lack of cricket knowledge was exposed. More telling, most players – including the senior members Rutherford, Crowe, Larsen and Morrison – expressed concerns about Howarth. There was a strong call for Warren Lees to be brought back. Howarth copped it for everything from grumpiness in the morning to poor practice structures. A separate report compiled by Bevan Congdon echoed these sentiments.

Howarth was interviewed on August 15, 1994. He said except for Mark Greatbatch (who'd apparently drifted away from the team) he'd had no problems with anyone on tour and defended his practice routines. On Crowe, he said: "We are not good friends, but we are not enemies. His regard for New Zealand cricket is more selfish than mine. He is an intellectual cricketer, but I am not interested in that. Martin is doing the fighting, not me."

Except for his sniping at Howarth, Crowe's contribution to the tour was commendable. John R. Reid, who was there for some matches, says Crowe's work with the younger players was excellent, and that he seemed a positive influence throughout. Of Crowe's criticism of Howarth, Reid says: "No, I damn well wouldn't have liked it if I'd been coach, but I'd have worked hard to find a way to get my best player on side."

Despite the concerns that had been raised, the same management structure was put in place for the tour of South Africa at the end of 1994, an indictment on New Zealand Cricket. This time, though, with Larsen unavailable, Crowe was elevated to the vice-captaincy.

In what had become typical Crowe fashion, though, there was a drama before the team left the country. The New Zealanders were to stop off in India for a week for a one-day tournament and Crowe sought permission to miss this segment because of his susceptibility to viruses and his desire to ensure his troublesome right knee was in the best condition to tackle the more important South African section.

This scenario suited Don Cameron, one of New Zealand's most experienced cricket writers, very well. He had warned during the tour of England that Crowe was so vital to his team's effort that he would have to be shepherded through the long 1994/95 season and suggested Crowe not go to India and restrict his appearances in the more physically demanding one-day matches. "There could, with care, be four or five more years of Crowe left for the benefit of New Zealand cricket. New Zealand cricket would be foolish if in the coming season it tried to burn the Crowe candle at both ends. He needs special treatment, and New Zealand needs Crowe."

Before leaving for South Africa, where he arrived early to train and await his teammates' arrival, Crowe explained to Lynn McConnell of the *Evening Post* how his troublesome knee restricted his batting: "I am conscious of it when I train, but once I set up for a test match and visualise what I want from the game, then the knee is not in my thinking. Obviously I can't do the silly ones and twos. My footwork is not affected at all, nor is my strokemaking. Basically it means that I am just not as quick as I was."

Crowe mentioned a couple more goals he had in the game. He left for South Africa on the brink of overhauling John Wright's tally of 5334 test runs to claim the New Zealand record. He needed a century against South Africa to make him the first player in the world to have test centuries against eight nations. And he said he was still eyeing 20 test centuries – he had 17 – which would put him in an elite group of history's greatest test batsmen. "It's always nice to have those little milestones to aim for. It would be nice to complete the set of centuries against all countries and to be the first to do that. There is nothing quite like the feeling you experience when you get a test century for your country. That feeling is what you play sport for."

The South African tour, so eagerly awaited, turned out to be a public relations nightmare. New Zealand won the first test, in which Crowe made a handsome 83, but the tour then went off the rails. New Zealand bombed out of the one-day tournament in mid-tour, then lost the remaining two tests. Crowe ended the tour on one leg again, having exacerbated his knee problem, and had double failures in the last two tests.

Crowe was also criticised for leaving the team in mid-tour. This was variously reported as a holiday and a chance to allow his knee to come right. Actually he asked to have a few days off. Rutherford, questioned about his vice-captain leaving the touring party, said: "I've got no problem with that. I've always said that, bar Hogan, the rest of the team pull the line."

Lance Cairns led the criticism of Crowe in his *Sunday News* column, writing: "When you're picked on a tour, you stay on a tour. You don't just wander off for a break when it suits. The only result of Crowe being allowed to take off is a divided team."

Crowe finished the test series with just 134 runs at 22.33 an innings. He trailed Thomson, Fleming, Young, Rutherford and even Doull in the averages. Geoff Howarth, in assessing the tour, said the batting disappointments were the opening partnerships and Crowe's output at No 4. "Martin Crowe's influence over the team as far as his batting skills are concerned was a deep disappointment. There has been no problem with input and contribution from him. It was just that his form for himself and for the team was very disappointing."

Crowe's knee got so bad he expressed doubts about his future as a one-day international, even when his knee had recovered.

But Crowe's knee was really only a small factor in this most unsatisfactory of tours. For legal reasons, it is not possible to detail all the misdemeanours, but they included the infamous party in which several team members smoked dope, regular bouts of late-night heavy drinking, Adam Parore smashing a Coke machine in a fit of temper, Ken Rutherford being suspended for two test matches for his behaviour in the third test (the suspension was suspended, so to speak).

New Zealand Cricket made the problems far worse when the team returned by naming, and suspending for a week, Stephen Fleming, Dion Nash and Matthew Hart, the only three members of the team with the moral fibre to admit they had smoked dope at the Christmas party. That matter had been dealt with at the time by manager Mike Sandlant, who fined each $250.

This double punishment of the honest players was reprehensible. It was reported that four other players (plus a team supporter) smoked dope, but refused to own up. One of them even offered Sandlant $250. New Zealand Cricket knew other players were involved, but elected to take the easy route and simply hang the three honest players.

Then there was the case of Chris Pringle, who was suspended for crimes unspecified. On further prompting a few days later, Pringle's suspension was also announced as a one-week job, and it was apparently for not preparing himself properly for a match and involved alcohol.

Sandlant's resignation on his return added to the dissatisfaction as it took an extraordinarily long time to get a satisfactory tour report out of him. Howarth was made the fall guy and there were two days of tense meetings between him and New Zealand Cricket before he "resigned", with a parting handshake of more than $150,000. John F. Reid was rushed in to replace Howarth as coach and Gren Alabaster was appointed manager for the domestic season.

Roddy Fulton's tour report, leaked in the *Sunday Star-Times* by that eager-beaver journalist Trevor McKewen (who these days works for the Super League organisation in Australia), laid a lot of the blame squarely on Rutherford, whose "personal example off the field needs improvement".

"The debacle which has occurred is a result of the captain, coach, vice-captain and physio failing to support the manager in terms of reporting lack of discipline and helping him maintain standards," concluded Fulton.

He said there was a lack of respect for New Zealand Cricket by some players and the management group, except Sandlant. His recommendation for the future was a complete change of manager, captain, coach and vice-captain with a review of the fitness procedures.

Dealing with Crowe's efforts as vice-captain, Fulton wrote that it was necessary to select a vice-captain "who has the strength of character to support his captain, manager and coach and ultimately lead his country at some stage." In view of the concern over Crowe's fitness and his "lack of support for management" Fulton recommended that he should not be vice-captain again.

Incidentally, Fulton recommended Gren Alabaster as manager, Glenn Turner or Mike Shrimpton as coach and Lee Germon as captain.

Germon, the Canterbury captain who was making his New Zealand debut, says Crowe was invariably helpful and that his work with two or three of the batsmen in particular was very good.

"It was the first time I'd toured with Martin and I had no problems with him. He obviously has the respect of the players through what he has done in the game. I'd heard he could be aloof and not really interact, but he did really well. He went out of his way to communicate. He's pretty astute. I found him really good to speak to in South Africa, especially about the one-day stuff. He's pro-active, not re-active, and is tactically an excellent captain."

Germon says any problems Crowe might have with teammates works the other way too. "It's hard for the guys to approach him, but in South

Africa he went out of his way to speak to people."

This defence of Crowe is interesting because over the years stories have circulated that Crowe has a snitcher on Germon. To listen to the scuttlebutt, he resented Germon's ability as a captain, and saw him as a potential rival. "I'd heard about him being resentful of my captaincy," says Germon. "That was a strain on us getting to know each other. Then, at the cricket academy, Martin spoke to us. Afterwards I thanked him and we had a chat. He brought up the rumours and said they weren't true. He was honest and able to talk about it. I mean, it's ridiculous. I hadn't played for New Zealand and it wasn't looking likely. But they're the sort of stories that seem to circulate."

Incidentally, Andrew Jones supports Germon's view of Crowe. "Martin hasn't put up a barrier," says Jones. "He has a very demanding, single-minded, critical, perceptive personality. That makes it difficult for some of the younger guys to deal with him, but it's a man's game. There are kids being put in the test team now when they haven't learnt the trade. Martin's a pragmatist. You don't often get a kid who's not up to it when he gets into the team, then comes good. They're either up to it or they're not. If anyone is game to ask Martin for advice, he's more than happy to help. I think people have had some difficulty in communicating with Martin, perhaps a tad more than with most team members. But he generally does his best in that regard."

Most observers felt Crowe was more relaxed in South Africa than he'd been for some seasons. Particularly until Simone arrived, he sought out the company of his teammates, and was something of a prankster. He spent a lot of time writing his autobiography. Often he'd be seen in his room tapping away on his lap-top. He was pleased when author Bryce Courtenay *(Power of One)* agreed to contribute a small section. Not so pleasing was the day he thought he'd inadvertently erased 20,000 words. Happily, he discovered them a while later. Crowe had various people read snippets of what he'd written. At that stage he planned for the book to be published after the West Indies tour in 1996, telling one journalist, "After this comes out, I won't be able to play any more." He mentioned how he'd returned fire to players and officials he had crossed during his career.

After the South African tour, Peter McDermott held his "full and open" (his words) press conference, in which he exposed the three dope smokers and Pringle, but not the others reported to be involved. Then the season went from bad to worse for New Zealand cricket.

On the field the New Zealand team was very poor, losing to the West Indies by a record margin, then to South Africa and Sri Lanka (Sri Lanka's first test victory overseas). In the one-day centenary quadrangular tournament, New Zealand sneaked into the final, where they were pummelled by Australia in embarrassing fashion.

There were other problems. They ranged from the most extraordinary run of injuries to key bowlers – New Zealand went into the last test against Sri Lanka without Morrison, Doull, Cairns and Nash, all out with injury – to the poor behaviour of various members of the test side. There were reports of late-night drinking by players during the Wellington test against the West Indies, which New Zealand lost; Murphy Su'a was suspended by the Auckland association for abusing an umpire in a club match; Rutherford at various times criticised the New Zealand selectors and announced the New Zealand public had been tricked into thinking Crowe would play in the one-day final to bolster gate takings; Kerry Walmsley was brought into the test team against Sri Lanka, a real dark horse selection, and within three days had been warned for abusing the opposition (he had already been suspended earlier in the season); Rutherford ran out Sri Lankan opener Samaraweera in the Napier test by firing the ball towards him, then did not recall Samaraweera when the batsman jumped to avoid the ball; Shane Thomson injured his leg on the eve of the Wellington test against the West Indies, but was played anyway and was a passenger throughout the match...

New Zealand Cricket made things worse. McDermott made some gaffes with his public utterances, and Su'a should never have been selected to represent New Zealand when suspended by Auckland. Throughout the New Zealand summer there was a rumbling Crowe story. How bad was his knee? Would he be able to play in the centenary one-day series? How many tests would he play?

Having gone through all this just the year before, Crowe was perhaps more prepared for the long slog back from injury through the summer of 1995. But the question which bubbled around in cricket circles was: how keen was he to come back? One former international had a bet that Crowe would play no one-day internationals and just one test, against South Africa, because he still wanted that elusive century to complete the set.

This seemed a ludicrous proposition. After all, how could Crowe hope to make the team for the South Africa match if he hadn't played some of the preceding internationals? Amazingly, it nearly happened that way.

He returned from South Africa, had the mandatory knee operation, then gradually got himself fit again. His first match was a Shell Trophy outing for Wellington against Canterbury on a featherbed at Lancaster Park. It became an historic match because it produced 1945 runs, a New Zealand record, and because Wellington's 475-4 was the highest fourth innings score ever to win a first class match in New Zealand. Crowe, who hadn't played for weeks, and had had surgery in the meantime, showed miraculous form and agility. He scored 50 not out and 193 not out, bowled 20 economical overs and fielded like a champion.

Wellington coach Bob Carter watched Crowe batting with disbelief. "He hadn't played for weeks and should have been trying to regain some form to get back into the New Zealand team. Instead he came straight in and batted superbly, especially when we were chasing that huge total to win in the fourth innings. I watched with mixed emotions because it was obvious he was batting so well he had to go straight back into the New Zealand side, and that we'd miss him for the rest of the season."

Carter is extremely praising of Crowe's contribution to the Wellington team over the past few years. "He's been very positive, especially as our captain. He is perceptive and knows a lot about the game. I suppose it could be a problem with him moving in and out of the team, depending on his availability through New Zealand commitments or injury, but he slips back in comfortably. Off the field I've never had any problems. He is willing to help, is keen to pass on his experience, and is generally very positive."

After his virtuoso display against Canterbury, Crowe was hurried into New Zealand's one-day line-up for the international at Napier against India. This tallied with what Crowe had announced a week earlier: that he could no longer pick and choose which matches he made himself available for. "I have got to be available and playing well in both forms of cricket to warrant selection for New Zealand – the criteria that all players must face. Exceptions have been made in the past, but now they should cease. Now I have to join the queue with the other players and prove myself physically. We are moving into a new stage of our cricket, and everything has got to be equal. That has probably been one of the problems over the last 12 months."

This caused more than a few wry smiles because the one player for whom exceptions had been made was Crowe himself. He ran his own schedule during the 1994 England tour, he did not have to tour India on the way to South Africa, he was permitted to take a break during the tour of South Africa, and he had questioned whether he would play one-day matches in future. Crowe duly came back for the one-dayer at Napier, but it was a short-lived comeback. He hurt a thigh muscle fielding, but still opened the batting, and was ░░░░░░░░░ ░eaply.

After this he mis░░ ░░ ░est of the one-day series, but there was just enough time for ░░ ░o recover before the test against South Africa. In this match, at ░░ ░ Park, he batted uncharacteristically poorly. In the first innings, ░ ░ked and prodded for nearly two and a half hours for 16, statis░ ░hich would be worse but for the six he hit off spinner Clive ░░ ░en.

Up in the TV commentary box, Glenn Turner said there could be two reasons for Crowe's strange innings: either he was out of form, or he was thinking too much about the century he wanted against South Africa. "I hope it's the former," said Turner. John Parker, John Morrison and Jeremy Coney all mentioned that he seemed unusually inhibited because he was so set on reaching what would be a record century.

In the second innings, when New Zealand were chasing victory, Crowe batted attractively, but briefly, for 14 before being caught in slips. And that was Crowe's lot for the season. The thigh muscle had apparently worsened again and he never did get back on the field. The former test player's predication had been eerily accurate – the test against South Africa was indeed the only one he played.

So the season ended with intrigue. Crowe supporters applauded his efforts at coming back and sympathised with his continuing injury problems; Crowe detractors scoffed and said it had been transparently obvious he'd wanted to play only against South Africa, and that he was selfish. One test player told me: "Martin found himself in a quandary. He likes the limelight, the spotlight. But he has walked away from the pressure of captaincy, so he keeps coming back in the side door to stay in the news. That's his dilemma."

While New Zealand Cricket, being leaned on heavily by the Hillary Commission and the Sports Foundation, reviewed itself ad nauseum in the off-season, the future of Crowe remained in doubt. There was ever-present speculation about his desire, his health, his goals. Few questioned his ability, but there was still a lot of talk about Crowe swirling about. ░hing had changed.

Chapter Thirteen

INFLUENCES OFF THE FIELD

MURRAY DEAKER:

> *"I'm sad this guy fell so badly. His self-analysis became atrocious. He started to blame everyone else. He and his advisors developed a siege mentality."*

Even Martin Crowe's staunchest backers find themselves asking where it all went wrong. How did the smiling, enthusiastic college boy become a man in his early 30s who seems to feel the world – or a goodly portion of it – is against him?

There is a well-known Jesuit axiom: "Give me the boy at seven and I'll show you the man."

"That might be true in most cases," says Murray Deaker, "but it's not true with Martin Crowe." Deaker has followed Crowe's career since Martin was 11, first as the First XI cricket coach at Auckland Grammar, then as a cricket fan, and more latterly as a radio and television sports broadcaster. He is a good friend of Jeff Crowe, whom he coached in the Grammar First XI, and knows Martin well. "I'm sad this guy fell so badly," says Deaker. "A couple of years ago I asked myself why the fascination of the public had moved from the cricketer to the image. People stopped considering his playing ability, and he became carried away with his image. I would think back to the lad I knew as a schoolboy and try to work out what happened to him.

"His self-analysis became atrocious. He started to blame everyone else. He, and his advisors, developed a siege mentality."

John Graham, who also knew Martin well in his formative years, says he often asks himself that very question. "I'm always defending Martin Crowe these days," says Graham. "He's a complex person, very intense. But at school, he was all boy, a superb role model, always grinning. He loved school and was very ambitious, pleasantly so. He was an outstanding young man. The Martin Crowe the public sees now is not the boy or young man I used to know pretty well. It's interesting looking at what's happened to Grant Fox and Marty. Both were outstanding at school and have become outstanding sportsmen. But one boy has handled it, the other hasn't."

Duncan Johnstone, who spent a year or so in the Grammar First XI with Crowe and these days is one of New Zealand's leading sports writers, is similarly bemused. "I can't figure it out, but it's sad," says Johnstone. "At school when I was there, he was the young guy, but he had the talent, more than everyone in the team. People recognised that. He'd be ribbed because he was young, but everyone respected his ability. I guess it was one of the things he's had to deal with through his career. He was selected for Auckland while at school and for test cricket while still a teenager. So he was a boy playing in a man's game, and it must have tested him, made it hard for him. It's made him single minded and more withdrawn.

"But at school Hogan never got up to mischief. He always had a smile on his face. He was very helpful, especially because he was a junior. He realised he was a third or fourth former and knew his place. Jeff had a touch of the larrikin element, but not Martin. There was always a serious side to Martin, but he's become consumed by that to a degree. He's complex now, but at school he was pretty straightforward, really.

"After I'd been a reporter a few years, I went overseas from 1982 to 1986. When I left he was the young guy, starting to score runs. When I got back, the whole thing had developed.

"I still find it a bit bemusing. Now he's someone whose feats you admire, but he has this image that's built up.

"Because of his talent, he is always going to get more media pressure than anyone. He's a rarity in New Zealand cricket terms. Initially he got the publicity because he was so good, but it's gone beyond that. He doesn't help himself in a lot of ways with some of the things he says and the way he's kept the rumours going by continuing to talk about them here and overseas. He'd be better to say nothing. My advice would be to say nothing, even in England, because it always comes back here and goes round and round again.

"I think it's sad. I feel sorry for the guy. When I talk to him now, I don't feel totally comfortable, perhaps because I'm a journalist. Yet we've known each other for years."

So what happened? Was there a blinding flash of light that changed Crowe irrevocably? Or has it been an evolutionary process?

Most people who know him – his friends, cricket teammates, the media – and many cricket followers who have never even met him have an opinion. He polarises opinion, a bit like Rob Muldoon once did in politics.

Both theories – the blinding flash and the evolution – have some basis of fact. Except there wasn't one flash of light, but several. Not a thousand points of light, as President George Bush was so fond of saying, but enough to alter Crowe's ideas and character markedly from the schoolboy to the adult. The key factors in this transformation, quite apart from his natural development as a professional cricketer, could be short-listed to his family, his decision to employ Darryl Sambell as his manager in the mid-1980s, his turbulent stint with Somerset in 1987 and '88, and his marriage to Simone Curtice in 1991. Outside his family, the three Ss – Sambell, Somerset and Simone – stand out.

Primarily, though, it's been his family. His parents, Dave and Audrey, and older brother Jeff have been very visible on the cricket scene since Martin began making his way in first class cricket. Earlier, Jeff's role was more as a competitor. Being older, he was better than Martin initially, and that drew the best out of Martin. Then they became sporting rivals as adults. As brother to brother they wished each other the best, but there was an edge there.

Keith Quinn recalls interviewing the pair of them before a Central Districts – Auckland Shell Trophy match when they were rival captains. "I got them into the studio for what I thought would be quite a nice story about two brothers," says Quinn, "but the whole thing never flowed. I wouldn't say I got the impression they didn't like each other, but there certainly wasn't a lot of warmth. The body language wasn't there; it was like they'd just had an argument. The rivalry was the big thing, plus the fact that they were treating each other almost exclusively as cricketers;

the brotherly feelings really didn't enter into it at all."

Martin and Jeff have grown closer over the past seven or eight years, as they've stopped competing so vigorously. Probably they're both more secure in their own achievements, too, so the need to score points off a brother does not arise any more.

Since Jeff succeeded John Morrison as Martin's manager a few years ago, the bonds have strengthened further, until today Murray Deaker observes, "Jeff Crowe is the best friend Martin has in the world. Jeff is there through thick and thin, which is a mark of the particular guy Jeff is. He has shown fantastic loyalty, almost blind loyalty, to his brother."

Audrey seems to be the typical utterly supportive sporting mother, doting on her sons' achievements, and with good reason. With Martin having achieved so much, that has meant a lot of doting.

It's Dave who has been the more intriguing influence on Martin.

He and Audrey have done their best to follow their sons around the cricket world, taking holidays to watch New Zealand touring England. So they've been a constant presence, at home and often overseas. But Dave is not the sort of father to sit back quietly and glory in Martin's cricket. He has shown himself to be very prickly whenever the boys have been criticised.

Dave Crowe has also written extensively on cricket. He had a major hand in two books, *The Crowe Report* on the 1986 England tour and, in 1987, *The Crowe Style*, about the lives of Jeff and Martin. In addition, he has contributed to various cricket magazines. Some of his writing is incredibly vitriolic, poisonous even.

In an article in the June 1994 issue of the English *Cricketer* magazine, he described Martin's entry into test cricket: "He had to learn how to play test cricket in the arena for he was mustered far too early, at age 19, when the incumbent, an average ex-county player named Parker was, allegedly, too scared to face Lillee and Thomson."

This, of course, is terribly insulting of John Parker, as well as being incorrect. "I retired from cricket just before I would have been dropped, after the tour of Australia in early 1981," says Parker. "By the time Thomson and Lillee toured here, my test days were long gone.

"As for being too scared, well, I played against the West Indies here in 1980, and in county cricket when every county side seemed to have a West Indies fast bowler. I was Worcestershire's player to combat the quicks. I never played the quicks as well later, when I was an amateur, that's true.

But fear doesn't come into it. I never played for New Zealand with a top five player who was frightened. Bob Willis once wrote that he hit more New Zealand batsmen than from any other country, which I suppose is a tribute to our willingness to stand there and take it. On our pitches, the ball does strange things, but no-one ever shied away from it."

Parker, who is very praising of Martin Crowe as a player and a person, is less enthusiastic about father Dave. "My parents were wonderful," says Parker. "One of the few things I said to them was not to say anything about cricket. They didn't know much about it, so were happy to go along and watch and support and leave it at that. For Dave Crowe to be making out like he's an expert . . . People think Martin has told him these things, so Martin cops it on the rebound. It's a terribly unfortunate situation because Martin is a great guy. I've always enjoyed his company."

Also in the *Cricketer* article, Dave wrote: "He is New Zealand's ace tall poppy. His public profile is staggering. He and Hadlee stand alone above all other New Zealand sportsmen. Their every move is news and if they aren't moving, someone will pretend they are. There is an insensate demand by our gutter press, including some electronic people, to level them...

"Only as I edit Martin's next book do I see all the stages of his career in perspective. In this fascinating account, he tells how he confronts the hacks who accuse him of having Aids, of being homosexual, of owning four homes (he has one) and who demand he divorce his wife . . ."

This might be great reading in England, where people would have little idea of the truth, but, when it bounced back to New Zealand, it had cricket people shaking their heads. For a start, Martin Crowe does not stand alone. He certainly is no taller, poppy-wise, than the likes of John Kirwan, John Walker, Susan Devoy, Sean Fitzpatrick and many others.

And as for Dave Crowe's regurgitation of the rumours . . . well, as Trevor McKewen says: "The Crowes' chief argument is lack of accuracy on the part of the media, facts wrong, stories embellished. Then you read rubbish like that."

Sometimes Dave takes things so far out of context it's difficult to know what he is actually on about. For instance, is his crack at the electronic media a criticism of Murray Deaker for suggesting during a TV3 panel discussion in 1992 that Simone Crowe should not be so prominent in the New Zealand team?

Is this what Dave Crowe is talking about when he accuses the electronic media of suggesting Martin divorce his wife? Deaker: "I was saying she should be excluded from a prominent role in the team. That has been completely and utterly distorted by Dave, but who takes anything Dave says seriously? I've read some of the things he's written in the English media. It's a figment of his imagination.

"My statement was a good one-liner and Simone was apparently furious. Debbie (Martin's sister) rang me and she got stuck in. She climbed all over me. She said she used to have respect for me, but that now I was despicable. My response was to say that I was sorry on a personal level, but my position was to say that Simone should keep her nose out of her husband's business."

There have been other Dave Crowe gaffes. He harked back 12 years to criticise Howarth's captaincy, at a time when Howarth had just taken over as New Zealand team coach and Martin was in the side as the senior player. This was hardly helpful for building good relations between Howarth and Crowe.

Andrew Jones (he and Martin had "an ambivalent attitude, ranging from friendship to distrust") and Ken Rutherford ("taking an age to become temperamentally attuned to test cricket . . . invariably gets out once he has reached his own private comfort zone . . . perhaps he will never mature, for as captain he deigned to criticise his colleagues from his comfortable cocoon") have also copped it. In fact, the Crowes have generally been critical of Rutherford. Don Neely suggests that at least part of the reason was that the family believed Jeff Crowe was dropped from the test team to make way for Rutherford.

The recurring themes in Dave's writing have been Martin's excellence and a distrust of the media which he describes as "fickle", "sheep", "local gutter tabloid press" and so on.

All in all, Dave Crowe has certainly not been reticent about voicing his opinions; whether they had much factual base is another matter. His barbs must have affected Martin, who is close to his father and naturally talks cricket with him.

So throughout Martin's career, there has been the ongoing influence of his parents and brother. The first major outside factor was probably Darryl Sambell, who in some ways replaced John Graham as the adult non-family influence in his life. After they left Auckland Grammar, Crowe and Grant Fox would sometimes return to the school to chat to John Graham. As an All Black captain and a fine loose forward in a great era of

New Zealand rugby, Graham knew a lot about top sport. He also understood boys, and young men, very well. He remains a man who commands respect because he tells it like it is, without fear or favour. In short, he offered budding sports stars like Crowe and Fox a healthy dose of reality.

Graham recalls advising Crowe and Fox to go to university when they left Auckland Grammar. "I spoke to them together and told them that a university degree was an international lifelong qualification. Martin was already talking about being a professional cricketer. My advice was to wait a few years, and to get a degree first. A Bachelor's degree would take just three years, a BCom four years. Pro cricket is a bit like schoolteaching. It's rather incestuous. You just don't get enough outside influence. Your vision can be restricted.

"At university Martin would have mixed with a whole range of minds. It would have broadened his mind and helped him mature. Instead, he went from an all-boys school to an all-male sport. There might be something there for the psychologists. He became focused on one thing very early and never really got into mainstream New Zealand people.

"Devoting oneself to one sport so young is not good. It's not just Martin; it's a problem with large numbers of very able sportspeople these days. A lot of top rugby players don't have outside jobs. But look at people like Martin Snedden, who got a law degree, or Olo Brown, who is an accountant. It's far more healthy to have a life outside your sport."

For some years Martin continued returning to the school occasionally to have a chat with Graham. "Sometimes Mark Greatbatch would come back with him. I'd get him to talk to the First XI or the hall. Marty loved coming back, he enjoyed that. He liked meeting the staff, and me, I believe. When he was having a bad trot we had a talk and he went out the next day and scored a century. After that it became a superstition almost that he would visit school during the Auckland test. Like putting your right boot on before your left for luck.

"When he spoke to the boys he was great. He didn't patronise them by saying Auckland Grammar was the greatest school in the world, but he talked about how he'd made it to where he was, what it had taken. It was always stimulating and the kids felt good. He'd tell them not to waste their days at school. It was quite a personal talk and it would fire up the kids.

"Then one year in the late 1980s he came back and spoke to the assembly. He was a different boy. It was the first sign of him getting into this intense self-analysis of performance and into sports psychology. He lost the kids in the first minute and didn't regain contact with them until he was saying goodbye. I listened and I had no idea what he was on about either. I asked him later what it was all about. He said, 'I'm thinking differently these days and thought I'd try it out on an audience.' I told him it hadn't worked and that it seemed there was some self-doubt creeping in, that he wasn't sure where he was going.

"He hasn't been back to school since. I've seen him on a couple of social occasions when he's been pleasant, but not at ease. He has that haunted look; his eyes are forever darting about the room."

Graham feels Crowe began to change, to become too introspective, in the mid-1980s, and wonders if the fact that he had employed Darryl Sambell as his manager had something to do with it. "Whatever it was, he's changed. When I think about Marty now, it saddens me. The lad either hasn't taken the right advice, or has got beyond taking advice. He was such an outstanding young man; you know them as boys and want to enjoy them for years. What is interesting is the way he and Jeff have swapped roles. At school Jeff was very relaxed, casual and easy-going – not really the Auckland Grammar model at all. He wasn't focused. But he has turned out to be a delightful, uncomplicated, mature person. Martin and Jeff have done a role change."

Deaker agrees. "Since school, Martin and Jeff have swapped characters. At school, Jeff was always on the edge of a scene. You'd see him coming back with Nicky Allen [later an All Black], and you just knew they'd been out for a smoke. I bailed them out and covered for them on heaps of occasions. Now Jeff has become popular and respected. And Martin, who was the good kid, is so divisive and gets so much criticism.

"Some people around him have given him advice to protect their own interests. It's a shame because the people who copped the blame were people who had tremendous admiration for him. Last year I went to dinner with Don Cameron and Audrey and Dave Crowe. I hadn't even had a chance to get the spoon up to my mouth when Audrey turned to me and said, 'Why do you hate my youngest son?' I told her I didn't. After the *Metro* article was published, Martin rang me to thank me for what I'd said. I told him, 'Don't thank me. I have been consistent all the way through. I don't believe you really know who your supporters are.'

"In my view it all started to go wrong when he employed as his agent Darryl Sambell, who introduced him to a lifestyle of gloss and glitter that was artificial."

Sambell these days lives on Queensland's Gold Coast and is the managing director of a company which designs and manufactures products for nursing homes and hospitals. In his time he has worked with Elton John, Rod Stewart, David Bowie and many other well-known musicians, as well as a variety of sports stars. Now though, he says, he has moved into another life. "I had a long look at myself and I came back to Australia. I was getting old and was sick of going to lunch all day." Even so, he remains an outrageous, larger than life character.

The first time I met him was during a Nutri Metics women's tennis tournament at Stanley Street. He was wearing white linen trousers, a billowing red shirt and enough gold chains to fund the national economy of a fair-sized country. He talked loud and seemed to delight in his camp image.

However, he was also a very astute person with a shrewd business mind. He was born in Gawler, South Australia, but had developed excellent business contacts in New Zealand, particularly in the music world. Then, during the 1980s, he got into sports management. Eventually he garnered a clutch of sports stars as clients, including Martin and Jeff Crowe, Possum Bourne, Peter Belliss, Simon Wi Rutene, Julie Richardson and Barry Griffiths. "It didn't matter what the sport was, the principles remained the same," he told me when I caught up with him one morning at Surfers Paradise. "If I became the manager of a sportsperson, I'd spend some time getting to understand their sport, whether it was skiing, table tennis or bowls. But the way you get publicity and negotiate deals doesn't alter from sport to sport."

Sambell's introduction to the cricket world came when he got chatting to John Wright about a rock-music fund-raiser. Wright recalls: "I met Darryl Sambell when I worked for the IHC at Pukekohe. We'd had the idea of putting on a rock concert and Sambell was the guy who did the big rock concerts in Auckland then, so I introduced myself and asked him for some advice. He was a funny guy, a character. I met him again at a race meeting soon afterwards."

Then, says Sambell, Wright suggested Sambell address the New Zealand team, which was then seeking an agent.

"It had reached the stage," says Wright, "where we needed a good, professional agent to look after our commercial interests. We'd done an advertisement for Morrison Mowers and got about $500 each. We were filling Eden Park by then, yet still regarded it as a triumph when Adidas gave us a couple of pairs of shoes free. Bob Vance [New Zealand Cricket Council chairman] agreed we could have someone, so one day at the Waipuna Lodge in Auckland we listened to submissions from Lindsay Singleton, TVNZ and Darryl. Singleton was managing Geoff Howarth and Lance Cairns and the vote went to him."

Sambell feels the New Zealand team were a bit frightened by his flamboyance. "They had Glenn Turner and some of the old brigade then. They were a conservative group. They've changed now, but have gone too far with the Young Guns and that face paint and so on.

"I was a bit nervous when I spoke to the team. Then before you know it, Martin rang me. It was the same day. He asked me if I'd manage himself and Jeff, whether the team took me or not." It was the start of an interesting few years, and a pivotal time for a young and easily-influenced Martin Crowe. While in his early 20s he had an agent with the contacts and the ability to earn him a very high profile. Crowe featured in countless magazine and newspaper articles and quickly became a national celebrity. At the comparative stage of his career, Richard Hadlee was still concentrating on learning how to bowl line and length, and not even contemplating life as a cricket pro. Hadlee, though he was New Zealand's No 1 bowler by his early 20s, was not nearly as commercially aware.

"Once I agreed to be the boys' manager, I set about learning about cricket," says Sambell. "I saw the potential in both boys. I also quickly learnt about the Crowe family and found that to be disastrous. They had a daughter no one seemed to even know about, called Debbie. I didn't get on well with Audrey, the mother, who was, to put it mildly, 100 million per cent behind Martin.

"Dave, the father, was rather harmless. He is a connoisseur of wines and knows about cricket. He seemed happy and cheerful, a slogger and a worker. I had a soft spot for Jeff, who seemed to play second fiddle to Martin from the family's point of view."

Sambell says he found it easier in some ways marketing Jeff than Martin, even though Martin was undoubtedly the better player. "I made more money for Jeffrey out of endorsements. He's a man's man, very approachable. Any managing director you took him to meet really liked Jeffrey. Martin was more reserved. He looked sly and wry. He had the runs on the board and gave the impression he didn't have to open his mouth. He seemed to think his runs were enough."

Sambell certainly involved himself in the brothers' cricket. Like most people on the PR scene, he was well–known for his habit of exaggerating his place in the scheme of things, but he did meet Somerset officials and lobby for the dismissal of Viv Richards and Joel Garner and their replacement by Crowe. "I pointed out that international cricketers rarely help county cricket teams. They generally don't give a damn. They aren't team people. They don't attend all the practice sessions. They don't get together after a game. Instead they drive off in their sponsored BMW. I suggested the club had to make drastic changes and said I was managing a person who could coach, work with the committee to make money, be a team player. It worked. They took Martin on board, and for that first year – 1987 – he did brilliantly. The next year, unfortunately, he seemed to become a lot of the things I had warned the Somerset officials about."

Besides his work with Somerset, Sambell says he was influential in Crowe opting to play for Central Districts. "This was a good move. You have to understand Martin to make him perform. He has an ego problem, but that comes with a lot of major stars. He needed to rule the roost wherever he was. He needed an audience and people to be there 100 per cent behind him. Otherwise he could get rather lethargic in his attitude. Moving to Central Districts was the challenge. I negotiated with the New Zealand Cricket Council for Martin to be able to play for Central Districts while still residing in Auckland."

As well as the cricket activities, Sambell says he did a lot for Martin commercially. "I believe I was a good influence. I took him from the beginning through the ranks. We set a lot of new rules for New Zealand cricket. We worked in with Mitre to market a new brand of cricket shoe, which appealed greatly to Allan Border and some of the other Aussies. I was able to get good commercial deals for Jeffrey and Martin.

"It wasn't hard to get them on magazine covers. There was lots of that. But in the first year or so, Martin got annoyed that I didn't do more deals for him. He didn't quite realise that I was resisting some petty offers, pathetic endorsement deals which would have set a precedent for future years. I pulled off some good commercials for Jeff, including a big one with Lucas, but with Martin I was waiting for the big one. I wasn't going to splatter his face around for five or six thousand dollars a time.

"I wanted to negotiate only with major companies. Martin was earning a lot of money, though. The Duncan Fearnley contract he had was the second highest in the world, behind Ian Botham, and even better than Border's."

Sambell also came up with the idea of Crowe Jewellery. He's still especially proud of one item. "It's a necklace with a small pendant on it that is a bat, ball and stumps. Naturally, part of the deal was that we got three complimentary necklaces. The boys, being cricket purists, wanted a red ball, a ruby. I took a white ball, a diamond. We sold those necklaces in solid gold and solid silver and did very well. In fact, the boys were very busy endorsing a lot of products. Mind you, it would have helped if Audrey had taken a very long holiday."

Martin found himself defending his business relationship with Sambell, a person who certainly did not fit naturally into the world of top sport. "Darryl's great. He's got all the contacts," Crowe explained one day to an inquiring John Graham.

So why did the partnership end?

Sambell's explanation: "I think at the end of the day Martin couldn't wait to make big bucks. John Morrison ran Brierley's New Zealand agency for Duncan Fearnley. He and Ron decided they would manage Martin and that suited me fine because I was just about over managing in general by then. I think it was the wrong move, going to Morrison. Clearly Martin needed direction and the stuff I saw made him look a bit of a dill."

Sambell says Martin had strengths and weaknesses as a client. "He was a good speaker at functions. Jeff was nervous. Yet Jeff is the one who gets on with people better. Neither Martin nor Jeff were whizz kids. In some things Martin surprises you, but I'd have to say he's not particularly bright. Jeff never asked till he had thought about it long and hard. Martin didn't think about things as much, perhaps because he regarded himself as the star."

It's become the fashion for anyone talking about Martin Crowe to blame Sambell for the Martin-is-homosexual rumour that did the rounds for a while and was kept alive by the Crowes for several more years. The theory is that Sambell was gay, and that Crowe got tarred with the same brush.

"I've watched everything Martin's been doing, and know what he's been saying," says Sambell. "Because I'm single, I don't need to tell everyone about my past, or what the deal is. I've always had lady friends. No one's ever seen me or caught me, or has had the guts to ask me to my face. If you're asking, I suppose I'm bisexual. I have my own set of friends."

Sambell, too, is sure the Crowe-is-gay stories began during their association, and feels he can pinpoint the reason.

"The first thing I'd say is that the stories were rubbish. Martin had many, many girlfriends. Then on one tour to Sri Lanka, or somewhere over that way, he had problems with two bad wisdom teeth. He'd chew on panadol or aspirins to kill the pain and by the time he had to get up he'd be overdosing on painkillers. I heard all this and thought it was time to put a stop to it.

"So the morning he arrived back in the country I had him booked into his local dentist at Titirangi. The parents popped in for a while. I waited in the car outside. Eventually the dentist came out and asked me to give him a hand with Martin because he was very groggy through painkillers.

"So I walked in and there's giggling Martin off his face with the injection. I helped the dentist take him to my car. At the time Martin and Jeffrey owned a house I'd negotiated for them in Remuera, and the upstairs had been done out for Martin. I drove him there. All the way he was giggling and saying stupid, dopey things.

"It was a hell of a job for me to get him from the car, because he's a big guy. I finally got him to the front door, then the stairs and pushed him up. When I got him to the bed, he flopped down. I was taking off his shoes when I heard a scream. Right behind me, her face just showing at the top of the stairs, was his girlfriend. She went crazy. She ran down the stairs screaming, and off up the road.

"Later in the day I rang her and told her Martin shouldn't be left alone, that he had to take painkillers and wouldn't know how many etcetera. A couple of days later, Martin dumped that girlfriend, who was part of the Auckland model set.

"Within a week the gay rumours had started. She'd gone and told people that he and I had been together. That was how all that stuff started. Mind you, if I was still managing Martin I'd have knocked it on the head from square one. I used to talk to the gossip journalists and feed them information, and also tell them when they'd got it wrong.

"I don't think it's right to say that just because I managed Martin, he got tagged a homosexual. Peter Belliss stayed at my house many times. Simon Wi Rutene and Possum Bourne were very good-looking guys, but there were no stories about them. No – it all started from that day in Auckland."

Sambell boasts, with typical extravagance, that he was the first cricket manager in New Zealand. Certainly he was among the first and, in Martin Crowe, he had the country's most marketable young player. But was it too much too soon? "I was probably a couple of years ahead of my time," Crowe said in early 1995. "It was just the volume, perhaps that was a problem."

Richard Hadlee, the other superstar of New Zealand cricket at the time – but 11 years older – says: "It can come too early. You have to earn it through consistency of perfomance. And you need a good manager. There's plenty available these days for the best performers – car, media exposure, clothing and equipment endorsements. There are public speaking opportunities, though if you speak a lot and you are playing, you have to be performing. It's hard to give a motivational-type speech if you're going through a rough patch yourself."

Peter Roebuck, Crowe's Somerset county captain and a very fine thinker about sport, stresses there is a fine line between making money and having marketing take over a sportsman's life. "A cricketer has to stay close to his game," says the Englishman. "That's what made him famous. And when he's an old man, it's his cricket deeds that will sustain him."

Besides the mountain of publicity he was getting, partly as a result of Sambell's work, Crowe had to put up with the unsavoury rumours, perhaps passed on gleefully by some people envious of the money he was making at so tender an age.

Certainly during his Sambell period, Crowe did some things which made regular cricket followers, people who knew him well, shake their heads in horror.

As an example there was the party the Crowes threw in 1984 at the Crowes Nest, the house Martin and Jeff owned on the slopes of Mount Hobson in Remuera. The party was for the New Zealand and visiting England cricket teams, and obviously made an impression because several members of the New Zealand side mentioned it to me during the course of my research for this book. Various cricketers recalled the good-looking women who attended the party, most with little or no interest in cricket. And there was Sambell, just being himself, the epitome of what the regular conservative cricketer is not.

Murray Deaker was at that party. "Jeff had scored a hundred against England," says Deaker. "He rang me and asked me to come to the party, saying it would be an interesting night. Well, when I got there and took it all in, it was like spew material. There was drinking, the women, and Dazza, as Sambell was called. I looked at Martin and Jeff and thought, 'These guys don't need this.' I came home really shattered. My wife said it was time I faced reality and that cricketers were like anyone else. But it was so

Lee Germon – "Martin went out of his way to communicate."

Richard Hadlee – "When your private life is being questioned, it must affect you."

Simone Crowe – feisty and ever-ready to wade into battle on behalf of Martin.

John Bracewell – "Martin cultivates that class thing with his talk about wine and fine restaurants. That irritates the hell out of everyone outside Auckland."

John Wright tries desperately to rally the troops during Inzamam's onslaught in the 1992 World Cup semi-final.

Choking back the tears during the lap of honour after the semi-final defeat by Pakistan at Eden Park in the 1992 World Cup.

Martin Crowe at his regal best.

Radio and TV man Peter Williams –
"He is certainly more sensitive as an
adult than as an adolescent."

Experienced Radio New Zealand
commentator Bryan Waddle (pictured with
Jeremy Coney, left, and John Parker) – "I've
never had the difficulties with Martin
others might have."

Grant Nesbitt (left) and Keith Quinn, two
veteran TV commentators, have both had
an amicable working relationship with
Crowe.

New Zealand v Australia Davis Cup tie, March 1990. Crowe and his lawyer, David Howman, watch proceedings. Or is Crowe in Brisbane to discuss a possible Sheffield Shield career? Oh, the intrigue!

John Morrison – "Martin says, 'I'm a great bat; why don't you love me?'"

Brett Steven – "It never worried me, but I felt sorry for Martin because rumours like that obviously upset him."

207

Bert Sutcliffe (left), John Reid, Merv Wallace and Walter Hadlee – four greats of New Zealand cricket who rate Crowe among the best ever.

Mark Burgess – "His record is fantastic."

Hanse Cronje – "It's very hard to plan against him."

artificial, set up by Sambell. I couldn't sleep when I came home that night, and it takes a lot to stop me sleeping."

Then came Martin's second stint at Somerset. As related in the chapter about his county career, he'd had a good season with the club in 1984. A couple of years later, Somerset took the brave, and highly controversial, step of sacking Viv Richards and Joel Garner and replacing them with 25-year-old Martin Crowe. Ian Botham, a good friend of the two West Indian stars, was so outraged he stormed off in protest.

Into this melting pot of boiling emotions stepped Crowe. He acquitted himself magnificently, steering clear of as much of the political ramifications as possible and playing sublimely good cricket.

But the vitriol, the wounded pride, the poison, remained on the other side. Supporters of Richards, Garner and Botham would not be mollified, no matter how many runs Crowe scored or how stylishly he batted. The club was split. Insults were hurled, stories were made up. Naturally a major, though innocent, target was the golden-haired New Zealand youngster. Roebuck, the county captain, was one of the other big victims of the slur campaign. "No one knew the pressure Martin and I were under," he recalls. "There were death threats and so on. People were very passionate. People think in names. Many members sensed the reasons we'd done what we did, but it was more puzzling to outsiders."

Don Neely watched these developments and detected a notable increase in the amount of anti-Crowe stories, or Crowe rumours, flitting about the country. "Perhaps they were there before," he says. "But they increased many times over during that Somerset period. There was some nasty stuff and it made its way back to New Zealand."

Roebuck: "It wouldn't surprise me if Don is right. Some of those people would stop at nothing. They made things very unpleasant for Martin and the whole thing rumbled on. There were gay rumours. The Somerset business was so nasty it is possible things could have started there. I always thought the interest Martin showed in leading the young players reflected very well on him."

Roebuck goes further and suggests some of Crowe's health problems, especially the salmonella he apparently contracted in Sri Lanka in 1984, were exacerbated by the Somerset furore. "If he felt low, all the rumours and the talk wouldn't have helped. Then Martin didn't endear himself to people by over-reacting. When I'm in New Zealand I still tell Martin to keep his head down and play his cricket, let these sort of things pass by outside the off stump. He seems to be fighting people all the time."

John Morrison and Crowe formally became business partners in 1989, forming Morrison, Crowe and Ray. Pauline Ray, the third partner, was a personnel specialist. The company's prospectus spoke of offering "a consultancy service focusing on how companies can get the best out of their prime resource, people". At the time Crowe was already under contract to Morrison through his use of Duncan Fearnley bats (for which Morrison held the Australasian franchise), so the business expansion had a certain logic.

Crowe initially seemed enthusiastic about the new company. He told Steven O'Meagher of *Sunday* magazine: "In essence, we're problem solvers. We get alongside companies, learn what their needs are or what particular problems they're having. We find out where we can help, then we try to correct the fault." Among the company's clients, Crowe mentioned the New Zealand Apple and Pear Board, Whitcoulls, the Rural Bank and the National Bank.

He said the business served two purposes – giving him a break from the cricket environment and leaving him with a ready-made career to step into when he retired. "When Greg Chappell, who is my role model, turned 27, he said he wanted an alternative career to cricket. He got involved in business and is now very successful. With John, things jelled just before I hit 27. Ours is an almost ideal relationship."

Despite the fine words, Crowe's involvement in the company was to be short-lived and negligible. Morrison explains: "The company of Morrison, Crowe and Ray was a front to develop Martin's other skills. Its formation coincided with him coming to Wellington. Pauline had a background in human resources and she and I had been running the company happily. I wanted Martin to be involved because I felt it was an opportunity to give him some credibility. I was marketing Martin at the time and wanted to portray him as more than just a cricketer.

"Hopefully his name would benefit our company, and he would have the opportunity to develop other skills. He had expressed an interest in this area. The reality was totally different. Martin never took any part in the company. It turned out that while the idea might have sounded fine to Martin, he never had any desire to get involved, and therefore Pauline and I had no desire for him to be there. The split was entirely amicably agreed because it was so obvious."

Morrison continued to manage Crowe and says that initially he had huge success. "In 1987 Martin was a very, very marketable product. He was buoyant, young, good-looking and a wonderful cricketer. I tried to line him up with top of the range companies. So he became involved with Brierley, the National Bank, DB, Ansett, Whitcoulls, Canterbury. I got his portfolio up to $150,000-plus a year, outside cricket. There was a very solid base there, and he was making good business connections with people like Ian Wells, John Anderson, Ron Brierley. It was a long-term thing and relationships with those sort of people should have secured his future. I'd shied away from the waterbed and roller-door type ads, not that there is anything wrong with those, but I was going for quality.

"The trouble was that the scene changed very quickly in 1990. He became New Zealand captain, and he got engaged to Simone. I don't think either development helped him in terms of marketing. I could see the beginning of the end when he was named captain and did the big tour spreading the gospel about the new era. Then Simone became a strong influence. Not long after, Martin and I parted company. Our philosophies were going in different directions. He'd changed. I don't think he quite realised what was happening."

Morrison says that nowadays Crowe would be a much harder person to market extensively. "He'd still have the cricket-related contracts with bat and shoe companies. But it would be very difficult to get major companies interested in him. There's a very big negative feeling surrounding Martin now, and companies avoid that like the plague. When they decide to back a person, they want only positives. You don't get that with Martin any more."

By the early 1990s, Crowe was getting far more negative publicity than other well-known New Zealand sports stars like Susan Devoy, John Kirwan, Sandra Edge, Ian Ferguson, Paul McDonald, Buck Shelford, Grant Fox, Erin Baker and John Walker.

There might be a bit of booing of Fox or Kirwan in some areas because they came from Auckland. Perhaps Devoy and Baker made themselves unpopular from time to time with their outspoken comments. But overall, there was general praise of most of them and a few, most notably Shelford, were legends about to develop into icon status.

Crowe, though, had changed. Sambell says: "He'd go underground and not know how to come out."

John Graham, while acknowledging the pressure a modern sports star is under, says it was different with Crowe. "Plenty of high profile people handle these issues confidently and without major problems. But with Martin the problems just got worse and worse."

Crowe's closer friends in the New Zealand team could see the difference. Ian Smith, the chirpy wicketkeeper who roomed with him through most of the 1980s, says that over the past few years there's been just as much written about Crowe as previously, but that less of it is about his cricket. "I'm pretty sure he is as resentful of that as anyone," says Smith.

Lance Cairns says Crowe has changed because of his image. "He thinks people are all against him, but a lot of it is his imagination. It's not fact. People do like winners, even if they are different. A lot of the time he assumes what people think and often he's miles off."

No one can say how Martin feels, except Martin himself, and he seems to chop and change. But there's general agreement, supported by the Crowes, that Martin is too wound up, that he complicates things, and can be obsessive. His intensity has helped make him the great batsman he is, but has also probably prevented him from enjoying other aspects of his life as he might have.

Very few of us can know what it's like to be a superstar cricketer in New Zealand in the television age. We've really only had one other: Richard Hadlee. And in the mid-1980s Hadlee got extremely depressed, when he felt the pressure of public expectation was becoming too much. I asked Hadlee to try to explain some of the problems Crowe has faced:

"The expectation to perform is greater, the better you do. The demands on your time are greater – interviews with the media, TV, radio. There's more likelihood of promotional activity, individually and as part of the team. So therefore you become more recognised in the streets.

"Then your private life tends to suffer. You are exposed far more to the public, so going out for a beer, or a quiet meal, is not as easy. People recognise you and want your autograph. You sit there and you know people are talking about you, so you become very self-conscious of the fact that you are exposed.

"There are times when you don't want to be on show. So you stay in your room, you become more aloof. Then you get criticised for being aloof. It's a Catch-22 situation.

"The publicity goes with the job. You don't go looking for it. You are expected to be available. You might say, 'It's my life; why should others know about it?' But as long as there is a reasonable balance, it's all right.

The thing is that some people will not accept 'No'.

"For a while there I said 'Yes' to everyone. I got physically sick. I hit a real low, got depressed, because I was flitting about the country trying to satisfy the needs of others. You become frustrated and irritable and are seen as arrogant because you have said, 'No'. That causes extra stress. At the end of the day, it's no one else's business."

Hadlee says he identifies very much with Crowe. "You're in a can't win situation. It goes with the territory. We had a chap like Wrighty. He had a clean cut image, was available, was known as a good old Kiwi bloke. He was liked. Martin and I get elevated above that, and become open to more criticism.

"For instance, I was criticised for setting goals. I always maintained if I was achieving those goals, it had to be great for the team. I'd be reminded by the media about targets, records approaching. That put more pressure on to perform, but at the same time it puts you more in the limelight. The media get a story either way: if you achieve or you don't. Then they want to know your next goal, so that's a third story!

"If you aren't performing the knives will come out. If you are, people will want more. There's always the jealousy that comes into it. There are knockers around. I call them would-bes-if-they-could-bes.

"I felt I was the target. I had no objection to people talking about me, criticising my ability if I didn't perform, if I was struggling to keep bowling well, or played a bad shot . . . no problem with that. I was disappointed when my private life was affected.

"Mind you, my situation is a little different from Martin's. Karen [Hadlee's wife] was very seldom seen publicly. She never sought out publicity at all. Simone is much more likely to do an interview or get photographed."

There must doubtless be times, says Hadlee, when Crowe wonders why he bothers. "You ask yourself if it's worth it. You think that having a quiet bach somewhere or going out in a fishing boat would be nice. For me, Hanmer Springs offers that sort of tranquility. There are no hassles. I can pop down to the pub, walk around the streets. That's my peace. Millbrook obviously fills the same role for Martin."

Hadlee feels Crowe's personality has changed over the years.

"It's understandable. All those rumours. He's supposed to have had marriage break-ups, Aids, homosexuality . . . that's a lot to cope with. You'd have to be talking murder, rape or embezzlement to be much worse. He's in the big league of rumours! That's tough to handle. When your private life is being questioned, it must affect you."

When he became captain of an under-strength New Zealand side in 1990, Crowe desperately needed good advice from people close to him, people he trusted. He handled the task of leading a young, inexperienced team superbly. Despite a series of widely expected beatings, Crowe batted commandingly and did all he could to hold the team together.

Then, in April 1991, he married Aucklander Simone Curtice, whom he'd known for five years. It was her 27th birthday and, appropriately enough for a Baradene girl, the ceremony took place at the Baradene Chapel. Mark Greatbatch was the best man and other well-known sports people in attendance included Ian Smith and Grant Fox. Simone was described variously as "a former international model" and "an interior designer".

In fact, she'd done quite a lot of photographic modelling work on leaving college, having been "discovered" by fashion photographer Des Williams. "It was about 1982 or '83," he recalls. "Simone was brought along to me to see if I thought she could be a successful model. She had that American look, blonde with classic features, and there was certainly some work about for her.

"She was never that keen on modelling. She'd only do the job if it suited her. Otherwise she was pretty forthright and would just say she wasn't interested. I'd say that overall she was not hugely successful, but moderately successful; there was some good work in there. She did some big knitwear fashion catalogues – she was good with knitwear – and one or two big jobs for companies like Zambesi. When she was good, she was very, very good, but she didn't suffer fools and often she'd simply be not interested in doing a particular job."

Angela Taylor, one of big names in the Auckland modelling scene and these days the managing director of Visage Models, remembers Simone as "a very successful model who got bored with the work".

"She was very beautiful and much sought after. I was modelling myself at the time," says Taylor, "and know that she got a lot of work, mostly photographic – she didn't like the catwalk. But she was always keen to get on and do her own thing, something more challenging, so she left modelling and went into interior design. Her heart was not really in modelling.

"But she was very respected, and turned out good quality work. In those days you had to do your own make-up and hair. She doesn't rave about her modelling, but she was good."

Simone dabbled in other things in Auckland – she tried her hand at selling advertising for the Boating World magazine for a few weeks – but it was and is the various strands of fashion which held most appeal for her. She worked at Mainly Chairs in Ponsonby for about a year, selling furniture and acting as an interior design consultant.

People who knew her at school and while she was living in Auckland portray her as a popular but strong-willed person. She has certainly retained that feisty spark and is ever-ready to wade into battle on behalf of Martin. For instance, during the 1993/94 summer, when Martin was out with his knee injury, she couldn't resist having a crack at the media – for doing nothing wrong! She told Martine Rule of *Woman's Day*: "I'm amazed that all the media comments have been totally on the level of cricket. We are so used to lies being printed about us and taken out of proportion."

Don't be surprised that she is quoted so often in *Woman's Day*. For a couple of years now Martin and Simone have had an exclusive contract with *Woman's Day*, which cuts out the other women's magazines. I was told the contract is worth $20,000 – either per year or per four stories – which would be about in line with what the various television celebrities receive.

On another occasion – in *Woman's Day* – Simone enlightened readers with her version of the tall poppy syndrome: "The most difficult thing is that Martin is very good at what he does and he puts everything into cricket for his country – and people constantly pull him down for that. I don't know if it is jealousy or their own inadequacies."

Simone has become a mini-celebrity in the women's magazine field. As a model, she never quite cracked it enough to enter the general public consciousness and so become standard magazine fare, but as the good-looking wife of a sporting celebrity, she is good copy, especially as she can usually be relied upon to speak passionately about a subject, be it the injustices being served on her husband, her love of Italy (her mother is Italian and Simone can speak some Italian herself) or her "dream hideaway" at Arrowtown. She told *Woman's Day* when their villa there was being built in 1993: "It is stunning, so peaceful, and we feel as though we are out there on our own. Our villa is being built amongst the golf course, away from the main hotel. I'm looking forward to going horse riding and skiing. It's the perfect place for me, where I can dabble with my paints, interior design and textiles." These interests are a natural progression from her work when she and Martin lived in Wellington, where she was employed in a gallery specialising in contemporary New Zealand art.

This, then, is the woman Crowe decided in 1990 to marry. He explained to me not long afterwards that actually making the decision to get married was the biggest part. "That was huge because I'd always put cricket first. I needed to have a bit more balance and decided in Pakistan [at the end of 1990] that cricket can't be the be-all and end-all. It was a brilliant decision. I have support and the ability to share in everything I do. I don't swamp myself with cricket all the time now. Simone likes watching, but the cricket lifestyle isn't that pleasurable." He spoke enthusiastically about the art gallery Simone was running in Wellington and how it was a new area of interest for him. "That and interior design. We're doing up our house. Really, it's nice just to do things not at all related to cricket sometimes."

They were words which those who'd known the young Martin Crowe never thought they would hear. But they were the signs, surely, of increasing maturity. Unfortunately, the marriage ran into a rocky patch very early on. For the next couple of years the New Zealand cricket world was abuzz with rumours about the state of the Crowes' marriage. In a familiar scenario, the family didn't help themselves.

In 1993 a front page article in the *Sunday Star* quoted Martin's mother, Audrey, confirming that Martin and Simone were "taking a breather" to try to work out their lives. They had been married two years. Mrs Crowe said that "all the recent nonsense about their relationship isn't helping them sort out their problems". She complained about the media interest, saying that when Jeff and Kathryn separated there was no media interest: "So why now?" There were the magazine articles, including a *Woman's Weekly* cover of Martin and Simone denying marriage problems. The stories, painting vastly different pictures, from various members of the Crowe family, only added to public speculation.

Further, Simone kept a very high profile. She was not backward in coming forward as far as the New Zealand team was concerned. She travelled with the team, sat with the team during matches, and appeared to enjoy being a media celebrity, even if it was only reflected glory. She often gave radio, television, magazine and newspaper interviews.

Of course, Simone spoke little about cricket because she knew little of the intricacies of the sport, so stories about her focused on the private lives of her and Martin: their homes, their travel plans, their hobbies and so on.

So still the media focused as much on Crowe the person as Crowe the cricketer. Think for a moment: how many stories have you heard or read about John Wright's wife, Danny Morrison's house or Adam Parore's hobbies? Very little. Yet the Crowes are like a cottage industry, feeding ever more information about themselves to an avaricious media. This is fine, but it becomes laughable when every now and then Martin unburdens himself at a press conference or to an overseas journalist and says he detests the way the media follows him, how he has no privacy. As Bruce Edgar, one of the most private modern sportsmen imaginable, says: "Martin has made his private life the media's business by drawing them in. In those circumstances, it is legitimate for the media to discuss and judge Martin as a person as well as a cricketer."

Crowe says this is no longer the case. He told interviewer Brian Edwards on TV3's *Sunday* programme in April, 1995: "I have to admit that for a long time in my career, until three years ago, I was the one who was telling the public about my style, with the amount of interviews I was doing and the amount of front covers I was featuring on. I was saying, 'This is what I'm like, what I wear; this is me.' You are going to get a little bit of criticism from that in terms of the volume of the profile that's coming in front of a lot of New Zealanders. In the last three years I've backed off from that. I realised that enough was enough and let the bat do the talking."

This might be the picture Crowe would like to paint, but the scenario falls down in two areas: his bat has done considerably less talking than previously over the past three years because he's been injured so often, and he has continued giving interviews, not only to cricket writers, but to the likes of Edwards and Ian Fraser on TV, in the women's magazines, to *Metro*, and to various overseas publications. The behaviour of someone shunning the spotlight?

Peter Roebuck: "He has become at war with his own publicity. He thinks that what is said in some places is what the public thinks. There are people out there in every country who appreciate the deeds of the players and aren't into politics. But Martin shouldn't portray himself as a saint; that's always dangerous."

Jeff, Simone and parents Dave and Audrey form Martin's closest advisers. When they look at Martin now, they must wonder about the quality of some of their advice.

Occasionally a piece of commonsense shines through. For instance, in February 1995 Martin was invited to be a guest on Ian Fraser's television programme. He had appeared on a similar show the season before and hardly covered himself in glory, bringing up himself the matter of all the rumours – "I did that because they were going to be brought up anyway," he told me – and casting doubts over the quality of Geoff Howarth as New Zealand team coach on the eve of the team's departure for their England tour.

Some of Martin's comments did not go down well with cricket officialdom. Yet when a request came for another appearance on *Fraser*, he agreed. What was the point? What could he talk about? Rutherford? His injuries? The rumours again, old and new? The dope-smoking scandal in South Africa? The sort of job New Zealand Cricket officials were doing? All great material for Fraser, but not the sort of areas Crowe should be exploring publicly. Eventually, at the 11th hour, Crowe pulled out on the sound advice of Jeff. Fraser talked Ken Rutherford into appearing as a replacement and there followed an uncomfortable 10-minute interview.

All too often though, Martin Crowe has lacked that sort of commonsense advice.

Chapter Fourteen

MARTIN AND THE MEDIA

JOHN COFFEY:

*"In hindsight it was rather a shame he became captain. Some of
the people looking at what went on during the centenary season are
aware the problem stems back further than that."*

Willie Watson's most enjoyable benefit year booklet, *Bouncers, Bottle
Tops and Bombs*, contains a page entitled "The Warren and Martin Show".
It is a tribute to, and an appreciation of, Warren Lees and Martin Crowe.
Unlike the rest of the booklet, the story, written by Watson himself, is
fairly serious in tone.

There, slipped in halfway down the second column, is a quote from
Martin: "In New Zealand, everyone knows you. Everyone knows what the
media says about you. I took a lot of stick. There was too much about what
I was doing and not what the team was doing…"

Watson picks up the thread, writing: "Martin, in the end, was forced
to confront certain journalists to stop the crap."

No doubt, Watson has written what he believes to be the truth, and
full marks to him for sticking by a player he clearly admires. But the trouble
is, this "confronting journalists to stop the crap" business is a myth, which
grows in the retelling. And Crowe has retold the story many, many times.

The episode he is referring to occurred at the Basin Reserve during
the test against Australia in 1993. Crowe, going through one of his low

patches, became the aggressor at the press conference on the Saturday evening, confronting Trevor McKewen, then sports editor of *Sunday News*, and Doug Golightly, sports editor of *Truth*.

As recounted in Chapter 11, he challenged both journalists about stories run in their papers the previous week.

Perhaps understandably, because of his emotional state, he got his facts wrong. He accused McKewen of implying in print he was a homosexual, which McKewen has never done. Then he took on Golightly, taking exception to criticism of the team morale.

As far as the two journalists were concerned, the attacks made no difference editorially, though Crowe lost a lot of respect in their eyes. McKewen carried on reporting cricket just as he had done. He continued to praise Crowe's cricket and report his injuries, always with impeccable accuracy. Golightly continued to champion Ken Rutherford as the better choice as New Zealand captain, a line he has not deviated from since.

The truth, unpalatable as it might be for the Crowe family, is that there was very little "crap" written about the Crowes, and most times various unsavoury rumours were publicised, either in print or via the elecronic media, it was one of several members of the Crowe family doing the publicising.

I asked Martin Crowe why on earth he had a problem with McKewen, who in my experience is about the fairest and most honest sports journalist you could hope to find. "He'd written the week before that I was suffering from a mystery virus. That was a smart bit of innuendo," said Crowe.

McKewen, for his part, was dumbfounded by Crowe's outburst at the Basin Reserve. "I rang Jeff Crowe to ask him what the problem was. I told Jeff I hadn't even realised Martin and I had a problem. Jeff said he didn't know that either, but would find out. He came back to me and said Martin felt I was suggesting in my match reports that he was homosexual. That staggered me. Unless he was taking a very strange connotation from an expression like 'getting on top of the bowling', I had no idea what he was on about. I invited Martin to come into our offices and said he could have all the files and papers available to him, and if he found one example of such a suggestion, I would apologise in print. Despite repeated invitations, he never took me up on that offer."

McKewen says that Crowe's claim of smart-alec innuendo is absurd. "We ran a photo of Crowe batting, with graphic boxes pointing to each of his injuries suffered during his career. One box was titled 'viruses' and read, 'He has been unusually susceptible to picking up viruses, particularly on the subcontinent. He had a five-year battle with a salmonella virus picked up in Sri Lanka in 1984, suffered tonsillitis during the 1987 Australian tour and glandular fever last year.'

"In the body of the copy, there is only one reference to viruses. That reads, 'His woes began in 1984 when he picked up a "mystery virus" on the tour of Sri Lanka, labouring under the debilitating illness for five years until it was finally diagnosed as salmonella.'"

Crowe was clearly wrong about McKewen. But rather than back down when challenged, he spread the myth around the world that he confronted McKewen and shut him up. His father added to the legend, and his wife chipped in as well. As late as 1994 Crowe was telling the same story to various overseas publications.

Things came to a head when Warwick Roger gullibly reprinted Crowe's assertions in *Metro* in 1995 without checking their veracity. When challenged, *Metro* backed down. A full page letter from McKewen was published, along with a note from the editor regretting the error. As a matter of interest, Roger tried to excuse himself by saying McKewen was in South Africa when the article was written. As the story contained description of cricket played in January 1995 and McKewen returned from South Africa the previous November, this excuse was fairly lame.

A few weeks later Auckland radio host Tim Bickerstaff challenged Crowe about the McKewen business. "Martin as good as said he was in the wrong. He backed right down," said Bickerstaff.

Crowe and his family have repeatedly claimed *Sunday News* rang him every week asking him to confirm rumours he had Aids. As McKewen wrote in his letter to *Metro*: "He was rung once, back in 1988, by a gung-ho reporter named Scott Cordes, who went against the advice of myself and the then sports editor Neil Harvey in making the call. No story was run. During the rest of my tenure at *Sunday News*, to my knowledge, none of the paper's other reporters rang Crowe and asked him that question, despite his claims to the contrary. If Crowe is so adamant they did, who are they, what are their names?"

Crowe is very much the modern sportsman in that his career has been recorded in great detail by the media, and he is used to being interviewed and appearing on television. The electronic media is so much a part of life now that we don't think twice about it. But consider this: when Lance Cairns made his test debut, he had never seen film of himself bowling, and had no idea his bowling action was so unusual. Crowe is one of the modern breed. He is used to being around microphones and cameras and has had very extensive dealing with the media.

When asked if he felt he had good relations with the media, Crowe said there was a certain section who were always having a go at him "...Coffey, Power, Bidwell, Romanos – you soon identify them. I'm not seeing the details come through. There are elements who want to have a dig for whatever reason." The four he named make a strange bunch. John Coffey followed the esteemed Dick Brittenden as cricket writer of the Christchurch Press, but has not written on test cricket for a couple of seasons, his place being taken by Geoff Longley. Coffey is regarded as New Zealand's most authoritative rugby league writer, and is a generally amiable personality. Power writes for the *Waikato Times* and various magazines, but is certainly not a high-profile cricket writer. Peter Bidwell, formerly sports editor of *The Dominion*, has been covering test cricket for the paper since the 1970s. He has not exactly gleaned a reputation as a controversial journalist, remorselessly chasing the big story and not caring who he upset. It is surprising that he should be mentioned by Crowe as being overly critical or negative.

I wrote the cricket for the *Evening Post* in the 1970s, and since then have covered cricket as a feature writer for *The Dominion* and the *Listener*, and in writing books. Crowe mentioned that he did not like the tone of the chapter on his family in *Great New Zealand Cricket Families*, a book I wrote in 1992. As the book was a celebration of cricket and contained virtually no critical content, I was dumbfounded to discover what the Crowes' reaction had been – his brother Jeff voiced similar sentiments to me while complaining about my writing a few weeks later.

Coffey says the Crowes' criticism of his writing stems from one article he wrote on February 26, 1993. "I saw recently where Jeff Crowe described it as 'scandalous'," says Coffey. "It's remarkable the things that stick in the mind after so many years. The background was that Martin had done one of those interviews in the English *Cricketer* magazine listing his favourite restaurants, drinks and so on. All his favourites were from overseas, and I had a bit of a go at him. It appeared in *The Press* alongside a cartoon of Martin sitting in the bath eating fish and chips."

The article was headed "Life of luxury charms Crowe". It said: "... One learns that Crowe drives a German car, and prefers Italian food, French champagne, Italian and German suits and jackets, Italian shoes and ties.

His favourite hotel is in Fiji, his favourite restaurant is in Florence. Clearly the New Zealand captain is not vigorously throwing his support behind any 'buy New Zealand-made' campaigns. He does, however, list 'collecting New Zealand contemporary art' as his hobby."

The article was critical of Crowe, listing various contretemps in which he'd been involved in preceding months, including chiding spectators in Zimbabwe for not giving his team due credit, arguing with the Zimbabwe umpires, accusing a Sri Lankan bowler of throwing, refusing to leave the crease when given out in a test in Sri Lanka, refusing to leave the crease during a one-day international against Pakistan when given out, and another run-in with an umpire, Graham Cowan, during a Shell match.

"I took over from Dick Brittenden during the Geoff Howarth era," says Coffey. "I found Howarth good to deal with. I was the new boy on the test cricket round, but, with Howarth there, I quite enjoyed it. I found Jeremy Coney, who followed him, to be a bit of a smart-alec with some, but fine with me. Jeff Crowe was next and he was good value. He was a nice guy and we all felt sorry when he was shown the door. Then came John Wright. That was the highlight of my time with the team. Wrighty was wonderful to deal with.

"But through the years I became more disillusioned with some of the players who became more and more aloof. Martin Crowe was one of them. The more senior and successful he became the more aloof he got. To score 299 in a test and then throw his bat against the dressing room wall, then apparently not be willing to come out for an interview was amazing. I got the impression he came out only because Andrew Jones, who was usually a quiet guy, was out there talking to the media and was all smiles. I think, to most of the media, it was a great relief when Martin Crowe got out of the job.

"He became stranger and stranger through the 1993 series against Australia. He claimed his wife was a victim of a sneak *Sunday News* photo, but in fact she posed for the photo for John McCombe. He didn't relate very well – he was always more involved in Martin Crowe than the team. He seems to be a big boy who hasn't grown up.

"In hindsight it was rather a shame he became captain. Some of the people looking at what went on during the centenary season are aware that the problem stems back further than that. If we'd had our eyes open a few years ago we'd have seen the deterioration in the team."

Coffey says Crowe does not compare well to the New Zealand

captains in the other big sport he covers – rugby league. "The league guys have been very helpful. Maybe they didn't have a privileged upbringing, or perhaps they weren't superstars as kids. But they've certainly been a lot more approachable. Mark Graham was marvellous, but all of them have been really helpful. The only one who could be even a bit sticky was Gary Freeman. He had a slight suspicion of the media, but I could understand that, as the Aussie journalists did tend to go after him. Gary was always very good with me."

Not all journalists feel as Coffey does. David Leggat, the New Zealand Press Association man in London for several years, has toured with Crowe to India in the 1987 World Cup, to Australia (1987/88), to England (1990), to Australia (1993) and to South Africa (1994), plus various internal tours.

"To be absolutely honest," says Leggat, "I've never had any problem with him. He's been fair and accessible, and I haven't encountered that prima donna side others talk about. In England in 1990 I do recall Bob Cunis remarking on one occasion that Martin wasn't contributing much as a selector. Martin had niggles with Bracewell and Thomson on that tour.

"But in South Africa, he was really good. For a start, he was the practical joker, the guy shoving the pie in someone's face. I felt he was right into the tour. When Simone came we didn't see as much of him, which would be natural. But he was very helpful towards the younger guys. I saw him behind the nets helping Harris and players like Thomson and Parore looked to him for advice. In South Africa he was the best I've seen him in terms of being relaxed.

"Of course, there are some guys he seems to get on with better than others. There was one night in Cape Town when Peter Williams was having a drink at the bar. Martin walked in and Peter said something like, 'Gidday, Martin. Can I buy you a drink?' Martin replied something along the lines of: 'Why is it, Peter, that you call me Martin and everyone else calls me Hoges or Crowey?'

"So they discussed that, and finally sorted it out. Then Martin talked about being New Zealand's most recent winning captain, mentioning the victory at Soweto when he'd captained New Zealand. Peter came back by claiming that hardly counted. And away they went again."

Williams, who has covered matches involving Crowe since Martin was 12th man for Auckland in the 1978 Shell Trophy final, says he's had a strange relationship with Crowe: "Things have changed considerably over the years. "When he got into the New Zealand team, he was a 19-year-old, a free spirit, relaxed and friendly. I used to play golf and tennis with him. I went to his parents' house for dinner. I don't know why he went off me, but he has. Now there's nothing like the relaxed relationship, a friendship really, there was at one stage.

"He has developed this persona where he is easily upset. He is certainly more sensitive as an adult than as an adolescent. He's one of the better interview subjects. Not as honest as Ruds, who speaks from the bottom of his heart, but still pretty good. You get a bit sick of Crowe doing the PR bit, mentioning DB on air and all that, but he's pretty good to interview.

"He would have to be the least relaxed as a captain of all the captains I've dealt with. When he became captain, you felt he seemed suspicious of you and you wondered why. He's very sensitive about any media criticism.

"I don't think I have ever criticised him, but I think because I have at various times been associated in the media with John Morrison and John Parker I am guilty by association. They are two people he looks down on.

"According to the Crowes, you are not fit to be a commentator unless you've been a very good test player, which would mean Turner, Coney, Smith and Wright would be okay.

"His father Dave put on a most outrageous performance at the end of the 1993 season, in the last one-dayer at Eden Park. He was hanging over the white rail shaking his head at me. He said, 'You and your friend Parker, you're tabloid on radio. You don't care what you say. You wreck people's lives and marriages, and what do you care?' I had no idea what he was talking about. I've never mentioned his marriage on air. But he must have known what he was saying, because he recalled the conversation a year or two later."

Dave Crowe makes no secret of his rating of Morrison and Parker as mediocre players. Parker: "There's no logic in that. Dave played a couple of first class games. By extension he would not rate his own knowledge or judgment on cricket. It's a stupid argument."

Williams says Crowe's attitude towards him in South Africa in 1994 exemplified their recent dealings. "He was strange. The only time he agreed to be interviewed by me was when he captained New Zealand at Soweto. I approached him on two or three other occasions to ask about his knee, the test century he was aiming for etcetera. He declined those requests. When he left the team in East London and went to Cape Town, I rang him in his room and asked if I could have a couple of minutes. He told me just to quote him and would not do an interview. Yet I was only two or three doors down the hall!

"It's unfortunate. He's too moody and sensitive as far as I'm concerned, and that makes his dealings with the media shaky."

Williams' fellow Radio New Zealand commentator Bryan Waddle has had a happier time of it with Crowe. "We've had a reasonably good relationship. There are moments when he's been reluctant to talk, but that's when he wants to concentrate on other things. Sometimes he's a bit unusual in his dealings with the media, but he's tried to be open and honest. I think he has sensed that openness and honesty has sometimes counted against him.

"He is generally wary, reticent about the media. He doesn't look at the media as though it's out to get him as such, but he is a victim of the personality cult. And he has interpreted things differently. He has seen things as negative publicity when maybe they're not. He has tended to be more open in his captaincy, but that had a lot to do with whether he was playing well.

"I never had any problems with him. If I desperately wanted to talk to him, he was always forthcoming and ready to answer questions. If he wouldn't, he'd explain why."

Waddle feels he may have had an advantage over most journalists because he has toured so often with Crowe. "I travelled with him a lot and he got to know me a little bit better and understood me as a person. We've eaten together on tours. In fact, in Australia one time he shouted some of the media for a meal.

"The more you're round a person the more they tend to open up. I've never had the difficulty with Martin others might have. He's never been slow to come to talk to me if I've been critical of him, and I have no trouble with that. It doesn't worry me.

"His performances at press conferences vary a little bit. He's never quite a Ken Rutherford. But I've never looked at Martin and felt he wasn't telling the truth. He was sometimes guarded, but you'd expect that."

Waddle says he got much closer to Crowe by touring countries like Sri Lanka, India and Pakistan with the New Zealand team. "They can be difficult places to tour and in a sense it's the New Zealanders against the rest. You're all part of the clan, and it draws you together."

One abiding Crowe memory for Waddle occurred in Lahore in 1990.

"The rest day occurred after the second day's play, and Martin was not out 17. On the rest day the team went down to the ground to practise. Martin got fully kitted up in pads, gloves and so on. He walked out to the middle, and just stood at one end, playing strokes for 20 minutes. Then he walked down to the other end and did the same thing. He was the only one there. It was total visualisation. Then he walked off the ground. That was his practice. The next day he scored a century against Wasim and Waqar.

"Some of us have debated the visualisation thing. If he'd been out straight away the next day, we'd have said he should have had a proper practice. And he's such a good player, he'd probably have scored a century anyway. He's always interesting though.

"It's the same over dinner. He looks at cricket from so many angles, and he's always thinking about the game. I find him very stimulating company at times like that."

Crowe gave an interesting insight into his view of a good cricket journalist when he said to Ian Smith as Smith walked out of the dressing room at the end of the 1992 World Cup (Smith had retired and it was no secret he was destined for a seat in the TV commentary box): "Stockley, be a good commentator."

TVNZ has a rather symbiotic relationship with New Zealand test cricket. They need each other in what, with the commercial sponsors also considered, is a multi-million dollar venture. Perhaps because of that, the TV commentators tend not to be very critical, though with the benefit of replays and close-ups, they are in the best position to offer harsh judgment. Glenn Turner and John Morrison are mild exceptions to this rule, though it would be stretching things to call them overly critical.

Two of the mildest TV media people, certainly when they are dealing with cricket, are Keith Quinn and Grant Nesbitt. Both obviously fit Crowe's requirements of what makes a good commentator.

Quinn says he's had an amicable relationship with Crowe. "I find him co-operative and friendly. I feel sorry for all the knocking he gets from the talkback callers. It got so heavy against him one summer that I said on air the difference between Martin and Ken Rutherford was that one was a lounge bar person and the other a public bar person. I was merely trying to illustrate the differences. But the talkback callers were really after him, particularly those who believed he didn't have the ability to captain the team. It got tiresome."

Quinn recounts a funny story about his dealings with Crowe during the World Cup semi-final against Pakistan in 1992. "I was the production assistant, and one of my jobs was to help Nisbo [Grant Nisbett] prepare the weather report before play. I rang the forecaster early on and he predicted rain later in the day. Martin came off the field and asked us for an exact forecast. So I wrote it on a note to the floor manager who passed it quietly to him. Before tossing, he came over and asked us again for the forecast. So I spoke to the forecaster again, and then told Martin rain was predicted for about 2pm.

"Martin won the toss and batted. At lunch he asked me again, so again I checked. Still rain was predicted. Well, that rain never came, and New Zealand lost. Later Martin jokingly asked me where was the bloody rain. I think he'd hoped it might rain and catch out Pakistan when they batted and began with a slow run-rate."

Nisbett too says he's had no problems with Crowe. "I did the frontman's job for a few years and always found Martin very helpful and willing. And we were a lot more demanding back then too. If I remember, we asked the captain or outstanding player to front up after each day's play, not just at the end of the match.

"Martin sometimes got himself into trouble through being too open. Probably to his own detriment, he has not mastered the Graham Mourie-Andy Dalton art of saying a lot without really saying anything. Then again, cricketers tend to be more honest. Allan Border was another who really spelled it out. Other people have told me of troubles they had with Martin, but I never struck it myself. He was always good value."

Crowe has not always endeared himself to the print media. In the days when Warwick Roger was editing *Metro* (and before he had his Road to Damascus conversion over Crowe), the magazine poked fun at Crowe by publishing an entry in its New English dictionary section. It said the verb "to Crowe" meant "to drink a particular brand of beer in an ostentatious way: eg 'as soon as the cameras began pointing in his direction, he began croweing'."

Some writers found he would not grant interviews and became snarky. In 1994 Margot Butcher wrote a piece on Ken Rutherford in *North and South* and made a point of putting in print the fact that Crowe had told her "politely but firmly that he was just not interested and that I could write whatever I wanted". Perhaps this was because in 1991 when *North and South* sought an interview with Crowe he demanded to be paid. Editor Robyn Langwell wrote: "I felt sad that he should be such a flawed hero."

These days, of course, the Crowes are off bounds to all the women's magazines except *Woman's Day*.

On the occasions I have spoken to Crowe I have found him to be very helpful. Whether discussing his plans to be a sports psychologist later in life, or his hopes for the World Cup, or his ideal New Zealand domestic cricket season set-up, he has been enthusiastic and lucid. In December 1994 I rang him in South Africa to ask him if he wanted to respond to some comments others had made about him in an upcoming *Listener* article. We spoke for 38 minutes, and I suppose it was a verbal joust. But, despite the fact that I'd woken him up, he was sharp and had a certain logic, even if I didn't agree with it.

The *Listener* article included some criticism of him. In April 1995 he was asked by Brian Edwards on *Sunday*, a TV3 programme, what he thought of the article. "They are only five or six people who don't agree with you," he replied, "who feel that way in terms of coming out in print and they've come out as a team, I suppose, and said those things."

Crowe once described newspapers as "only good for wrapping up fish and chips. They destroy society". Yet Crowe himself has made considerable money through the media, not only by charging for interviews, but by writing (or having ghost-written) columns in five newspapers, the Ansett magazine and having spots on various electronic media outlets.

In his relations with the media, and his views on journalism, Crowe is clearly as enigmatic as ever.

Chapter Fifteen

ABOUT TALL POPPIES

JOHN MORRISON

"The New Zealand sporting public admires and respects ruggedness, durability and humility. But mainstream New Zealand doesn't see Martin as having those qualities. He believes New Zealanders knock him for his cricket ability. In fact, they admire him for that, but only that. They knock him for his behaviour. The public believes he is a prima donna, spoilt and pampered, neurotic."

Martin Crowe has an unusual relationship with the New Zealand public. While it's clear they do not warm to him, they want to know about him. He is an unusual, intriguing case study, and there's always a fascination reading about him, or listening to him.

Early in 1995, when Crowe was no longer New Zealand captain – indeed, when he was out of the national team through injury – he was still the most talked about cricketer in the country. I wrote a cover story for the *Listener* entitled "Martin Crowe: I'm a great bat; why don't you love me?" A few weeks later Warwick Roger followed it with an 11,000-word story in *Metro* entitled "The Twilight of the God" (referring, I assume, to Crowe, not Roger), in which he discussed Crowe's complexities and insecurities with the man himself and a few other people.

The stories were written because the magazines' editors recognised that Crowe is a figure who tantalises the public, that people want to know more about him. They appeared about the time news of the drugs scandal in South Africa broke. Four members of the New Zealand cricket team were suspended for their behaviour in South Africa; the manager, Mike Sandlant, resigned on his return; the coach, Geoff Howarth, followed a few days later. All this was bubbling along, with the promise of more drugs revelations to come, and still Crowe, who wasn't even playing, was the most talked about cricketer in the country.

Shortly afterwards, New Zealand and the West Indies were preparing to do battle in the second test at the Basin Reserve. For the two days before the match began, the two Wellington newspapers, the *Evening Post* and *The Dominion,* ran four photos of cricketers. Three of them featured Crowe, either playing golf with Brian Lara or practising in the nets in preparation for another comeback from injury. Merely by his presence in Wellington, Crowe overshadowed 22 players about to play the decisive test of a series.

Such is his dominance. We've had great cricketers over the past 30 years, including Bevan Congdon, Glenn Turner and Richard Hadlee, but you have to go back to 1965, when John Reid retired, to find a cricketer who bestrode the national stage as Crowe has these past few years. Reid had a larger-than-life personality, was outspoken and was so much better than everyone else in the country at cricket that he ruled the show. But he played before television made superstars of top players. Crowe, in his own way, is at least the equal of Reid as a player, and has been followed around by a much bigger publicity machine.

He is to the sports pages what Rachel Hunter and Princess Diana are to the women's magazines: always worth a story. I've never had more reaction to a story than I did to the Crowe *Listener* cover. Newspapers up and down the country reported it. I was invited to discuss the story by several radio stations and the personal feedback was incredible.

Keith Quinn, one of the hosts of *Sports Round-up*, says of all the cricketers in the test team, it is Crowe who inspires the most comment from talkback callers. Some are for him, some agin. But everyone seems to have a strong opinion. He polarises people. The odd thing about this is that I doubt Crowe wants to divide opinion. He wants to be "liked, loved, adored" as he told *Metro*. It's just that he has developed the ability to put his foot in it, to turn a triumph into a disaster.

Examples? Well, to be honest, there are dozens. The *Listener* article listed a few.

- In the television interview which followed his record 299 against Sri Lanka, the day he and Andrew Jones set a world record with their partnership of 467, Crowe three times drew attention to the can of beer he was drinking. He said later that his actions were "just an instinctive action after a hard day's work". His "gesture" would certainly have pleased the team's official sponsors, DB, but it provoked complaints that broadcasting advertising standards had been breached and there was a flurry of letters to newspapers on the subject. The Alcohol Liquor Advisory Council criticised him for prominently endorsing the beer in television news bulletins. When the country should have been rejoicing in Crowe's superlative batting, they were debating the rights and wrongs of his blatant advertising of DB.
- The 1992 World Cup was a Crowe benefit. He batted magnificently, led New Zealand with flair and initiative and was rightly named Player of the Tournament. Yet the evening after New Zealand were so unluckily eliminated by Pakistan in the semi-finals, Crowe appeared on *Crowe on Crowe,* the televised interview of Martin by older brother Jeff, which returned fire at the national selectors who earlier that season had contemplated taking the captaincy off him.
- Crowe in 1991 offered to take part in a Ministry of Transport safety campaign. The gesture seemed generous until his letter to the MOT was leaked and it was revealed that the offer was conditional on the MOT waiving payment for two speeding tickets. He did not take part in the campaign. He said his request to the MOT was no different to writing seeking to be excused for the same sort of offences. "I guess because I'm a high profile New Zealander, someone saw it as a chance to have a crack at me."
- Crowe stood down from the New Zealand captaincy in March 1994 in a gutsy decision to put the team above national pride. But he undid that good work by then criticising New Zealand coach Geoff Howarth repeatedly to the media.
- During the tour of South Africa in 1994-95, Crowe had to battle hard to combat his worsening knee problem. He limped through the first few one-day matches, even opening the innings. But his batting was overshadowed by controversy over his leaving the team in mid-tour.
- In the *Metro* article, Crowe opened by saying he did not wish to go over old ground again – the unsavoury rumours, his disputes with Ken Rutherford and Geoff Howarth, and so on. Yet during the article he

went right through the rumours again, had another crack at some New Zealand journalists, questioned Rutherford's loyalty as his vice-captain and again cast doubts on Howarth's ability to coach a New Zealand team.

Jeff Crowe, as Martin's manager, must have been shaking his head at his brother's incredible ability to put his foot in it time after time. And if Jeff wasn't, he should have been.

Obviously not everyone in the country feels negatively about Martin Crowe, but there is an anti-Crowe element out there, as Jeff conceded in that same *Metro* story.

The Crowes write it off as the tall poppy syndrome. It's an interesting concept, the tall poppy syndrome. Stars from all over the world seem to feel their country is unique in having a crack at high profile performers. Gordon McLauchlan made a good point in his *New Zealand Herald* column when he wrote in March 1992: "I am always suspicious of those who complain about New Zealanders' lack of adulation of the rich and famous. These complainants are so often minor celebrities themselves, poppies not much above average height. What they usually want is their insecurities bolstered, their vanity pandered to. They'll get respect when it's due."

This is not a view with which the Crowes agree. "New Zealanders don't relate to excellence," Jeff Crowe told *Metro*.

This may be convenient, but it's not true. Of course we admire Martin's excellence as a batsman, as we admired Sutcliffe's and Donnelly's, and as we admired the excellent bowling of Cowie and Hadlee. We salute the All Blacks when they play excellently, revelled in the excellence of Hillary's ascent of Mt Everest, and still bask in the reflected glory of Kiri Te Kanawa's excellent voice. And then there was the great outpouring of national pride when the excellent Team New Zealand campaign brought home the America's Cup. Would the yachties claim their excellence was not appreciated or applauded?

If we don't admire Martin Crowe, it has nothing to do with not recognising excellence. New Zealanders are excellent at all sorts of things, from fixing their own cars to running small businesses. We relate to that.

New Zealanders like to idolise their sports stars. We have a Sports Hall of Fame to recognise the great ones and every year one of the big events on the sporting calendar is the Halberg Awards dinner, honouring the top sportsmen, sportswomen and teams of the previous year.

Many, possibly most, of New Zealand's icons are sports stars. People like Bob Charles, Sir Edmund Hillary, Ian Kirkpatrick, George Nepia, Colin Meads, Brian Lochore, Bob Scott, Norman Read, Peter Snell, Wilson Whineray, Yvette Williams, Buck Shelford, Murray Halberg, Jack Lovelock, Denny Hulme, Ivan Mauger, Richard Hadlee, Lois Muir . . . icons, all of them. Today we have sports stars who have not yet reached icon stage, but surely will. How will Michael Jones, Sandra Edge, John Kirwan, Barbara Kendall and Grant Fox be regarded in another decade? They'll be heroes. There'll be no talk of tall poppies, or of them being resented for their excellence.

The tall poppy theory is a popular one among some sports stars, but the New Zealand public is reasonably discerning. They admire the courage and humility of people like Meads, the class and dignity of Whineray and Muir. What they detest is self-promotion and puffery, false modesty and smart-alec behaviour.

The New Zealand public gets a little testy when sports stars are outspoken. We like the strong silent types. So when we get a John Walker, Rod Dixon, Susan Devoy or Erin Baker, there is less than total adoration. New Zealanders still admired Walker's running, Devoy's squash ability and Baker's phenomenal results as a triathlete, but a percentage of the public felt, rightly or wrongly, they talked too much. Similarly, yachtie Chris Dickson is often seen as being too clever by half.

Then there are other stars who simply dared to be different, such as Arthur Lydiard, an outspoken athletics coach, and Glenn Turner, a professional cricketer dealing with an amateur set-up. Both are very obliging, personable characters, but they've stood up against the tide and again New Zealanders don't necessarily like that.

The point is that if Devoy, Baker, Lydiard, Walker or Turner ran into public profile problems, it was not because they were good at a particular sport. New Zealanders admired them for that, totally. It was the other stuff that rankled with some.

But no sporting figure has had so much "other stuff" as Martin Crowe. You will never hear anyone criticise his cricket. He is peerless in that regard. But he has copped it for being variously a wimp, arrogant, outspoken, disloyal . . . you name it, he's been it.

John Morrison sums it up nicely: "The New Zealand sporting public admires and respects ruggedness, durability and humility. But mainstream New Zealand doesn't see Martin as having those qualities. He believes New Zealanders knock him for his cricket ability. In fact, they admire him for that, but only that. They knock him for his behaviour. The public believes he is a prima donna, spoilt and pampered, neurotic. They see these emotional press conferences and interviews, Martin looking like a five-year-old, pouting. It's like something out of *Monty Python*.

"He doesn't understand the public. He says, 'I'm a great bat; why don't you love me?' The trouble is, no-one has ever been able to explain it to Martin. As soon as you get into a debate with him, he says you're knocking him. He's had bad advice from people close to him, and New Zealand Cricket has allowed him to run rampant. The whole thing's gone so far, the public has got fed up. I believe he doesn't understand the reasons and the tall poppy thing justifies to him the reaction he gets. It doesn't happen overnight. It builds up."

These things tend to snowball. England had it with Ian Botham. For a while there in the 1980s, it was simply Botham-bashing season, and the media had a feast. Tabloid journalists felt they could write anything and get away with it because there was enough fact mixed in with the fiction.

Ironically, the New Zealand sporting figure who copped it most severely, before Crowe, was not a player at all, but rugby commentator Keith Quinn. Anyone who knows Quinny will tell you he is a generous, affable, open person. Yet for a while there it became the vogue to criticise his rugby commentating. He was called "the screaming skull", there were newspaper cartoons about him, campaigns to get him off air. The attacks got so vitriolic that he had to have an unlisted phone number, and was even taken off air for two or three seasons until the furore died down.

Since then, of course, he's bounced back and is now somewhat of a cult figure, figuring not only in rugby commentating, but on *Sports Round-up* and as a public speaker and MC. Quinny smiled through the worst of the criticism and has won over nearly all his critics.

Crowe is in a different class to most New Zealand sportsmen and sportswomen because he has such a high profile. He would receive a lot of exposure anyway, because he plays our national summer game, and because he is so good at it. But he has also worked assiduously to build that profile, and it has paid off because he is a wealthy person.

His problem is that as people have come to know him, through various television programmes and interviews, magazine articles and books written about him by his father Dave, they have not necessarily liked what they've seen.

Some sports stars of previous generations were not very nice. In fact, some were absolute ratbags. But the public never got to know them, except for their sporting deeds. They received no bad publicity; on the other hand they made no money from their sporting ability.

Crowe is a modern phenomenon, a cricket equivalent, in New Zealand terms, of John Kirwan, except that Kirwan is Saint John to a lot more people than Crowe is Saint Martin. In a sense one has to admire Crowe for his openness. He says things which cannot help but grate on people, yet says them anyway. Many of his teammates say nothing, and suffer none of the vilification. With Crowe, the good, the bad and the ugly have all been exposed.

It should not surprise if many of our greatest sportspeople have not been particularly nice. To be the very best in any field requires a certain ruthlessness and selfishness, and at times these traits do not translate so well when taken outside sport.

Some sports stars have been involved in shonky business deals, others have been dishonest with teammates. But this has never come out. The public's perception of these people bears little relation to reality.

The flood of sports biographies over the past 15 years has not helped. Occasionally, a sports biography is produced which is honest and incisive. Chris Laidlaw, Graham Mourie and John Wright should be proud of the books they wrote. But hardly any others offer any insight into the real person. Some are unashamedly shallow. Phil Gifford wrote Alex Wyllie's biography and even called it *Grizz: the Legend*. It enhanced the legend, but never dug below the surface. But the Wyllie book was better than several others of a recent vintage, which have offered no insight into the subject.

There is a fine line reporters have to walk between writing exposés and maintaining contacts within the sports they cover. But sometimes this getting alongside sportsmen can go too far.

Crowe has quite often turned personality problems around so they become cricket problems. The classic case is his letter to John Bracewell telling him that once Crowe became New Zealand captain, Bracewell would no longer be part of the team. There are many others, including Shane Thomson, Mark Priest, Rutherford and Howarth, whom Crowe has taken exception to publicly. He got the pip with Don Neely, after having his position as New Zealand captain questioned, to the extent of not talking to him. In view of this, it is impossible to agree with the point of view put forward by Lynn McConnell in the *Evening Post* last season. Defending Crowe on the grounds that anything outside cricket is out of bounds,

McConnell wrote, "But just as Bert Sutcliffe, John Reid, Stewie Dempster, Jack Cowie and others were ahead of their time, so, in his own way, was Crowe. While New Zealand's attitudes have changed, largely as the result of Government freeing up of restricted aspects of life, they have not changed quickly enough for New Zealanders to accept Crowe's tastes, interests and attitudes outside cricket. Not that they are of particular importance to anyone but Crowe, but the instant society retains its own borders and Crowe sits outside them.

"Like Sir Richard Hadlee, life at the top for Crowe has brought rumour, scuttlebutt and frustration. Like Hadlee, his every moment has been scrutinised. Instead of reflecting on deeds of greatness, fans have picked at the man, overlooking the sheer skill he possesses."

McConnell is wrong on several counts. First, Crowe has made his private life the public's business. His various homes have featured photographed in magazines. Crowe's wife Simone is no recluse. She often travels with the New Zealand team, gives plenty of interviews and is not adverse to posing for photographers. Crowe's brother and business manager Jeff is a television commentator and part-time interviewer, and their father Dave writes for magazines. The Crowes have written two books. In view of the very public life they, and particularly Martin, lead, it would be remarkable if their actions did not provoke comment.

Crowe has made it his business to involve the public in his private life. It is unreasonable, therefore, for him to expect, and for writers like McConnell to suggest, that the public not form views on what they see and read.

But the public's views of Crowe as a person and as a cricketer should not be confused, as McConnell did. The public most certainly do reflect on his greatness as a cricketer. When the New Zealanders were in South Africa, and the test matches were beginning quite late in the evening, cricket followers were in a quandary: to stay up and watch the action on TV3, or to go to bed and have a reasonable amount of sleep. A straw poll reveals that many people covered both bases by staying up until Crowe was dismissed. They might not have all liked what they'd seen of Crowe as a person, but they acknowledged his greatness as a player. It is a pleasure to watch him bat, worth any loss of sleep.

There is a frostiness towards Crowe; people dislike him for all sorts of reasons. Keith Quinn once came up with a theory on why people didn't like his rugby commentating. "Imagine a public bar the day after a big rugby test," he said. "Six blokes might be sitting around discussing the game. One of them will say he didn't like something I said, another will chip in with something else I said which had annoyed him. Eventually all six would be able to point to an example from my commentary of something which grated on them. It might be six different statements, but the thing they would eventually agree on is that Quinn is a bum commentator."

So it is with Crowe. There are people who say he is vain, precious, a wimp, that he is a skite, that he's crass, that he's too outspoken, that he's not injured as badly as he says he is, that he's class conscious. There is no one who thinks Crowe is a vain, precious, wimpy, skiting, crass, outspoken, class-conscious sook. Rather, people have their own reasons for not liking him, but agree simply that they don't like him.

Murray Deaker, a long-time supporter of the Crowe family, tells of a "perfectly normal sounding" female caller to his Newstalk ZB sports show. "She said Martin should be out of the team. I asked her why. 'It affects all the other boys,' she said. I pointed out that Richard Hadlee did too, and that he was a terrific asset to the team. 'I just don't like him. There's always something wrong with him. He's always injured. And all those gold chains.' I asked again why she didn't like him. 'He's arrogant.' I pointed out that had nothing to do with cricket. 'I just don't like him. He shouldn't be in the team,' she said. I've had many, many callers like that. They knock Martin Crowe more than anyone else."

The class thing is interesting. John Bracewell's theory is that we like to grab our heroes from the working class. "People would have loved Andy Earl to be captain instead of Gary Whetton. Martin cultivates that class thing with his talk about wine and fine restaurants etcetera. That irritates the hell out of everyone outside Auckland. JK is another example. He was everyone's hero when he was a butcher's boy, but by the time he was selling Italian lights it was a different story."

Doubtless there's a degree of truth in this. Yet it's not the complete answer. We love Mark Todd, yet he competes in a sport which is strongly associated with high society and money. People aren't resentful of Todd for that. What wins for Todd is his humility. Remember watching him in Seoul, in 1988, after he'd retained his Olympic three-day equestrian title? It made Kiwis glow to hear a New Zealander speaking as he did; he was genuinely humble, quick to thank the people who had helped him, relieved, clearly proud to have won for New Zealand. It was a winning mix, but the overriding factor was how genuine he was.

Sure, the class thing has a bit to do with it, but there's more to it than that. As John Graham says: "It's not just a money thing. Most New Zealanders think 'good on them' when sports stars make some money. If Martin thinks people have a go at him because of his wealth, it's merely his rationalisation of his inability to make life work."

Crowe has a pride in his appearance that some would regard as vain. At school he was always immaculately turned out, and ever since he has displayed a sharp dress sense. He follows fashions and styles closely. He's spoken of the fact that he is losing his hair: "It's part of the reason I wear hats during media interviews," he told his brother during *Crowe on Crowe*. "I know when I get to your stage I'll accept the fact that I am bald and I'll enjoy it, but it's hard going through the phase."

He thinks too much is made of his liking for a good wine, even though he is the one who harps on about it. "I can have a pie and a pint with the best of them," he's said. "But I've chosen to focus on my job and there's where I stand out over some of the players I've played with over the years."

What about the wimp aspect? Is he as injured as he says? Last season Auckland doctor Barry Tietjens took the unusual step of issuing a press release about the state of Crowe's knee; unusual because Tiejens is, understandably, incredibly reluctant to discuss his patients. (A story about Michael Jones' remarkable comeback after knee surgery couldn't contain anything from Tietjens until okayed by a hand-written note from Jones.) So to see Tietjens issuing the release was a jolt. Clearly the knee specialist believes Crowe is suffering from a severe knee problem which will never really be right. That ties in with what another of Crowe's doctors said months earlier: that he would be most surprised if Crowe got through the 1994 England tour, so bad was his knee.

There's no doubt Crowe's knee is bad. And some days it's clearly better than others. But it hasn't just been the knee. There was the salmonella he picked up in Sri Lanka in 1984 and which affected him for years. And the fainting, the dizzy spells. He's missed matches because of flu, because of hamstring, shin, thigh, knee, ankle, thumb and finger injuries. His back has caused him problems for virtually his whole career. He's had treatment for shoulder pain.

There's been more, but that's enough to make the point.

Ian Smith says it's unfair to look at this catalogue of injuries and say Crowe could have played through some of them. "Only one person knows the extent of an injury, and what the rest of us say is only speculation," says Smith. "If one person is injured more often than others, then there is a lot of talk about it. And Martin's place has been so vital that people almost resent him being injured. If it was a lesser player injured, he would be easier replaced. I would say he has been very unlucky. For instance, if he's fielding under the helmet in close and the batsman belts one towards him, it'll hit his hand and dislocate a finger. With another fieldsman it might just leave a bruise."

Others, though, don't think it's that simple. Two New Zealand Cricket officials said privately he was starting to be distinctly unwilling to play during the summer of 1994. Eventually New Zealand Cricket invoked a clause in its contract whereby Crowe was not to be paid if he did not play for more than three months. Within a short time he announced he would be available to tour England, though not as captain. The officials felt the pressure that was put on Crowe financially influenced his decision to play. Yet, as Smith says, who can really say, except the man himself?

Chatting to some former internationals, teammates of Crowe, it's surprising to find they believed he could have played more often if he'd wanted.

To outsiders, it has always been assumed Crowe was such a magnificent player, and has batted so brilliantly against test attacks from every country, that he would be eager to front up if he could. In fact, some test players said they felt he had become a most reluctant player at home. Some suggested Glenn Turner got that way towards the end of his career, too. The theory is that the pressure of performing at home is very much greater than when you are away on tour. It is great if you do well, but the build-up to a big match, the well-wishers, the media attention, can be overwhelming.

John Parker says he always found it harder to play at home. "Most New Zealanders do. New Zealanders are all behind you, but it can come out in negative ways . . . perhaps a sarcastic comment. Yet everyone is behind you. Martin hasn't come to grips with that. I don't believe his father has done him any good at all in that area. Martin could feel these days that he would rather not be playing at home, but I'm sure that situation could be overcome quickly if the environment around him was changed."

In truth, Crowe is no wimp. He has a severe knee injury and has batted bravely in spite of it. His batting in Perth in 1993, when he played Shane Warne on one leg to save the test, and again in South Africa at the end of 1994 are examples. Neither is he a wimp in that he is scared of fast bowling; he has batted too well too often against the West Indies and Pakistan pacemen for that accusation to have any credibility. But perhaps he has felt the pressure of public expectation at home.

He is precious. He gets very upset about all the rumours, about any publicity that is not glowing. I was surprised, when speaking to him while he was in South Africa, to hear him reciting details of stories I'd written about him over the past several years. The stories were generally vastly complimentary, but Crowe recalled any criticisms, even the exact wording. Then he started on about Rutherford, complaining, for instance, about a statement Rutherford had made in *Woman's Day* eight months earlier. Far from being numbed by the constant exposure he gets, Crowe seems to have become ever more prickly, to the point where he doesn't seem able to be objective about any criticism.

The vicious rumours have obviously upset him, and they've obviously been hurtful. But I believe he has over-reacted, and exacerbated the situation. For example, in 1989 he and Brett Steven spent quite a lot of time together. They met at the Institute of Sport gym where they were training as they recovered from injury. They got talking and the next thing, they were playing a bit of tennis together.

Soon after, according to the rumour mill, they were having an affair. "I thought it was funny," says Steven. "It never worried me at all, but I felt sorry for Martin because rumours like that obviously upset him. Hell, how can you be pissed off though? That rumour was so ridiculous; the next week it was me and Ron Brierley, or him and Ron Brierley, I forget which."

The rumours have certainly been many and varied.

The Aids and homosexuality stories, you had to shrug your shoulders. Other prominent New Zealanders have been subjected to stupid rumours, too. There were so many stories about the state of Murray and Lorraine Mexted's marriage that they eventually had to hold a press conference to set the record straight. One *Truth* front page talked about Chris Lewis having Aids, turning to religion and losing his money on the share market. A rumour involving Ken Rutherford's wife with a prominent Dunedin citizen gathered such momentum that Karen Rutherford was forced to confront the issue with denials in the city's newspaper. And so it goes.

You can be sure there are other stories about other stars and their families, all of them equally absurd. But it's doubtful if many treated the rumours as seriously as the Crowes. Martin himself has spoken endlessly about the stories, on the *Fraser* TV programme, to Michael Parkinson in the *Daily Telegraph,* to South African *Sports Illustrated,* at press conferences, to *Metro.* His father has written about them in the *Cricketer.* Simone has talked about them in the *Sunday News,* on Radio Pacific. If you didn't know better, you'd think the Crowes were deliberately keeping the stories alive. By not giving a once-and-for-all denial then shrugging their shoulders and simply getting on with life, the Crowes, particularly Martin, have opened themselves up to the accusation that they are precious.

Of course, few people know what it is like to have an unsavoury rumour about them sweeping the country. If someone accuses an accountant, lawyer or typist of having an inter-office affair, only a few people hear of it. But to be discussed from North Cape to Bluff must be galling. After the *Listener* story was published, Keith Quinn asked me on *Sports Round-Up* about the rumours. Quinn felt Crowe has had to put up with some vicious stories and did not agree with me that he should have done his best to ignore them, or at least stopped talking about them. It was interesting that the next day Quinn received a letter from Mexted, congratulating him for taking the line he had.

And how has Crowe handled the adverse publicity over the years? It's not hard to find out, as he has seldom stopped talking about it. Here are a few examples:

To *Sunday* magazine's Steven O'Meagher in October 1990: "I don't know whether it has affected me. Perhaps I've gone into myself a bit, but overall I think I cope well. I've certainly had a lot of practice . . . I found people forming attitudes who were turned off by me. It's the old tall poppy story – I don't think there's anything you can do about it. They've [the rumours] never got to me, but have to my family. It is something you have to put up with."

To Jeff Crowe in *Crowe on Crowe,* in March 1992: "If it's a personal thing, it doesn't worry me because it's rubbish. It's floating around in restaurants and it gets back to my wife and friends. It's a nuisance. Early on, I started to wonder, but I'm past that now. I've heard so many rumours, from homosexuality to Aids, to marriage, divorce. That's all part of the deal, part of the psyche out there. You've got to laugh and get on with it. When you get knocked you say it's the tall poppy syndrome, the knocking machine. It gives you a bit of comfort to say it's the knocking machine. You can then get on with it."

At the infamous Basin Reserve press conference in February 1993: "It just doesn't seem to stop. Every day there is something. My wife is demoralised by the whole thing . . . There are lies being written and a lot of innuendos which affect me personally – my marriage and all that sort of thing. I really do wonder if it's all worthwhile."

To Ian Fraser in *Fraser,* April 1994: "I do probably show my feelings. I'm a sensitive, complex person who goes through moments where I express disappointment, frustration and elation. When you get attacked for your private life – homosexual, gay, bankrupt, divorced – they hit home. They are sensitive issues . . . private things I think are sacred. It's a time to become low key and get out of the spotlight. I've had 10 years facing the music, but it's my choice. Now I want to get on with finishing my career."

To Michael Parkinson in England's *Daily Telegraph,* 1994: "Since Richard Hadlee's retirement, I've dominated the cricket scene in terms of having a high profile presence, endorsements, publicity and all that. Critics have tried to undermine my position. It's a difficult problem being famous in New Zealand. I took a lot of stick . . . The tabloids are the dark element in the situation."

To South African *Sports Illustrated's* Niall Piper, in November 1994: "It [the tall poppy syndrome] is a common disease in New Zealand. We're a tiny nation, 3.5 million people, and we tend to pull ourselves down. A person is not allowed to stand above the crowd, especially in sport."

To *Metro,* in February 1995, after listing all the rumours and giving his version (subsequently shown to be incorrect) of the steps he'd taken to stop them: "It's part of the Martin Crowe folklore that it's going to be brought up whatever we do. I don't want to bring it up all the time – but it's just become part of my life."

Few cricketing people care about the rumours or the endless prattle about enjoying the finer things in life.

What annoys is how transparent Martin is. This comes out in all sorts of ways. After he scored his 299 against Sri Lanka in 1991, the DB line he plugged simply did not ring true. It was obvious he was going out of his way to advertise his and New Zealand's sponsors. I suppose what made it worse was that this is the man who has turned boasting about liking fine wines into an art form. Crowe's gesture had a cheapness to it which soured the moment.

The other thing about Crowe is his evident willingness to talk about himself ad nauseum. He says, "I'm not running to the media. I don't ring a media person. I don't have a column any more. I don't even speak to the media any more. I do a PR job for New Zealand Cricket part of the year. What happens is that when I go to a different country, they want to know a bit more about me. They want to get into my psyche. So I talk to them."

The point is that, at a time when he says he wants to be merely a player, to get out of the limelight, he gave extensive interviews to Michael Parkinson in England, South African *Sports Illustrated,* to Warwick Roger in *Metro* and featured in New Zealand women's magazines. In each he regurgitated all the stories about the rumours and what a tall poppy he is. It was odd behaviour from a shrinking violet.

The way Crowe describes himself brings to mind those film stars on the *David Letterman* show. Pure ego, they sit on the couch and talk all night about themselves. As John Morrison says, "Martin's like a Hollywood star. Great actor, but you have to put up with all the crap."

Martin, and the other Crowes, will read all this and shrug and say it's another example of tall poppy bashing. And they'll get plenty of support. Journalists I respect, such as Keith Quinn and Murray Deaker, believe there is an element of the knocker in many New Zealanders. They say they've sampled it often in their talkback shows. Deaker says Crowe is "the most extreme case of a tall poppy being subjected to constant attacks that we have had in New Zealand sport".

Quinn and Deaker are partially correct, of course. We aren't a nation of perfect people. Some strange people will delight in having a crack at big achievers – whether in politics, sport or business.

But to simply write off any criticism as the tall poppy syndrome is naive. Why don't people bash Edmund Hillary, or Brian Lochore, or Wilson Whineray? There has to be something there to criticise first, something which gets right up the nose of the average New Zealander. Good advice to people who claim they are tall-poppy victims is to look to themselves first.

A few years ago, Martin had a painting by a young Auckland artist named Wayne Young. He called the work "Tall Poppies". "The painting has green for envy in the stalks, bright yellow for jealousy, red for the poppy and blue and purple for strength. That's my interpretation of it and I feel it strongly because I'm suffering from the tall poppy syndrome," he told *New Zealand Woman's Weekly.*

Yet John Graham, who knows him better than many, says: "It's not a tall poppy thing with Martin, or most New Zealanders. If you mix easily and are available and don't put yourself beyond the reach of normal New Zealanders, you're fine. I played alongside great All Blacks like Colin Meads and Wilson Whineray and they were not tall poppies. On the other hand, the All Blacks went astray in 1991 because they got beyond normal people and became arrogant. The public saw that. If a sports star lets people down in terms of his personal life, that's when the public reacts: the public hates arrogance."

The point about a person putting himself beyond the reach of normal New Zealanders is a good one. John Morrison sums it up like this: "When Ewen Chatfield was asked what his favourite restaurant was, he'd talk about the fish and chip shop in Dannevirke. Martin says his is some restaurant in Italy. The public sees through that sort of stuff."

The final word on tall poppies can go to John Wright, a pretty tall poppy himself, and an eminently sensible person: "The New Zealand media falls over itself to praise New Zealand players. Coping with any criticism is part and parcel of performing in the public arena. In England the reporting is ruthless. But back here, the media, and the public, give us a good ride. I never had any problems at all with the media. I think New Zealanders are very fair and usually looking to praise their sports stars. The tall poppy thing is bullshit."

Chapter Sixteen

CROWE ASSESSED

WALTER HADLEE:
"Martin has succeeded for a decade, and has scored runs against the very best bowlers in the world."

John Arlott, that brilliant English cricket commentator and perceptive writer on the game, wrote *100 Greatest Batsmen in* 1986. In the introduction he grumbled about the problems of sifting through the many great batsmen down the ages and restricting the final choice to just a hundred. "Only as this preface was being written was the final alteration made. One man had to go in, and it was a heart-searching business to decide who to leave out of what had been the 'final' list."

That hundredth man was Crowe, as Arlott later confirmed privately. In 1986 Crowe was in only the early stages of his test career. By the end of the 1985/86 New Zealand summer – Arlott's cut-off point – Crowe had scored 7483 runs at 48.20 in first class cricket. In test play – the true yardstick for the great – he had scored 1601 runs at 36.38, with four centuries. They were good figures, but hardly overwhelming evidence that he had to be included, especially when Arlott was forced to omit such fine batsmen as Cyril Washbrook, Percy Holmes, Seymour Nurse, Mohammad Azharuddin, Dilip Vengsarkar, Bill Edrich and Alan Kippax.

Arlott mentioned the case of Graeme Hick, then in the embryonic stages of his career. "We all look forward to Hick's achievements, which are, surely, a cricketing certainty." But Arlott dismissed Hick on the grounds that "promising" did not equate to "great".

He found room for Crowe, though (as well as Bevan Congdon, Stewie Dempster, Bert Sutcliffe, Martin Donnelly, Glenn Turner and John R. Reid from New Zealand). Arlott described Crowe as a "tall, strong, personable batsman, who, before he was twenty-one, had played cricket for New Zealand and made himself a considerable reputation in English county cricket".

Since then, of course, Crowe has gone on to more than justify Arlott's faith in him. Despite an incredible run of illnesses and injuries, he has scored runs consistently and attractively and clearly rates among the game's best batsmen. But how good? Before moving to the world stage, let us look first at New Zealand. It would be stretching credibility to try to rank New Zealand's best players before 1930, when we played no test cricket. Therefore Daniel Reese and Sid Hiddleston do not enter these calculations.

Since 1930, by general consent our best batsmen have been the seven players Arlott sorted out for his book, plus perhaps Roger Blunt, Merv Wallace and John Wright. With no disrespect to great players like Jeremy Coney, John Reid (the younger) and Andrew Jones, the Top Ten stand supreme.

Naturally, there must be some notes made about these bald statistics. Blunt, Dempster, Wallace and Donnelly had very little time to establish their test careers. For instance, if Crowe's career had been cut off after 13 tests, his record would have been 429 runs at 21.45 with one century. This must always be taken into account. Wallace and Donnelly lost the best years of their careers to the Second World War, yet each twice thrived on tours of England. Dempster and Blunt played in an era when New Zealand engaged in very few official tests. So, in that sense, Turner, Congdon, Wright and Crowe have been particularly fortunate; they have had the chance to make slow starts to their test careers, then redeem themselves.

Sutcliffe and Reid were New Zealand's key batsmen from about 1949 to '65. Most of the time they played, there were few other New Zealand batsmen of test class, let alone world class. That must have had an effect. Crowe, by comparison, often batted with Wright, Edgar, Howarth, Reid, Coney and Jones around him, and all-rounders like Ian Smith and Richard Hadlee to bolster the lower order. That must have been comforting.

On the other hand, Crowe scores well in that he has fronted up to the best bowlers of his era, notably the West Indian pacemen, and scored runs attractively and heavily (two centuries and an 83 in three tests against the West Indies in 1987). Turner missed several years of test cricket by choice and Congdon became a world class performer only from 1972, his eighth year of test cricket. Wright was always gritty, and had some great days, but in terms of both style and output falls just below our very best.

The first class figures are interesting. All 10 players had plenty of matches in which to overcome poor starts to their careers, or to atone for a falling off in productivity at the tailend. Crowe's figures are notably superior to everyone else's, even Turner's.

Here is how their figures stack up, in first class and test cricket:

| | **First class** | | | | **Test** | | | |
	M	Runs	Ave	100s	M	Runs	Ave	100s
Blunt	123	7953	40.99	15	9	330	27.50	0
Dempster	184	12,145	44.98	35	10	723	65.72	2
Wallace	121	7757	44.32	17	13	439	20.90	0
Donnelly	131	9250	47.43	23	7	582	52.91	1
Sutcliffe	233	17,447	47.41	44	42	2727	40.10	5
Reid	246	16,128	41.35	39	58	3428	33.28	6
Congdon	241	13,101	34.84	23	61	3448	32.22	7
Turner	455	34,346	49.70	103	41	2991	44.64	7
Wright	366	25,073	42.35	59	82	5334	37.82	12
Crowe	242	19,333	56.03	69	74	5394	46.10	17

It is impossible to be definitive merely by looking at statistics, but, on figures alone, Crowe stands at least the equal, and probably the superior, of the best New Zealand can offer.

Of course, statistics do not take into account intangibles like style, determination, big match temperament, selflessness and courage. No one should be dogmatic in this regard. The best solution is to offer a range of opinions from New Zealand cricket followers whose judgement is respected.

Walter Hadlee, in his book *The Innings of a Lifetime*, selected Crowe to bat at No 4 in his all-time New Zealand team, saying, "His compactness of style and execution of stroke put him in world class, where he has been since the mid-1980s."

Hadlee feels Crowe compares favourably with any New Zealand batsman. "He has a good range of strokes, is technically fairly sound and there is no better hooker of the ball."

Comparing him with other top New Zealand batsmen, Hadlee says Crowe has a more comprehensive range of strokes than Glenn Turner. "I don't know that I ever saw Turner hook, but then that's not necessarily a bad thing. Walter Hammond never hooked either. I'm an admirer of Turner and Crowe as far as their application and technique are concerned.

"Bert Sutcliffe was lighter and quicker on his feet than Crowe, a more agile batsman. In his peak years, from 1947 to '53, Bert was probably a better bat than Crowe. Bert's record in those years was comparable with Bradman's. Martin Donnelly, too, was in that very highest class from the end of the war through to 1949. Bert and Martin Donnelly were different sorts of players, but they were arguably the best two left-handers in the world.

"Purely as a batsman, I'd put Martin Crowe above John Reid. Martin has good flair and is very good off the front foot through the off and straight past the bowler. John had quite a lot of failures early on, as did Martin. But I don't want to write off John. He was a powerful batsman, a brilliant batsman on his day, and one of the best we've produced."

Hadlee points out it is important to consider the quality of the opposition when rating a batsman. "Stewie Dempster was a very good player. He did well on his two England tours and at the time was rated among the best in the world. His test average is extraordinary, but against that you have to remember that the England team he played against in 1930 had a very mediocre attack, not really of test class. And Stewie played only a few tests. Turner played for a long time, but if you study his record, you will not find any instances where he succeeded in test matches against teams with genuine pace bowlers.

"Martin has succeeded for a decade, and has scored runs against the very best bowlers in the world.

"Bevan Congdon was a good player, but Crowe is more complete and I'm sure a bowler would fear Crowe more than Congdon. I would put Blunt and Wallace about on a par, and very much enjoyed watching them bat. They did not get the opportunities at test level that Crowe has had, but certainly approach him in quality."

One other aspect of Crowe's batting has impressed Hadlee. "When he started he didn't respond well to being hit. Later he overcame that and he deserves a lot of credit. I've seen him play big test innings where he has been hit quite badly, yet come back and batted very well."

Merv Wallace, who coached New Zealand to their first-ever test win, against the West Indies in 1956, was not only one of New Zealand's best batsmen for 20 years, but is also regarded as perhaps the best coach the country has produced. People say that cricket is a complex, complicated game, but after five minutes with Wallace, it all seems fairly straightforward.

"I rate Martin pretty high, as you'd expect," he says. "He is fairly sound technically. But he has the modern tendency of turning balls pitched on the middle and leg around the corner past square leg. These days, with only two fieldsmen allowed back there, there are plenty of gaps. Batsmen tend to play across the line on the leg side, using a lot of bottom hand. Martin is a lovely driver, off and straight, but you don't see him on-drive much. He turns that one around the corner.

"Also, Martin struggles a little against good spinners. Like most of today's batsmen, he hasn't faced a lot of spin over the years. In his time it's been mainly medium-pacers and quickies or perhaps an orthodox spinner. Only since Shane Warne arrived have the leg-spinners come back in vogue. Martin doesn't have the quick footwork to allow him to move out to play the spinners. He plays them from the crease. But he's not alone – except for the Aussies, who have always been good at using their feet, you don't see many batsmen able to get down the wicket quickly enough to get the ball on the full. Martin plays the quicker bowlers well. He plays straight. And he moves into a good position early for the hook shot.

"He's a class batsman. He has made runs against good opposition consistently. Balancing that, you have to say they play more test matches these days. It's a bit like us playing club cricket in our day. These days they play so many tests and one-day internationals they know their opposition very well and are used to playing at that level."

Along with Hadlee and Sutcliffe, Wallace felt Crowe would have benefited greatly from being in a team like the famous 1949 New Zealand side to England. That team was packed with big-name players, everyone was very supportive and no cliques developed.

"I've never played with Martin," Wallace says, "but he's never had to work in his life outside cricket. In those conditions I would imagine he is a little self-centred and worrying about himself first, and then those around him, like an individual playing a team game. He's been in a side that he has dominated. Often it has reached the stage where, without him, the test side is lost.

"It would have helped him to be in a side where he is only one of seven or eight top players. There would be no room to be a prima donna. It would be 'we' not 'I'. When you have one outstanding player, you have to hope he has the sort of personality that fits happily into the team, otherwise it can be a problem. You need a very strong management unit in that situation."

Bert Sutcliffe says Crowe stands out like a beacon among New Zealand batsmen since the war. Sutcliffe is not the sort of person to mention himself – there has never been a more modest personality. But of other New Zealand batsmen, he says Crowe would be a "must" selection for any New Zealand all-time team. "I don't think he is a fluent or graceful batsman. He hits the ball hard and he plays straight, presenting the full blade. He plays the shots he knows best; he's sensible about that."

Sutcliffe says it's difficult to compare Crowe with John Reid. "Bogo was a real clubber of the ball. When he got angry he hit the ball as hard as anyone ever. But he left himself a bit open. Perhaps Martin plays straighter and is a bit tighter."

John R. Reid: "He is still one of the best players in the world, knee and all. He's better than the Englishmen and Aussies. There are others as talented. For instance, Mark Waugh has all the hallmarks of class. The difference is that Crowe has better concentration and can therefore make bigger scores.

"Looking back through the years, I'd put him ahead of Turner, who improved during his career, but remained a selfish player, and about on a par with Donnelly and Sutcliffe. Merv Wallace has a special place in my memory and I would rank Crowe below him."

Frank Cameron: "The ones who stand out in my time are Bert Sutcliffe, John Reid, Glenn Turner and Martin Crowe. Bogo was inclined to throw his wicket away, but he was doing a lot of bowling, and captaining the side too. He was potentially a hell of a good bat. You would put Martin on a level with Sutcliffe and Turner, not better or worse. Sutty was a cavalier, Turner was an opener. I would regard Martin as in the mould of Greg Chappell – he looked good and scored his runs well."

Barry Sinclair, New Zealand's leading batsman in the mid-1960s, is reluctant to compare players of different eras. "The amount of cricket they play now makes comparisons very difficult," he says. "But Martin was and is a superb player, world class. Technically he's as good as anyone we've had and he's had a burning desire to succeed. I played with Sutcliffe, but not in his prime. If Sutcliffe and John Reid had had the same opportunities, maybe they would have been up there in terms of runs and centuries."

Sinclair says, technically, Reid and Crowe are poles apart. "Martin is a stylist. He caresses the ball to the gaps, plays fine tickles, things like that. Martin destroys an attack subtly. With John there was a lot of strength and power. John destroyed attacks brutally; he stood there and smashed them. I have a huge amount of respect for Bogo's batting, but Martin is a bit tighter.

"Turner was different again. But, like Martin, he was a true professional, and they have the edge. All they do is play cricket."

Mark Burgess: "I never played with Martin. Our careers had a slight overlap, but we never actually played in the same match. But from what I've observed he is clearly one of our best ever. His record is fantastic. He and Turner of my time belong in that top bracket. Looking overseas, you have to wait for someone like Lara to come along to find a player as good. I rate Martin above Richie Richardson, for instance.

"The best I played against were Greg Chappell, Barry Richards and Geoff Boycott and Martin is in that league. Since then, you'd put Allan Border up there too. Most great batsmen – with the exception of Boycott – aren't great leavers of the ball. They look to go to the ball, to dominate the game. And with Martin, I think he has had an additional pressure that some others haven't faced. He's been the only outstanding batsman in the test team at times, which must create its own difficulties."

John Parker: "Martin hasn't changed technically. One of his strengths is that he hasn't changed. When he is in form, his backlift is getting up and there is a full arm swing. Martin is a full extension driver. That's his strength.

"He's as good as anyone in the world. He reminds me of Pete Sampras. His game is well organised. Sampras's coach spent his early years working on his game from the back of the court. Later he worked on his volleying. Now he has the complete game. Crowe is a powerful driver and a vicious puller, the best in world cricket. He has a well-organised game. When he's going well, he crushes attacks. Where can you bowl?" Parker scoffs at any suggestions of emotional frailty in Crowe's batting. "If there is, it is covered up by his skill and his desire and his love of run-scoring."

Parker categorises batsmen into three types – those who want to play all the shots, those who just want to score runs, and those who want to do both. "Only the very best go in the third category, and that's where you find Martin. Batsmen like Border and Gavaskar went into the second category. I put Crowe in the class of Greg Chappell, a wonderful player. He is a better bat than Tendulkar. Lara is a higher run-scorer, but Martin is the better batsman. With Viv Richards, you'd say he was the best slogger, but Crowe is the better batsman. He's up there with Turner, and I saw Turner play some of his best innings, in county cricket. They are different types, one an opener, the other a middle-order batsman. But they are at the top of the tree. You can add 10 runs an innings to their average to find how they compare with Australians. So if Martin played for Australia, his test batting average would be around 56. The wickets there are better and there are so many good batsmen to support a player."

Richard Hadlee: "Well, I never got him out. He often reminds me of that. There was one match, Somerset against Notts at Trent Bridge, on a green wicket. He got 90-odd. Clive Rice broke his thumb. I was beating him a lot, getting edges, hitting his pads and so on. Dickie Bird, the umpire, said if it was a boxing match, he'd have stopped the fight!

"Martin knows where his off stump is. He's technically correct, with a good concentration level. And he has an intense desire to prove a point. You have to rate him very, very highly.

"He is one of the best batsmen New Zealand has produced. His record speaks for itself. Turner and Crowe were different players. Glenn was technically efficient, and his batting improved as he met the demands of the one-day game. He played within his limitations. He had his own style and grip . . . he was a fine player. But Martin is a better all-round player. He hooks, cuts, deflects. He's more dominant in general terms."

Hadlee disputes the contention that Crowe was an emotionally fragile batsman. "He never gave any sign to me of not being in control. Actually, he had a commanding presence about him at the crease. He is a big man and has an upright stance and is an imposing character. With a shorter person, you might be more inclined to think you had a physical ascendancy."

Jeremy Coney: "Martin is a world class player, obviously. But I must say I always felt slightly frustrated because he didn't wring the best out of himself. Now, of course, he's had health problems, but before that he went through a period when he should have still been playing down the line and he wanted to play square of the wicket. He was not quite stable emotionally at the wicket. He'd be very, very tight, then he'd push things and play a stroke out of character.

"I was probably slightly envious – if I had had the amount of ability to play strokes that he did, perhaps it could have been utilised a bit better."

John Wright: "I wouldn't say I've seen any batsman better than Martin. Once you get to that level – Greg Chappell, Martin, Brian Lara – it comes down to individual preference. Personally, I always especially enjoyed watching Greg Chappell bat. But Martin is as good as anyone I've seen."

Bruce Edgar: "Martin is good against pace and spin. He worked hard in Pakistan, concentrating on soft hands to develop the technique against spin. He probably plays the fast bowlers better. He always has time. He is an excellent judge of line and length and not afraid of the quickies, as he showed when he came back after being hit on the jaw against the Aussies. The crux of the thing with Martin is to get inside his mind and manage him effectively. I know Brian Lara is a fantastic player, but I prefer to watch Martin bat. Lara has a great eye, but Martin has the classic style. I'm more of a perfectionist and enjoy watching Martin build his innings."

Ian Smith: "Martin always looks at ease batting. He always has plenty of time. Even when he gets out he looks good. He's never in a real mess. Not many people look good getting out! Like all great players, he seems to know where the bowler is going to bowl. He picks up the fact that it is short of a length and doesn't get hit on the crease so often."

Don Neely: "Martin has proved himself over and over. He has gutsed it out. Against the West Indies he scored two centuries and an eighty in three consecutive tests against the quickest and best attack in the world. He was fighting all the way, yet he got them in style. Once he got past his first season [in test cricket] he has always been the equal of any batsman in the opposition. I get the feeling with Martin that he would really want to play the perfect innings. He has his own standards as well. Excellence and Crowe go together.

"Without the salmonella and knee problems, he'd be up to 25 hundreds and would be ranked among the all-time greats."

Neely points out that Crowe not only scores runs, but that he gets them in an entertaining manner. "He's a stylist, correct and at the same time entertaining. He's like a coaching book, but could you watch Allan Border bat for 10 hours? Border would guts it out. With Martin, you never had that feeling. Even that 299 against Sri Lanka… at no stage were you aware of how long he'd been going."

Pressed to make comparisons with former New Zealand greats, Neely concedes that Dempster, Donnelly, Sutcliffe and Turner all have claims. But he points to their lack of opposition, to Crowe's average of a century every four and a half tests, of his ability to win matches for New Zealand. "Test cricket is the yardstick. Martin is almost exclusively a test player. A quarter of his hundreds are in tests. His record stacks up against anybody."

On a world scale, Crowe rates fairly well statistically.

These averages of various batsmen down the years are not a definitive list, but are provided to give an indication of where Crowe fits in. The figures for current players are as recent as available:

	First class				Test			
	Matches	Runs	Avg	100s	Matches	Runs	Avg	100s
David Boon	239	17,165	46.89	52	97	6959	44.89	20
Allan Border	374	26,462	51.78	70	156	11,174	50.56	27
Geoff Boycott	609	48,426	56.83	151	108	8114	47.72	22
Don Bradman	234	28,067	95.14	117	52	6996	99.94	29
Greg Chappell	321	24,535	52.20	74	87	7110	53.86	24
Ian Chappell	262	19,680	48.35	59	75	5345	42.42	14

Denis Compton	516	38,942	51.85	123	78	5807	50.06	17
Colin Cowdrey	692	42,719	42.89	107	114	7624	44.06	22
Mike Gatting	474	31,785	50.93	82	79	44.9	35.56	10
Sunil Gavaskar	348	25,834	51.46	81	125	10,122	51.12	34
Graham Gooch	525	40,174	49.23	112	118	8900	42.58	20
David Gower	448	26,339	40.08	53	117	8231	44.25	18
Tom Graveney	735	47,793	44.91	122	79	4882	44.38	11
Gordon Greendige	481	34,440	46.04	83	108	7558	44.72	19
Wally Hammond	634	50,551	56.10	167	85	7249	58.45	22
Desmond Haynes	351	24,219	46.04	59	116	7487	42.29	18
Hanif Mohammad	238	17,059	52.32	55	55	3915	43.98	12
Neil Harvey	306	21,699	50.93	67	79	6149	48.41	21
George Headley	103	9921	69.86	33	22	2190	60.83	10
Graeme Hick	276	23,124	57.23	77	32	1933	35.79	2
Jack Hobbs	825	61,237	50.65	197	61	5410	56.94	15
Len Hutton	513	40,140	55.51	129	79	6971	56.67	19
Rohan Kanhai	416	28,774	49.01	83	79	6227	47.53	15
Brian Lara	85	7569	56.48	22	21	1975	58.08	4
Clive Lloyd	490	31,232	49.26	79	110	7515	46.67	19

Stan McCabe	182	11,951	49.38	29	39	2748	48.21	6
Peter May	388	27,592	51.00	85	66	4537	46.77	13
Vijay Merchant	146	13,248	71.22	44	10	859	47.72	3
Javed Miandad	402	28,647	53.44	80	124	8832	52.57	23
Arthur Morris	162	12,614	53.67	46	46	3533	46.48	12
Norman O'Neill	188	13,859	50.95	45	42	2779	45.55	6
Graeme Pollock	262	20,940	54.67	64	23	2256	60.97	7
Bill Ponsford	162	13,819	65.18	47	29	2122	48.22	7
Barry Richards	339	28,358	54.74	80	4	508	72.57	2
Viv Richards	507	36,212	49.33	114	121	8540	50.23	24
Richie Richardson	191	12,280	41.91	32	76	5445	45.75	15
Bobby Simpson	257	21,029	56.22	60	62	4869	46.81	10
Gary Sobers	383	28,315	54.87	86	93	8032	57.78	26
Herbert Sutcliffe	748	50,138	51.95	149	54	4555	60.73	16
Mark Taylor	166	12,248	44.37	30	62	4853	46.21	13
Clyde Walcott	146	11,820	56.55	40	44	3798	56.68	15
Steve Waugh	187	11,402	48.72	33	72	4011	44.56	7
Everton Weekes	152	12,010	55.34	36	48	4455	58.61	15
Frank Worrell	208	15,025	54.24	39	51	3860	49.48	9

| Zaheer Abbas | 459 | 34,843 | 51.54 | 108 | 78 | 5062 | 44.79 | 12 |

As a reminder:

| Martin Crowe | 242 | 19,333 | 56.03 | 69 | 74 | 5394 | 46.10 | 17 |

On statistics, then, he falls below the all-time greats, batsmen like Bradman, Hammond, Headley, Hobbs, Hutton, Lara, Miandad, Ponsford, Sobers, Herbert Sutcliffe, Weekes, Worrell and Walcott.

He is about the equal of Boycott, McCabe, Morris and Bobby Simpson – good company. And he rates above such fine players as Boon, Ian Chappell, Cowdrey, Gooch, Gower, Graveney, Lloyd, May, O'Neill, Richardson, Steve Waugh and Zaheer.

Overseas, Crowe is very highly thought of, as this smattering of opinions tells:

Greg Chappell: "He's been one of the players of his generation, good against all types of bowling. You have to put pressure on him early, otherwise it becomes a long and protracted exercise. Glenn Turner was a more defensive player, more into occupying the crease and scoring runs by accumulation. Martin is more dangerous. He can tear you apart. It is harder to dominate Martin. He would walk into any test side of his era and make runs.

"You try to isolate a class batsman like Crowe. He tends to dominate Australian thoughts before a match – he and Hadlee were the key players in the New Zealand team. Once Martin has settled in, you have to hope he makes a mistake.

"He suffers from the expectations of the New Zealand public. If he was playing in a side where there was a more even spread of talent, he would have less expected of him, and more support."

Hanse Cronje: "He is a world class batter, technically very, very good. In South Africa we had to study him very hard to find flaws and couldn't. He's very determined and doesn't give his wicket away. The knee injury must be very frustrating for him. He already has an impressive test record and has a fantastic one-day record as a player and captain.

"As with Steve Waugh, it's very hard to plan against him. You have to try to frustrate him. We thought in South Africa we'd try spin against him, but he destroyed our provincial attack when we put on the spinners.

Yet he's very polished against pace. He cuts, hooks, pulls. He's the best New Zealand batsman I've seen and is up there with the best in the world."

Tony Greig: "He'd have to be a bit of a disappointment. He looks like the best bat in the world; you don't get much better than him. Yet over the years, if you look at his whole career . . . I don't want to be too detrimental, but he's a bit like Hick. There's a lot of talent there, but the runs don't always come. The comparison isn't quite fair, though, because Crowe hasn't had a lot of back-up. It's very difficult to be the number one batsman without much support. You need to be a Boycott or a Turner to be really successful for New Zealand – blinkered. A strokemaker is better off in the Aussie team. He'd have had a better reward with the Aussies."

Mohammad Azharuddin: "The best thing about Martin's game is that he makes it look so easy. That's very important, the sign of a class player. He has stood out along with Richard Hadlee in the New Zealand teams I've played and has been definitely the best New Zealand batsman, followed by John Wright. Sometimes Martin gets a little impatient and gets himself out; otherwise there are no obvious faults."

Ian Chappell: "He's very good technically. The only query has been over his mental approach. There was a period in Australia a few seasons ago when he had cut out a lot of his horizontal bat shots and he is so good he should never think of doing that. He would have been the best bat in Australia in the mid-1980s. Well, there was Border, but he is a different sort of player, not such a strokemaker. Martin found it a burden holding the batting together. It's always more difficult for a Crowe than a Border to do that, because Border was a grafter, not looking to get after the bowling. Crowe wanted to get after it, but couldn't afford to get out. When that happens a batsman starts to play against his natural instincts, and that's a burden."

David Houghton (Zimbabwe captain): "Before all the injuries, Martin was among the top three batsmen in the world. There's really only one place for Martin, and that's right at the top. He just doesn't make a mistake. With him batting at four, you have to hope he gets into the middle in the first five or six overs when your bowlers have their tails in the air."

Bill Lawry: "Crowe is technically fairly sound, the best bat to come out of New Zealand in my time. He has a good defence. His strength is his on-side shots, but he is a capable all-round player. I'd never put him in the Boycott class technically, though. Crowe is a different type of player to Turner, but for me, they'd be on a par. It's a different era now, with more hurly-burly. From what I've seen, Turner and Crowe would be about equal, but Crowe has been unlucky with injury."

How does he compare with Greg Chappell? "Well, they both bat right-handed! Seriously, Crowe does play very straight in defence, like Greg, but he's not as good, not in the class of Greg Chappell. In form and fit though, he is in the top bracket. He'd be good enough to get into the Australian side even today, but he'd have to be fit. You don't want to be picking crocks."

Peter Roebuck: "Martin would have been the best player in the England team during most of his career. He has been a major batsman over the past 20 years. But he's had a few problems. Martin probably puts too much pressure on himself to get results.

"I've played with Viv Richards and Sunil Gavaskar and Martin at his best was as good as them. He lacked internal solidity emotionally. It was always an internal journey with Martin. He had to get things right around him. Sunil was a great player who thrived on conflict and Viv . . . well, there was no one like him. He was immune to other factors.

"If Martin had been more secure mentally, he would have been a truly great player. As it is, he has been a remarkable player and one of the 10 best over the past 15 years. He is very respected by other players."

Bobby Simpson: "We've always thought he was a fine player. The tragedy is that he can't get on the paddock as much. He was in the top two in the world at one time. I've always thought he gives you a chance of getting him lbw because he sometimes plays back too much and gets caught in front. But he would have walked into our side, or any side."

Courtney Walsh: "I don't like making comparisons, but he is a very fine bat, among the top five or six in the world."

Ashley Mallett: "Crowey was the most positive New Zealand batsman I've seen, a world class player. The only time I ever saw him struggle a bit was when a spin bowler, a leggie in particular, bowled to him. He absolutely murders bowling not up to the mark. He would have walked into the Australian team. Boon at No 3 is a very compact, safe player, but Crowe is the better bat. Boon doesn't have Crowe's flair. Crowey can decimate an attack, any attack.

Allan Donald: "He has a lot of time and I'd put him in the top six in the world. The guys worked him out a bit in South Africa. They bowled just outside his off-stump, where he doesn't move his feet. He doesn't get forward sometimes and can nick them to the slips."

Mark Taylor: "In the games I've played against New Zealand, he's been the pick of the batsmen, the one wicket we've really wanted to get. If we can get Martin cheaply, we feel we're on our way. He's a confident all-round player with no obvious weaknesses, though Shane Warne has had a bit of success against him."

By the judgement of his peers and commentators, both domestic and international (with the notable exception of Tony Greig), Crowe's place in cricket's pantheon is secure. As if there was any doubt . . .

STATISTICALLY SPEAKING

(to end of 1994-95 season)
Compiled by Peter Marriott

FIRST-CLASS CAREER RECORDS

		BATTING & FIELDING										*BOWLING*				
		M	I	NO	Runs	Ave	HS	100	50	Ct	Wkts	Runs	Ave	Best	5WI
1979-80	Auckland	2	4	1	68	22.66	51	—	1	4	0	10	—	—	—
	Young New Zealand	2	3	0	70	23.33	47	—	—	—	2	70	35.00	2-14	—
1980-81	Auckland	7	12	3	303	33.66	81	—	3	7	2	48	24.00	2-8	—
1981-82	Auckland	7	13	1	525	43.75	150	1	3	12	0	26	—	—	—
	NZ in NZ	4	5	0	57	11.40	37	—	—	3	0	33	—	—	—
	North Island	1	—	—	—	—	—	—	—	1	—	—	—	—	—
1982	DB Close in England	1	1	0	104	104.00	104	1	—	2	—	—	—	—	—
1982-83	NZ in Australia	2	4	0	49	12.25	27	—	—	2	0	37	—	—	—
	Auckland	9	16	2	736	52.57	119	3	3	5	12	220	18.33	5-69	1
1983	NZ in England	11	19	5	819	58.50	134	3	3	13	12	284	23.66	3-21	—
1983-84	Central Districts	6	10	1	501	55.66	151	2	1	13	9	354	39.33	5-18	1
	NZ in NZ	3	4	0	148	37.00	100	1	—	3	0	93	—	—	—
	NZ in Sri Lanka	5	7	2	109	21.80	45	—	—	1	3	76	25.33	1-6	—
1984	Somerset	25	41	6	1870	53.42	190	6	11	27	44	1353	30.75	5-66	1
1984-85	NZ in Pakistan	4	7	1	294	49.00	71	—	3	5	6	181	30.16	2-29	—
	Central Districts	3	5	0	246	49.20	143	1	—	1	7	145	20.71	5-51	1
	NZ in NZ	3	5	0	295	59.00	84	—	3	5	—	—	—	—	—
	NZ in West Indies	5	9	0	396	44.00	188	2	1	7	3	55	18.33	2-25	—
1985	Rest of World in England	1	2	0	13	6.50	7	—	—	—	—	—	—	—	—
1985-86	NZ in Australia	4	7	2	562	112.40	242*	2	1	4	0	55	—	—	—
	Central Districts	1	2	0	139	69.50	97	—	1	1	0	6	—	—	—
	NZ in NZ	3	4	1	179	59.66	137	1	—	—	0	8	—	—	—
1986	NZ in England	12	18	6	787	65.58	106	2	6	10	2	190	95.00	1-37	—
1986-87	Central Districts	8	15	2	1348	103.69	175	6	5	11	13	293	22.53	4-26	—
	NZ in NZ	3	6	1	328	65.60	119	2	1	6	1	35	35.00	1-13	—
	NZ in Sri Lanka	1	1	0	27	27.00	27	—	—	1	0	13	—	—	—
1987	Somerset	18	29	5	1627	67.79	206	6	6	15	0	100	—	—	—
1987-88	NZ in Australia	5	9	1	715	89.37	144	3	4	4	—	—	—	—	—
	Central Districts	1	2	1	133	133.00	119*	1	—	—	—	—	—	—	—
	NZ in NZ	3	5	0	216	43.20	143	1	—	2	—	—	—	—	—
1988	Somerset	5	9	1	487	60.87	136	2	2	4	—	—	—	—	—
1988-89	Central Districts	7	11	1	373	37.30	141	1	2	2	0	34	—	—	—
	NZ in NZ	2	4	1	261	87.00	174	1	1	—	—	—	—	—	—
1989	World XI in England	1	1	1	138	—	138*	1	—	1	—	—	—	—	—
1989-90	NZ in Australia	3	5	0	332	66.40	143	1	2	2	—	—	—	—	—
	Central Districts	6	10	2	559	69.87	242	2	1	3	—	—	—	—	—
	NZ in NZ	3	3	0	161	53.66	113	1	—	1	—	—	—	—	—
1990	NZ in England	9	13	3	537	53.70	123	1	5	5	0	20	—	—	—
1990-91	NZ in Pakistan	5	9	3	356	59.33	108	2	1	10	1	68	68.00	1-22	—
	Wellington	2	3	0	126	42.00	101	1	—	—	—	—	—	—	—
	NZ in NZ	2	3	0	365	121.66	299	1	—	1	—	—	—	—	—
1991-92	Wellington	2	3	0	31	10.33	23	—	—	—	0	10	—	—	—
	NZ in NZ	3	6	1	212	42.40	56	—	1	2	—	—	—	—	—
1992-93	NZ in Zimbabwe	2	4	0	249	62.25	140	1	1	1	0	15	—	—	—
	NZ in Sri Lanka	2	4	0	137	34.25	107	1	—	1	0	10	—	—	—
	Wellington	3	6	1	438	87.60	152	2	1	—	0	16	—	—	—
	New Zealand Board XI	1	2	0	179	89.50	163	1	—	—	—	—	—	—	—
	NZ in NZ	3	6	0	186	31.00	98	—	1	1	—	—	—	—	—
1993-94	NZ in Australia	4	8	1	238	34.00	105	1	—	3	—	—	—	—	—
	Wellington	1	2	0	27	13.50	16	—	—	3	—	—	—	—	—
	NZ in England	9	16	2	654	46.71	142	3	3	6	2	81	40.50	2-81	—
1994-95	NZ in South Africa	5	9	1	350	43.75	124*	1	2	7	0	16	—	—	—
	Wellington	1	2	2	243	—	193*	1	1	—	0	55	—	—	—
	NZ in NZ	1	2	0	30	15.00	16	—	—	1	—	—	—	—	—
Totals		**242**	**406**	**61**	**19333**	**56.03**	**299**	**69**	**80**	**219**	**119**	**4010**	**33.69**	**5-18**	**4**

SUMMARY:

BATTING & FIELDING / BOWLING

	M	I	NO	Runs	Ave	HS	100	50	Ct	Wkts	Runs	Ave	Best	5WI
Auckland	25	45	7	1632	42.94	150	4	10	28	14	304	21.71	5-69	1
Other:														
In New Zealand	4	5	0	249	49.80	163	1	—	1	2	70	35.00	2-14	—
In England	3	4	1	255	85.00	138*	2	—	3	—	—	—	—	—
Central Districts	32	55	7	3299	68.72	242	13	10	31	29	832	28.68	5-18	2
New Zealand in New Zealand†	33	53	4	2438	49.75	299	8	7	25	1	169	169.00	1-13	—
New Zealand Overseas†	88	149	27	6611	54.18	242*	23	32	82	29	1101	37.96	3-21	—
Somerset	48	79	12	3984	59.46	206	14	19	46	44	1453	33.02	5-66	1
Wellington	9	16	3	865	66.53	193*	4	2	3	0	81	—	—	—
Totals	**242**	**406**	**61**	**19333**	**56.03**	**299**	**69**	**80**	**219**	**119**	**4010**	**33.69**	**5-18**	**4**

† *includes Tests*

SUMMARY OF HOW DISMISSED

Bowled	57	16.52%
Leg before wicket	59	17.10%
Caught	199	57.68%
Caught and bowled	9	2.61%
Run out	10	2.90%
Stumped	9	2.61%
Hit wicket	2	0.58%
Total	**345**	**100.00%**

BOWLERS TAKING HIS WICKET MOST OFTEN

8 : S.L. Boock
6 : P.A.J. DeFreitas, C.W. Dickeson, M.D. Marshall
5 : M.G. Hughes, Iqbal Qasim, C.A. Walsh
4 : N.G.B. Cook, N.G. Cowans, P.H. Edmonds, J.E. Emburey, M.W. Gatting, E.E. Hemmings, Salim Jaffer, C.J. McDermott, G.R.J. Matthews, R.G.D. Willis
3 : Abdul Qadir, J.P. Agnew, A.M. Babington, G.C. Bateman, S.M. Carrington, E.J. Gray, S.J. Maguiness, N.V. Radford, J.R. Ratnayeke, M.C. Snedden, P.C.R. Tufnell

FIVE WICKETS IN AN INNINGS (4)

5-69	Auckland v Central Districts	Napier	1982-83
5-18	Central Districts v Auckland	Auckland	1983-84
5-66	Somerset v Leicestershire	Leicester	1984
5-51	Central Districts v Northern Districts	New Plymouth	1984-85

CENTURIES (69)

150	Auckland v Central Districts	New Plymouth	1981-82
104	DB Close XI v Pakistanis	Scarborough	1982
119	Auckland v Otago	Auckland	1982-83
108	Auckland v Northern Districts	Gisborne	1982-83
100	Auckland v Wellington	Auckland	1982-83
134*	New Zealand v Middlesex	Lord's	1983
116*	New Zealand v Essex	Chelmsford	1983
110*	New Zealand v DB Close Int. XI	Scarborough	1983
119	Central Districts v Northern Districts	Whangarei	1983-84
151	Central Districts v Auckland	Auckland	1983-84
100	**NEW ZEALAND v WEST INDIES**	**Wellington**	**1983-84**
100*	Somerset v Oxford University	Oxford	1984
125	Somerset v Middlesex	Bath	1984
113	Somerset v Lancashire	Bath	1984
152*	Somerset v Warwickshire	Birmingham	1984
190	Somerset v Leicestershire	Taunton	1984
108	Somerset v Gloucestershire	Bristol	1984
143	Central Districts v Northern Districts	New Plymouth	1984-85
118	New Zealand v Shell Award XI	Kingston	1984-85
188	**NEW ZEALAND v WEST INDIES**	**Georgetown**	**1984-85**
242*	New Zealand v South Australia	Adelaide	1985-86
188	**NEW ZEALAND v AUSTRALIA**	**Brisbane**	**1985-86**
137	**NEW ZEALAND v AUSTRALIA**	**Christchurch**	**1985-86**
100*	New Zealand v Essex	Chelmsford	1986
106	**NEW ZEALAND v ENGLAND**	**Lord's**	**1986**
160	Central Districts v Wellington	Levin	1986-87
154*	Central Districts v Auckland	Palmerston North	1986-87
175*	Central Districts v Canterbury	Christchurch	1986-87
151	Central Districts v Northern Districts	Morrinsville	1986-87
144 ⎫	Central Districts v Canterbury	New Plymouth	1986-87
151 ⎭	Central Districts v Canterbury	New Plymouth	1986-87
119	**NEW ZEALAND v WEST INDIES**	**Wellington**	**1986-87**
104	**NEW ZEALAND v WEST INDIES**	**Auckland**	**1986-87**
148	Somerset v Surrey	Taunton	1987
102*	Somerset v Middlesex	Bath	1987
100	Somerset v Essex	Chelmsford	1987
206*	Somerset v Warwickshire	Birmingham	1987
105	Somerset v Worcestershire	Worcester	1987
148	Somerset v Glamorgan	Weston-super-Mare	1987
119	New Zealand v West Australia	Perth	1987-88
144	New Zealand v South Australia	Adelaide	1987-88
137	**NEW ZEALAND v AUSTRALIA**	**Adelaide**	**1987-88**
119*	Central Districts v Canterbury	Christchurch	1987-88
143	**NEW ZEALAND v ENGLAND**	**Wellington**	**1987-88**
132	Somerset v Worcestershire	Worcester	1988
136*	Somerset v Lancashire	Manchester	1988
141*	Central Districts v Wellington	New Plymouth	1988-89
174	**NEW ZEALAND v PAKISTAN**	**Wellington**	**1988-89**
138*	Michael Parkinson's World XI v MCC	Scarborough	1989
143	New Zealand v South Australia	Adelaide	1989-90
138*	Central Districts v Northern Districts	Rotorua	1989-90
242	Central Districts v Otago	New Plymouth	1989-90
113	**NEW ZEALAND v INDIA**	**Auckland**	**1989-90**
123*	New Zealand v Essex	Chelmsford	1990
105*	New Zealand v Karachi	Karachi	1990-91
108*	**NEW ZEALAND v PAKISTAN**	**Lahore**	**1990-91**
101	Wellington v Sri Lankans	Wellington	1990-91
299	**NEW ZEALAND v SRI LANKA**	**Wellington**	**1990-91**
140	**NEW ZEALAND v ZIMBABWE**	**Harare**	**1992-93**
107	**NEW ZEALAND v SRI LANKA**	**Colombo**	**1992-93**
152 ⎫	Wellington v Canterbury	Christchurch	1992-93
137* ⎭	Wellington v Canterbury	Christchurch	1992-93
163	New Zealand Board XI v Australians	New Plymouth	1992-93
105	New Zealand v Tasmania	Launceston	1993-94
102*	New Zealand v Somerset	Taunton	1994
142	**NEW ZEALAND v ENGLAND**	**Lord's**	**1994**
115	**NEW ZEALAND v ENGLAND**	**Manchester**	**1994**
124*	New Zealand v Orange Free State	Bloemfontein	1994-95
193*	Wellington v Canterbury	Christchurch	1994-95

TEST CAREER RECORDS

BATTING & FIELDING / BOWLING

		M	I	NO	Runs	Ave	HS	100	50	Ct	Wkts	Runs	Ave	Best
1981-82	v Australia	3	4	0	20	5.00	9	—	—	3	0	14	—	—
1983	in England	4	8	0	163	20.37	46	—	—	5	2	58	29.00	2-35
1983-84	v England	3	4	0	148	37.00	100	1	—	3	0	93	–	—
1983-84	in Sri Lanka	3	5	1	98	24.50	45	—	—	1	1	60	60.00	1-21
1984-85	in Pakistan	3	5	0	173	34.60	55	—	1	4	6	165	27.50	2-29
1984-85	v Pakistan	3	5	0	295	59.00	84	—	3	5	—	—	—	—
1984-85	in West Indies	4	7	0	216	30.85	188	1	—	6	3	55	18.33	2-25
1985-86	in Australia	3	5	1	309	77.25	188	1	1	4	0	55	—	—
1985-86	v Australia	3	4	1	179	59.66	137	1	—		0	8	—	—
1986	in England	3	5	2	206	68.66	106	1	—	4	0	51	—	—
1986-87	v West Indies	3	6	1	328	65.60	119	2	1	6	1	35	35.00	1-13
1986-87	in Sri Lanka	1	1	0	27	27.00	27	—	—	1	0	13	—	—
1987-88	in Australia	3	6	0	396	66.00	137	1	3	2	—	—	—	—
1987-88	v England	3	5	0	216	43.20	143	1	—	2	—	—	—	—
1988-89	v Pakistan	2	4	1	261	87.00	174	1	1	—	—	—	—	—
1989-90	in Australia	1	2	0	92	46.00	62	—	1	—	—	—	—	—
1989-90	v India	3	3	0	161	53.66	113	1	—	1	—	—	—	—
1990	in England	3	4	0	96	24.00	50	—	1	1	—	—	—	—
1990-91	in Pakistan	3	6	2	244	61.00	108	1	1	7	1	44	44.00	1-22
1990-91	v Sri Lanka	2	3	0	365	121.66	299	1	—	1	—	—	—	—
1991-92	v England	3	6	1	212	42.40	56	—	1	2	—	—	—	—
1992-93	in Zimbabwe	2	4	0	249	62.25	140	1	1	1	0	15	—	—
1992-93	in Sri Lanka	2	4	0	137	34.25	107	1	—	1	0	10	—	—
1992-93	v Australia	3	6	0	186	31.00	98	—	1	1	—	—	—	—
1993-94	in Australia	1	2	1	73	73.00	42	—	—	—	—	—	—	—
1994	in England	3	6	0	380	63.33	142	2	1	2	—	—	—	—
1994-95	in South Africa	3	6	0	134	22.33	83	—	1	6	—	—	—	—
1994-95	v South Africa	1	2	0	30	15.00	16	—	—	1	—	—	—	—
Totals		**74**	**128**	**11**	**5394**	**46.10**	**299**	**17**	**18**	**70**	**14**	**676**	**48.28**	**2-25**

AGAINST EACH COUNTRY

BATTING & FIELDING / BOWLING

	M	I	NO	Runs	Ave	HS	100	50	Ct	Wkts	Runs	Ave	Best
England	22	38	3	1421	40.60	143	5	3	19	2	202	101.00	2-35
Australia	17	29	3	1255	48.26	188	3	6	10	0	77	—	—
South Africa	4	8	0	164	20.50	83	—	1	7	—	—	—	—
West Indies	7	13	1	544	45.33	188	3	1	12	4	90	22.50	2-25
India	3	3	0	161	53.66	113	1	—	1	—	—	—	—
Pakistan	11	20	3	973	57.23	174	2	6	16	7	209	29.85	2-29
Sri Lanka	8	13	1	627	52.25	299	2	—	4	1	83	83.00	1-21
Zimbabwe	2	4	0	249	62.25	140	1	1	1	0	15	—	—
Totals	**74**	**128**	**11**	**5394**	**46.10**	**299**	**17**	**18**	**70**	**14**	**676**	**48.28**	**2-25**

IN EACH COUNTRY

BATTING & FIELDING / BOWLING

	M	I	NO	Runs	Ave	HS	100	50	Ct	Wkts	Runs	Ave	Best
New Zealand	32	52	4	2401	50.02	299	8	7	25	1	150	150.00	1-13
England	13	23	2	845	40.23	142	3	2	12	2	109	54.50	2-35
Australia	8	15	2	870	66.92	188	2	5	6	0	55	—	—
South Africa	3	6	0	134	22.33	83	—	1	6	—	—	—	—
West Indies	4	7	0	216	30.85	188	1	—	6	3	55	18.33	2-25
India	—	—	—	—	—	—	—	—	—	—	—	—	—
Pakistan	6	11	2	417	46.33	108	1	2	11	7	209	29.85	2-29
Sri Lanka	6	10	1	262	29.11	107	1	—	3	1	83	83.00	1-21
Zimbabwe	2	4	0	249	62.25	140	1	1	1	0	15	—	—
Totals	**74**	**128**	**11**	**5394**	**46.10**	**299**	**17**	**18**	**70**	**14**	**676**	**48.28**	**2-25**

HOME AND AWAY

		BATTING & FIELDING										*BOWLING*			
	M	I	NO	Runs	Ave	HS	100	50	Ct	Wkts	Runs	Ave	Best
Home	32	52	4	2401	50.02	299	8	7	25	1	150	150.00	1-13
Away	42	76	7	2993	43.37	188	9	11	45	13	526	40.46	2-25
Totals	**74**	**128**	**11**	**5394**	**46.10**	**299**	**17**	**18**	**70**	**14**	**676**	**48.28**	**2-25**

AS CAPTAIN/NOT CAPTAIN

		BATTING & FIELDING										*BOWLING*			
	M	I	NO	Runs	Ave	HS	100	50	Ct	Wkts	Runs	Ave	Best
Captain	16	31	4	1466	54.29	299	4	4	13	1	69	69.00	1-22
Not Captain	58	97	7	3928	43.64	188	13	14	57	13	607	46.69	2-25
Totals	**74**	**128**	**11**	**5394**	**46.10**	**299**	**17**	**18**	**70**	**14**	**676**	**48.28**	**2-25**

SUMMARY OF HOW DISMISSED

Bowled	15	12.82%
Leg before wicket	21	17.95%
Caught	74	63.25%
Caught and bowled	2	1.71%
Run out	2	1.71%
Stumped	2	1.71%
Hit wicket	1	0.85%
Total	**117**	**100.00%**

BOWLERS TAKING HIS WICKET MOST OFTEN

6 : P.A.J. DeFreitas
4 : M.G. Hughes, Iqbal Qasim, C.J. McDermott, M.D. Marshall,
    Salim Jaffer, R.G.D. Willis
3 : Abdul Qadir, N.G. Cowans, G.R.J. Matthews, J.R. Ratnayeke,
    C.A. Walsh
2 : I.T. Botham, D.S. de Silva, P.S. de Villiers, G.R. Dilley,
    P.H. Edmonds, J.E. Emburey, M.W. Gatting, M.A. Holding,
    S.D. Jack, P.W. Jarvis, C.C. Lewis, D.K. Lillee,
    B.M. McMillan, M. Muralidharan, A. Ranatunga,
    P.L. Sleep, A.J. Traicos, P.C.R. Tufnell, Waqar Younis,
    C. White

ONE-DAY INTERNATIONAL CAREER RECORDS

BATTING & FIELDING **BOWLING**

		M	I	NO	Runs	Ave	HS	100	50	Ct	Wkts	Runs	Ave	Best
1981-82	Australia in NZ	3	2	0	10	5.00	7	—	—	3	2	9	4.50	2-9
1982-83	Australia in Australia	1	1	0	66	66.00	66	—	1	1	2	30	15.00	2-30
1982-83	Sri Lanka in NZ	2	2	2	50	—	43*	—	—	1	3	81	27.00	2-30
1983	England in England	2	2	0	117	58.50	97	—	1	—	0	51	—	—
	Pakistan in England	2	2	0	77	38.50	43	—	—	1	0	12	—	—
	Sri Lanka in England	2	2	0	8	4.00	8	—	—	1	1	47	47.00	1-15
1983-84	England in NZ	3	3	1	113	56.50	105*	1	—	—	—	—	—	—
1983-84	Sri Lanka in Sri Lanka	3	3	0	106	35.33	68	—	1	—	1	32	32.00	1-19
1984-85	Sri Lanka in Sri Lanka	2	2	1	75	75.00	52*	—	1	1	2	38	19.00	2-20
1984-85	Pakistan in Pakistan	4	4	0	122	30.50	67	—	1	1	5	97	19.40	2-17
1984-85	Pakistan in NZ	3	3	0	111	37.00	59	—	1	2	—	—	—	—
1984-85	West Indies in Australia	2	1	0	8	8.00	8	—	—	—	—	—	—	—
	Sri Lanka in Australia	1	1	0	22	22.00	22	—	—	1	—	—	—	—
	India in Australia	1	1	0	9	9.00	9	—	—	—	—	—	—	—
1984-85	West Indies in West Indies	5	5	1	88	22.00	41	—	—	—	—	—	—	—
1985-86	Australia in Australia	5	5	0	116	23.20	71	—	1	3	1	51	51.00	1-16
	India in Australia	5	5	0	214	42.80	76	—	2	3	2	98	49.00	1-20
1985-86	Australia in NZ	4	4	0	101	25.25	47	—	—	4	5	109	21.80	2-23
1985-86	Sri Lanka in Sri Lanka	1	1	0	4	4.00	4	—	—	—	—	—	—	—
	Pakistan in Sri Lanka	1	1	0	75	75.00	75	—	1	—	0	20	—	—
1985-86	India in Sharjah	1	1	0	1	1.00	1	—	—	—	1	16	16.00	1-16
	Pakistan in Sharjah	1	1	0	9	9.00	9	—	—	—	—	—	—	—
1986	England in England	2	2	1	102	102.00	93*	—	1	—	1	51	51.00	1-36
1986-87	West Indies in NZ	3	3	0	102	34.00	53	—	1	—	1	71	71.00	1-26
1987-88	Zimbabwe in India	2	2	0	130	65.00	72	—	2	3	—	—	—	—
	India in India	2	2	0	30	15.00	21	—	—	—	—	—	—	—
	Australia in India	2	2	0	62	31.00	58	—	1	1	—	—	—	—
1987-88	Australia in Australia	5	5	0	139	27.80	48	—	—	2	—	—	—	—
	Sri Lanka in Australia	4	4	0	159	39.75	52	—	1	3	—	—	—	—
1987-88	England in NZ	3	3	0	33	11.00	18	—	—	1	—	—	—	—
1988-89	Pakistan in NZ	5	5	2	196	65.33	87*	—	1	1	—	—	—	—
1989-90	India in NZ	2	2	0	122	61.00	104	1	—	2	—	—	—	—
	Australia in NZ	2	2	1	68	68.00	51*	—	1	1	—	—	—	—
1989-90	Australia in Sharjah	1	1	0	41	41.00	41	—	—	—	—	—	—	—
	Bangladesh in Sharjah	1	1	0	69	69.00	69	—	1	—	—	—	—	—
	Pakistan in Sharjah	1	1	0	5	5.00	5	—	—	1	0	5	—	—
1990	England in England	2	2	0	53	26.50	46	—	—	2	—	—	—	—
1990-91	Pakistan in Pakistan	3	3	0	88	29.33	46	—	—	—	1	64	64.00	1-24
1990-91	Australia in Australia	6	6	0	198	33.00	81	—	2	5	0	54	—	—
	England in Australia	4	4	0	207	51.75	78	—	2	4	—	—	—	—
1990-91	Sri Lanka in NZ	3	3	0	98	32.66	64	—	1	2	1	12	12.00	1-12
1990-91	England in NZ	3	3	0	24	8.00	13	—	—	3	—	—	—	—
1991-92	England in NZ	3	3	0	66	22.00	31	—	—	2	—	—	—	—
1991-92	Australia in NZ	1	1	1	100	—	100*	1	—	—	—	—	—	—
	Sri Lanka in NZ	1	1	0	5	5.00	5	—	—	1	—	—	—	—
	South Africa in NZ	1	1	1	3	—	3*	—	—	1	—	—	—	—
	Zimbabwe in NZ	1	1	1	74	—	74*	—	1	1	0	6	—	—
	West Indies in NZ	1	1	1	81	—	81*	—	1	—	—	—	—	—
	India in NZ	1	1	0	26	26.00	26	—	—	—	—	—	—	—
	England in NZ	1	1	1	73	—	73*	—	1	—	—	—	—	—
	Pakistan in NZ	2	2	0	94	47.00	91	—	1	—	—	—	—	—
1992-93	Zimbabwe in Zimbabwe	2	2	0	134	67.00	94	—	1	1	—	—	—	—
1992-93	Sri Lanka in Sri Lanka	1	1	0	1	1.00	1	—	—	—	—	—	—	—
1992-93	Pakistan in NZ	3	3	2	132	132.00	57*	—	1	2	—	—	—	—
1992-93	Australia in NZ	5	5	1	195	48.75	91*	—	2	4	—	—	—	—
1994	England in England	1	1	0	0	0.00	0	—	—	—	—	—	—	—
1994-95	South Africa in South Africa	2	2	0	15	7.50	9	—	—	—	—	—	—	—
	Sri Lanka in South Africa	1	—	—	—	—	—	—	—	1	—	—	—	—
	Pakistan in South Africa	1	1	0	83	83.00	83	—	1	—	—	—	—	—
1994-95	India in NZ	1	1	0	7	7.00	7	—	—	—	—	—	—	—
Totals		**139**	**136**	**17**	**4517**	**37.95**	**105***	**3**	**33**	**65**	**29**	**954**	**32.89**	**2-9**

AGAINST EACH COUNTRY

BATTING & FIELDING											*BOWLING*			
	M	I	NO	Runs	Ave	HS	100	50	Ct	Wkts	Runs	Ave	Best
England	24	24	3	788	37.52	105*	1	5	12	1	102	102.00	1-36
Australia	35	34	3	1096	35.35	100*	1	8	24	10	253	25.30	2-9
South Africa	3	3	1	18	9.00	9	—	—	1	—	—	—	—
West Indies	11	10	2	279	34.87	81*	—	2	—	1	71	71.00	1-26
India	13	13	0	409	31.46	104	1	2	5	3	114	38.00	1-16
Pakistan	26	26	4	992	45.09	91	—	7	8	6	198	33.00	2-17
Sri Lanka	21	20	3	528	31.05	68	—	4	10	8	210	26.25	2-20
Zimbabwe	5	5	1	338	84.50	94	—	4	5	0	6	—	—
Bangladesh	1	1	0	69	69.00	69	—	1	—	—	—	—	—
Totals	**139**	**136**	**17**	**4517**	**37.95**	**105***	**3**	**33**	**65**	**29**	**954**	**32.89**	**2-9**

CENTURIES

105*	v England	Auckland	1983-84
104	v India	Dunedin	1989-90
100*	v Australia	Auckland	1991-92

SUMMARY OF HOW DISMISSED

Bowled	24	20.17%
Leg before wicket	10	8.41%
Caught	65	54.62%
Caught and bowled	6	5.04%
Run out	13	10.92%
Stumped	1	0.84%
Total	**119**	**100.00%**

Bibliography

A Century of Great New Zealand Cricketers, Joseph Romanos; David Bateman Ltd, 1993.

An Opener's Tale, Bruce Edgar and David Roberts; Bootsie Books, 1987.

Botham: My Autobiography, Ian Botham; Collins Willow, 1994.

Christmas in Rarotonga, John Wright and Paul Thomas; Moa, 1990.

Cricket Almanack of New Zealand (various editions), Arthur Carman and Noel MacDonald, Ian Smith and Francis Payne; Sporting Publications, Moa, Moa Beckett.

Great New Zealand Cricket Families, Joseph Romanos; Random House, 1992.

Men in White, Don Neely, Richard King and Francis Payne; Moa, 1986.

New Zealand Cricket Annual (various editions), Don Neely, Lynn McConnell; Moa, Moa Beckett.

Passing Shots, Frank Keating; Robson Books, 1988.

Rhythm and Swing, Richard Hadlee and Richard Becht; Moa, 1989.

The Crowe Style, Dave and Audrey Crowe; Moa, 1987.

The Innings of a Lifetime, Walter Hadlee; David Bateman Ltd, 1993.

The Wisden Book of County Cricket, Christopher Martin-Jenkins; Queen Anne Press, 1981.

Willie's Tail; Willie Watson, 1994.

Wisden Cricketers' Almanack (various editions); John Wisden and Co Ltd, Macdonald and Jane's.

100 Greatest Batsmen, John Arlott; Macdonald Queen Anne Press, 1989.

The author also referred to the *Cricketer*, the *New Zealand Listener*, the *New Zealand Woman's Weekly*, *Woman's Day*, *Metro*, *North and South*, the English *Daily Telegraph*, *South African Sports Illustrated* and various New Zealand daily and weekly newspapers.

Three television programmes, *Crowe on Crowe* (1992) and the Ian Fraser interview with Martin Crowe (1994), both on TVNZ, and the Brian Edwards interview with Crowe on *Sunday* (1995), on TV3, provided further information.